One Foot in Front of the Other

One Foot in Front of the Other

Daily Affirmations for Recovery

Tian Dayton, Ph.D.

Health Communications, Inc.
Deerfield Beach, Florida

www.hcibooks.com

Library of Congress Cataloging-in-Publication Data
is available through the Library of Congress

ISBN-13: 978-0-7573-1788-0 (Paperback)
ISBN-10: 0-7573-1788-X (Paperback
ISBN-13: 978-0-7573-1789-7 (ePub)
ISBN-10: 0-7573-1789-8 (ePub)

Health Communications, Inc.
201 S.W. 15th Street
eerfield Beach, FL 33442–8190

rissa Hise Henoch
rmatting by Lawna Patterson Oldfield

To Mom

with love

for showing us how

to put one foot

in front of the other . . .

Either we have hope or we don't;
it is a dimension of the soul, and it's not essentially
dependent on some particular observation of
the world or estimate of the situation.

Hope is not prognostication. It is an orientation
of the spirit, an orientation of the heart; it transcends
the world that is immediately experienced, and is
anchored somewhere beyond its horizons . . .

Hope, in this deep and powerful sense,
is not the same as joy that things are going well,
or willingness to invest in enterprises that are obviously
heading for success, but rather the ability to work for
something because it is good, not just because it
stands a chance to succeed. The more propitious
the situation in which we demonstrate hope,
the deeper the hope is.

Hope is definitely not the same thing as optimism.
It is not the conviction that something will turn out well,
but the certainty that something makes sense,
regardless of how it turns out.

It is hope, above all, which gives us
strength to live and

continually try new things.

—Vaclav Havel,
Czech playwright, poet,
dissident, and former president
of the Czech Republic

Introduction

God grant me the serenity to accept the things
I cannot change; courage to change the things I can;
and wisdom to know the difference.

—Reinhold Niebuhr

There is an awakening of consciousness that happens when we learn to put words to feelings and feelings to words. A part of us that was unavailable becomes available. Through articulating our deepest feelings we're able to use the unique brilliance of our thinking minds to bring order and clarity to our feeling/sensing minds; we can shed light where there was darkness and restore voice and sensation to those parts of ourselves that have been emotionally mute or numb.

Life is a challenge for even the strongest among us; we all need tools for living that help us to face each and every day. This is one of the reasons that those who suffer from various forms of addiction, or have lived with the collateral damage that surrounds addiction, come to bless the very disease that got them into recovery. Simply put, the tools of living that we learn in recovery and Twelve-Step rooms, along with the positive attitudes for living a day at a time, provide us with a foundation for living that strengthens each and every day. These perspectives and tools also give us something of lasting value to pass on to our children and grandchildren.

Life is also full of little fears and anxieties that undermine our ability to breathe into the day, to take life a moment at a time—fears and anxieties that are mostly unnecessary and become self sabotaging; in other words, that lead us to create the very problems that we're trying to avoid. We need help and guidance to turn this vicious circle into a virtuous circle. This is why we need support each and every day, we need a wholesome, grounded, and spiritually alive basis for living that can strengthen our resolve and our resilience.

Recovery, whether from living with addiction, process addiction, childhood trauma, dysfunction, or relationship loss issues, is a process of putting one foot in front of the other. It's an experience of deep, inner growth that challenges us to become fuller, deeper, and wiser people. One of its many treasures is that we do not have to do it alone. This book is meant to accompany you on your journey, to serve as a pocket companion filled with tiny bits of inspiration, motivation, tools and research to return to throughout your day, to help you consolidate your "experience, strength, and hope" a day at a time.

The Format

I have written this book in the first person, the "I" format, because I feel that makes the information in it more personal, intimate, and digestible. An excellent body of research on emotion, interpersonal neurobiology, trauma, and attachment has developed over the past three decades. I have woven this research into each daily affirmation, alongside time-honored program wisdom, tools, and slogans as an intimate and informative way of addressing issues of personal growth. *One Foot in Front of the Other* is a composite of recovery struggles, aspirations, experience, strength, and hope. It's what underlies the small and big miracles that I hear in my groups and in my travels while doing this work. In these pages you will find:

- **Tools of the program:** I have incorporated the tools of the program into affirmations so that they can be remembered and brought into daily focus.
- **Scientific Information:** Neuroscience has "proven" much of what we in recovery have long known about positive thinking, faith, and prayer. Where appropriate I have included brief research insights and information.

- **Inspirational quotes and readings:** We who walk the path of recovery have long sought beautiful quotes and readings to guide and inspire us. I include many of the favorites that I know others love, and my own as well, in these pages.

For more information about interactive ways of processing emotions to use as a companion to this book, plus training that includes this research, visit my online membership site at *tiandayton.com.*

JANUARY

Sanskrit Prayer

Look to this day
For it is life
The very life of life.
In its brief course lie all
The realities and verities of existence
The bliss of growth
The splendor of action
The glory of power—
For yesterday is but a dream
And tomorrow is only a vision
But today, well lived
Makes every yesterday a dream of happiness
And every tomorrow a vision of hope.
Look well, therefore to this day

One Foot in Front of the Other

All I need to do today is to put one foot in front of the other. I can only walk this walk a step at a time. Each time I take a step, I will trust that the next will follow, along with the next, and the next, and the next. What I know today is that no matter what does or does not come my way, I will wake up each morning to one more day of my spiritual journey—nothing more, nothing less. I will keep putting one foot in front of the other. Occasional leaps of faith and periods of unusual progress will no doubt happen as will slips and backslides. But no matter what comes along, I have the gift of recovery in my life, a gift that I can rely on, a gift that means that I never have to struggle alone again. I place my hand in the hand of my Higher Power and together we walk a path of recovery one step at a time.

I embrace a community of recovering people

May today there be peace within.
May you trust that you are exactly where you are
meant to be. May you not forget the infinite possibilities
that are born of faith in yourself and others. May you use the
gifts that you have received, and pass on the love that has been
given to you. May you be content with yourself just the way you
are. Let this knowledge settle into your bones, and allow
your soul the freedom to sing, dance, praise and love.
It is there for each and every one of us.

—St. Theresa's Prayer

Keeping My Soul Alive

Today I choose to what I need to do to keep my soul alive, to stay awake to life and to this new day with all of its potential. If I walk by this day without seeing it, I will miss what the day has to offer me. If I rush through it with a preoccupied, distracted mind, I will just get from one thing to the next and the next, till it is over. But if I look, if I understand that being alive in the moment brings unexpected gifts; if I recognize that simply being alive is a gift, then the moments in my day will expand, they will have a feel of something subtle and alive, I will be aware of a deeper pulse of living.

I will stay on the path for one more day

There also exists a sleeping sickness of the soul.
Its most dangerous aspect is that one is unaware of its coming.
That is why you have to be careful. . . . You should realize that
your soul suffers if you live superficially. People need times in
which to concentrate, when they can search their inmost selves.
It is tragic that most men have not achieved this feeling of
self-awareness. And finally, when they hear the inner voice they
do not want to listen anymore. They carry on as before
so as not to be constantly reminded of what they have lost.
But as for you, resolve to keep a quiet time. . . .
Then your souls can speak to you without being drowned
out by the hustle and bustle of everyday life.

—Albert Schweitzer

Keeping It Simple

I understand that the quality of my week is influenced by how I live the hours of my day. I will keep it simple today. I cannot solve all of the problems I am becoming aware of overnight, nor do I wish to try. Awareness can hurt. It asks me to become responsible for what I now see, to stop living mindlessly, and to recognize that if my life isn't working the way I want it to, I may need to pull up my shirt sleeves and get messy, to dig my hands into the soil of my day. Awareness can empower me. If I try to make all my life changes at once I may get overwhelmed and want to quit, give up, run away, or self-medicate. Today I will take baby steps. I'll have a simple plan for my day and trust that today well lived will create a better tomorrow.

I will keep things simple today

The ability to simplify means to eliminate
the unnecessary so that the
necessary may speak.

—Hans Hofmann

Emotional Sobriety

Just for today, I can sit with what I am experiencing right now, I can live my life a feeling at a time. I am learning what it means to live an emotionally sober life. I used to think that emotional sobriety sounded dull, flat, and unexciting. I thought that living in the emotional extremes was living life to the fullest. But today, when I feel the beauty of feeling my feelings without acting out, I have a kind of peace inside that feels good. When I can allow my emotions to fill and inform me, but not control me, I feel my life as it's happening. I experience a new choice. There is a space where I can reflect on what I am feeling before I swing into action. Doing this expands my sense of self and my confidence that I can manage my own inner world. It allows me to live in the moment and to be more spontaneous and adaptable. Living in emotional extremes is a form of acting out or running away from what I feel, running from my manageable feeling center. Emotional balance and sobriety actually allows me to experience a deeper, wider inner world.

Emotional sobriety allows me to be more of who I am

The truth is that our finest moments are most likely to occur when we are feeling deeply uncomfortable, unhappy, or unfulfilled. For it is only in such moments, propelled by our discomfort, that we are likely to step out of our ruts and start searching for different ways or truer answers.

—M. Scott Peck

My Only Job

My only job today is to have faith, to stay positive, and put one foot in front of the other. When I slip into negativity, I head down a slippery slope. I make things important that I could just as easily release and allow to move past me. I obsess, argue with myself, and convince myself that there is something wrong in my life that needs fixing, something wrong with my relationships that makes me dissatisfied with them, or something wrong with me that I need to hide or run from. Just for today I am going to try to live the principles of the program in all of my affairs, not just in some of them. I am going to live one day at a time and surrender my resistance to change and my need to control to my Higher Power. I am going to live a clean and wholesome life and I am going to love the life I have. I am grateful for the gift of one more day of recovery.

Life is a gift and I will not devalue it with negativity

Plant seeds of expectation in your mind;
cultivate thoughts that anticipate achievement.
Believe in yourself as being capable of overcoming
all obstacles and weaknesses.

—Norman Vincent Peale

A New Design for Living

The world is opening up to me in a whole new way. Thank God I learned to reach out and ask for help. Thank God I came to understand that I cannot, nor need not, do it all alone. Thank God I became humble enough to let something in. My best thinking got me this far. But whatever got me here, I am grateful because recovery brings grace. I can, with the support of others traveling this path, learn new ways of being. I can surrender, let go and let God, and live life a day at a time. Life, lived like this, takes on whole new meaning and purpose for me, simplified, distilled, and manageable. It is enough. It is emotionally sober. Today I feel blessed and even thrilled to be learning a new design for living. A new design for living that certainly beats the old one.

I embrace a new design for living

The belief that unhappiness is selfless and happiness is selfish is misguided. It's more selfless to act happy. It takes energy, generosity, and discipline to be unfailingly lighthearted, yet everyone takes the happy person for granted. No one is careful of his feelings or tries to keep his spirits high. He seems self-sufficient; he becomes a cushion for others. And because happiness seems unforced, that person usually gets no credit.

—*Gretchen Rubin,* The Happiness Project: Or Why I Spent a Year Trying to Sing in the Morning, Clean My Closets, Fight Right, Read Aristotle, and Generally Have More Fun

The Experience of Being Alive

I cannot fit more life into the day than the day will naturally hold. Experience unfolds a moment at a time. When my mind is always on where I can get and what I can become, I walk right by the moment as if it were nothing to savor or cherish or even notice. When I can allow myself to sink into the here and now, everything I need for this moment is right here, the moment expands, and actually fills up of its own accord. I am learning that being in my life is better than piling up evidence of being in my life, that being in my day is better than thinking about being in my day, and that experiencing the quiet radiance of God at work in all things gives each moment, each day, and each circumstance its own quiet meaning and purpose. The purpose is to see, to sense, to be in this experience called life rather than avoid it, medicate it, overthink it, or overlive it.

I am alive in this day

I don't believe people are looking for
the meaning of life as much as they are looking
for the experience of being alive.

—Joseph Campbell

Respecting the Gift of My Life

God has given ME to ME to look after. No one is with me twenty four seven; if I want to be help-able, it has to begin with me. I am my own responsibility. If I don't care for me, if I don't hold me up, if I don't sustain and nurture myself, there will be no way for another person to be able to do that for me. Today I will take care of the gift of ME, knowing that this is my right and responsibility. I will get the rest, nutrition, exercise, and companionship that I need to feel good. I will find something constructive to occupy my time. I will be aware of my mood and my attitude, and I will do my best to keep them heading in a positive rather than a negative direction. I am responsible for seeing to it that I am well cared for; if I do not take care of ME, no one else will, no one else can.

I will sustain and respect the life I have been given

We do not receive wisdom, we must
discover it for ourselves, after a journey through
the wilderness which no one else can make for us,
which no one can spare us, for our wisdom is
the point of view from which we come
at last to regard the world.

—Marcel Proust

JANUARY 9

Leaving the Disease Behind Me

I am leaving this disease behind me. I cannot get where I need and want to go dragging it along anymore. What I used to accept as business as usual, I see today as a legacy of dysfunction, a legacy that I don't need or want to continue. I have been trying to fix this long enough—it's unfixable. I have been trying to spackle in the ever widening cracks between myself and this disease, but it never really holds. I have had enough. I am not bigger or more powerful than this disease. I will allow myself to move forward into my own psychological health, with or without anyone else. Today I see that the only person I can change is myself, and that trying to fix everyone else only causes them to make me the problem. They will change in their time, not mine. I have a right to wriggle loose and lead my own life whether or not they see the disease as I am now learning to see it. I have a right to be free. I surrender; I release and let go of what is binding me.

I respect the power of the disease to hold me, or anyone I love, in its grip

Be patient. Your skin took a while to deteriorate. Give it some time to reflect a calmer inner state. As one of my friends states on his Facebook profile: "The true Losers in Life, are not those who Try and Fail, but those who Fail to Try."

—*Jess C. Scott,* Clear: A Guide to Treating Acne Naturally

Boundaries

I can set a boundary. It may not be easy and it may not feel great, but I can do it. I can sit with the reality of the boundary I have set so that I don't boomerang into action to undo it when it feels unfamiliar, scary, or anxiety provoking. I have a right to do what I need to do to keep myself sane and balanced. I will not use my boundaries to bully others nor to punish them. When I set a boundary it will be sincere and only with the best intentions. If I have set my boundary too firmly, I can amend it. If I need to set it more firmly, I can do that, too. Nothing is permanent. When I sit with the feelings that setting a boundary bring up in me, I learn things about myself, about why I was not able to set it sooner—and I see more clearly what not setting it cost me.

I am worthy

When you know who you are;
when your mission is clear and you burn
with the inner fire of unbreakable will;
no cold can touch your heart;
no deluge can dampen your purpose.
You know that you are alive.

—*Chief Seattle*

I Begin Now

I will start where I am. I take responsibility for my state of mind, the state of my relationships, and the state of my life. I will start from today, from this minute and the one that follows. And when I fall down, disappoint myself, or let others down, I will pick myself up, promptly admit it, reassess, and start again. I will reflect on why I fell where I fell, make some mental, physical, and emotional adjustments, and move on. I'll take the next step, do the next right thing, and keep my focus on moving forward. Life is full of opportunities if I am willing to see them; it's filled with unlived potential if I am willing to live it; it's full of promise if I am willing to have faith. Anything is possible if I believe it is.

I start here and now

It's never too late, or in my case too early,
to be whomever you want to be.
There's no time limit.
Start whenever you want.
You can change or stay the same.
There are no rules to this thing.
We can make the best or the worst of it.
I hope you make the best of it.
I hope you see things that startle you.
I hope you feel things you never felt before.
I hope you meet people who have
a different point of view.
I hope you live a life you're proud of,
and if you're not, I hope you have the
courage to start all over again.

—*Eric Roth*

A Day at a Time

I can only live one hour at a time. This hour. All I have to do is to live this hour well and let the rest take care of itself. All I have to do is not self medicate, act out, or sink into despair or emotional drunkenness this one day. I can do, a day at a time, what might frighten or overwhelm me if I thought I had to it for the rest of my life. I will live the life I want to have today, knowing that this is my best assurance of a good tomorrow. There is such a thing as time. Life unfolds in moments and hours. Today surrounds me. Everything is alive and so am I. A God of my understanding is alive in this moment and I am being held by this Higher Power whether I know it or not. Today I am alive and I know it.

I change the world by changing me

Never doubt that a small group of
thoughtful, committed citizens can change the world.
Indeed, it is the only thing that ever has.

—Margaret Mead,
American anthropologist (1901–1978)

Principles, Not Personalities

Today I am part of a community of recovering people that is bigger than me, bigger than anyone. I am benefiting from a collective wisdom that has developed slowly and over time, that has been passed with love, commitment, passion, pain, sweat, and deep joy from one hand to another, from one heart to another. This is a journey with fellow journeyers, owned by no one and affiliated with nothing outside of itself. I owe my recovery to no person, place, or thing. I am here like so many others, taking my turn in these beautiful rooms, seeking Good Orderly Direction a day at a time.

I allow the grace of this collective wisdom to enter me each and every day

Do not believe in anything simply because you have heard it. Do not believe in anything simply because it is spoken and rumored by many. Do not believe in anything simply because it is found written in your religious books. Do not believe in anything merely on the authority of your teachers and elders. Do not believe in traditions because they have been handed down for many generations. But after observation and analysis, when you find that anything agrees with reason and is conducive to the good and benefit of one and all, then accept it and live up to it.

—Buddha

My Reservoir of Peace

There is nothing in my day that is more important than my serenity, and it is my responsibility to maintain and attend to it. Whatever I do in the world, my serenity comes first. I owe it to no one. I will pay attention today to the myriad of ways in which I am thrown off balance and I will take a moment to center myself, to breathe, to remember that when I can calm my body, mind, and spirit, I interact differently with the people, places, and things of my day. I will work daily to build my serenity muscles so that I stay strong and flexible. Serenity isn't something that I can just grab and have. I need to nourish it through quiet and reflection and come back to it when I lose it. My serenity is mine to look after. I give myself the gift of my own serenity today and every day.

I let go and let God

For peace of mind, we need to resign as
general manager of the universe.

—Larry Eisenberg

Beating Myself and Others Up

Today I will be less hard on myself. I will realize that the world isn't out to get me, I am not the center of everyone's universe, and most people are too busy thinking about themselves to want to spend their time focusing on me. Everyone makes mistakes, so what. I will let mine go, knowing I will make more, and will let those go, too. If I feel bad inside about something I did, I will be less critical of myself. I cannot change all at once. When I beat myself up on the inside, eventually I look for a culprit. I can't bear the feelings I am having, so I want to blame them on someone else. Do I feel my indiscretions are unforgivable? Why? Why do I go to such a self-blaming place? It's as if the child inside of me who felt bad gets warmed up and cannot get out of my own self-centeredness and breathe some fresh air. Just for today, I can allow myself to make mistakes and I can allow others to make them, too.

I am only human, and only human is good enough for me

Let me never fall into the vulgar mistake
of dreaming that I am persecuted
whenever I am contradicted.

—Ralph Waldo Emerson

Terminally Unique

My pain is not so very unique after all; it looks a lot like everyone else's. In the rooms I become right-sized. I have a place to share what is inside of me, what I have carried in silence. I hear other people's experiences and I find myself in them, too. I share my own and people identify with me. I feel less alone, less terminally unique. I get out of myself and into the world. My head stops spinning and my heart opens up. For a moment I am present in the here and now; my thoughts aren't racing towards the future or churning on the past. Today I will remind myself that pain is part of life. I recognize that what causes people to become crazy or dysfunctional is running from pain. Actually feeling pain takes a few minutes, a few hours, a few days, or a few months. Running from pain takes a lifetime.

No matter what my life is handing me, I am part of creating it, even if all I am creating is my reaction to it. If I don't like what is around me, if something is bringing up feelings of pain or frustration, then life is trying to teach me something that I need to learn. Today I will hold the problem I am experiencing in the palms of my hands and ask my Higher Power to reveal the answers to me, to give me insight.

Pain is part of life, I can feel it and let it go

We either make ourselves miserable
or we make ourselves strong.
The amount of work is the same.

—Carlos Castaneda

JANUARY 17

Standing on My Own Two Feet

I will not take the fall for anyone anymore. If I misbehave I will promptly admit it and I will take steps to rectify things. I will keep my side of the street clean. If someone else misbehaves, it's theirs to correct, not mine. I cannot manage a relationship conflict from both ends. When I try to do that, I wind up feeling and looking crazy. If I am sincerely trying my best today, that is all that I will ask of myself. I cannot resolve everything; with some things I simply need to do my best and then move on. I will make sure I am practicing the principles of the program and release what I have no control over. Today I can take a risk, I can do what I thought yesterday would be too much for me to do, and I can try new things, knowing that my growth is in the doing, not in the result.

I let go of control over people, places and things and keep the focus on myself

If you hear a voice within you say
"you cannot paint," then by all means paint,
and that voice will be silenced.

—Vincent Van Gogh

Living the Life That Is Mine to Live

I have a right to my own life. If I don't live my life fully, it will simply not be lived, because no one else can live it for me. I cannot bequeath it to anyone else to live on my behalf. If I don't sing my song it will remain unsung, because no one can sing it for me. If I don't dance my dance, however clumsy, it will remain still, frozen in place, because no one can dance it for me. If I don't find the poetry in my day, in my own soul, it will not be found, because it is mine to search out and speak out. Life is a spiritual gift and my life is my personal gift from God, from the Universe, from someplace much bigger than me. If I don't live it, no one else will, no one else can.

I will use the life I have to actualize myself

Don't die with your music still in you.

—Wayne Dyer

Detaching with Love

I need to detach with love from those I care about who are still mired in this disease. I will tolerate the pain of watching. When I detach with resentment, it is not detachment; it keeps me preoccupied and connected. When I amputate, it is not detachment; I develop phantom limb. I still hurt where that part of my heart used to be and am haunted by something missing. When I detach by ignoring, shunning, or running, it is simply the other side of enmeshment, and eventually I get hooked in all over again. Today I will detach with love and I will allow others the dignity of their own path. I am grateful to have found recovery. If I teach, it will be by example. When I see someone I care about locked in this disease, I want to run and help. I want to tell them what to do to get better. But time and again, this hasn't worked. In fact, it usually blows up in my face. Today my emotional sobriety allows me to have perspective and to let someone else recover at their pace, not mine. Today I can model recovery quietly and steadily.

Other people have their own Higher Power and it's not me

It is impossible for a man to learn what
he thinks he already knows.

—*Epictetus*

First Things First

My only job is to stay on my own path. I cannot help anyone who doesn't want my help. If someone wants what I have they will also want to find it in their own way. I cannot really teach anyone. I cannot really save anyone. My feelings of disgust at their blindness and frustration, with their seeming unwillingness to get with the program, color my message. And so often, I help because I feel so much survivor's guilt. What I really want to do is run the other way but I feel too guilty to do that. What I really want is the family I lost to this disease or the family I never had to begin with. Today, I will allow myself to have what I have, to live well, to follow my own path of recovery.

I can mind my own business

Then, without realizing it, you try to improve yourself at the start of each new day; of course, you achieve quite a lot in the course of time. Anyone can do this, it costs nothing and is certainly very helpful. Whoever doesn't know it must learn and find by experience that a quiet conscience makes one strong. . . . How wonderful it is that nobody need wait a single moment before starting to improve the world.

—Anne Frank

Hiding Pain

Pain grows in hiding. Recovery teaches me not to hide my pain and suffering from myself or from my Higher Power. When I bring my most honest and pure self to the fore, when I am truly willing to turn over my angst to a power greater than myself, something changes. I let go and create space for a shift in perception. I experience a quiet awakening in my life, and forces that I did not allow to enter my life before, come in to heal me. I will open the door today and let the parts of me come forward into my own consciousness that I too often shove away and shut down. After all it's only more of me. Once these parts of me find legs, they walk; once these parts of me find a voice, they share and speak, they find words. And once they find words, I understand.

I open my heart to my Higher Power

You think your pain and your heartbreak are unprecedented in the history of the world, but then you read. It was books that taught me that the things that tormented me most were the very things that connected me with all the people who were alive, or who had ever been alive.

—James Baldwin

The Three Cs

I didn't cause it, I can't control it, and I can't cure it. I didn't cause it, I can't control it, and I can't cure it. I didn't cause it, I can't control it, and I can't cure it. I need to repeat and repeat this to myself in order to deal with my codependency that actually makes me feel that I did cause this disease, I can control it, and I can cure it. When I get into this trap I lose myself all over again. I get into fights that cannot be won, I alienate others, I give away my power, and I wind up feeling terrible about myself. Today I will not try to do the impossible. I will remember that my only job is to get better myself.

I didn't cause it, I can't control it,
and I can't cure it

There is a power under your control that is greater
than poverty, greater than the lack of education,
greater than all your fears and superstitions combined.
It is the power to take possession of your own mind
and direct it to whatever ends you may desire.

—Andrew Carnegie

When Things Aren't Holding

This disease is traumatizing. It is shocking. It takes away my sense of normal. It makes people I love unpredictable and scary. It undermines my trust and faith in an orderly and predictable world and in my primary relationships and even in myself. Sometimes the earth beneath me can feel unsolid, shaky, and unreliable. And when I feel like this, I want to hold on tighter, to control, to fix and pin things down so I won't have to feel this way anymore. Today I will accept these feelings as natural, and I will breathe through them and give them space to move through me, knowing that there is a new kind of solidity growing daily within me. The power of presence is enough.

Past trauma need not rule my present and future

Change will not come if we wait for some other person
or some other time. We are the ones we've been waiting for.
We are the change that we seek.

—Barack Obama

Waking Up

I am carrying something inside of me that is undermining my happiness and stealing my joy. I am sick and tired of holding onto this pain no matter where it started or who it belongs to. It belongs to me now, lives inside of me, disturbs my peace of mind, and exacts a heavy price. And I am just as sick of my own self-recrimination, of holding something against myself, of hurting my own inner world because I can't let myself, or someone who is living in my head and heart, off the hook. I am blocked in some way that I don't fully understand; but today I'm willing to take a leap of faith into my inner world to look for some answers. I'm slowly coming to the conclusion that whatever grudge or resentment or wound I'm carrying is costing me more than I want to pay. I am waking up; seeing things differently, willing to take a deeper look.

I am willing to feel what I have been blocking

Self-trust, we know, is the first
secret of success.

—*Lady Wilde*

Strong At the Broken Places

I will develop strength from facing challenge. I will become resilient by solving problems and developing strategies for handling what is tough in my life. I will find and hold onto faith knowing that sometimes faith is all that I have. I will meet my life head on rather than run from it. I need to remember that emotions can run high when I am growing and changing inside, when I am challenging myself to stretch, but today I will see this as an opportunity to stretch my ability to tolerate inner turbulence without blowing up or cutting off. In a healing process, my joys are higher and my longings are stronger. The world is more intense than it usually is. When I forget this, I start to feel out of step if I'm not where I think I should be, I compare my insides with everybody else's outsides and use that to make myself wrong. I want to push away my inner world and I get a little afraid of what I'm experiencing if it doesn't fit my image of what I'm supposed to be feeling. Then I engage in a cover up. When I do that, I am only half there and when all is said and done, the only person I am covering up is me. Today I will let myself have my full range of feelings, knowing that they may, at times, be a bit of a roller coaster. But I know, that I will land comfortably at the end of the ride, and each time I land, I will be stronger and more resilient where I stretched.

I am willing to see more of me

The world breaks everyone and afterward many are strong at the broken places. But those that will not break it kills. It kills the very good and the very gentle and the very brave impartially.

— *Ernest Hemingway,* A Farewell to Arms

Emotional and Psychological Trauma

I have found living with addiction to be confusing, painful, and even traumatizing. Not knowing when the next crisis will erupt—wondering if this family event will actually happen, will blow up, will pass by as if no one had ever heard of it, or just be an empty ritual—has been painful, mortifying, and scary. Life feels so unpredictable when addiction has us all by the tail. I find myself living on the edge emotionally, going from zero to ten and ten to zero with no speed bumps in between. Too much stress, too much fear, pain, anger, or anxiety makes me want to shut down. I go from emotional and psychological overwhelm to numbness. It's my body's and mind's way of protecting me from either exploding or melting down. Today when I feel on the edge and flooded with more emotion than I can handle, I will pick up the phone, go to a meeting, or take a break. I will breathe. I will remember that I am on a path of recovery and I will use the tools of the program.

I rely on program tools, wisdom and camaraderie to get me through

Tears, sorrow, and disappointment are bitter,
but wisdom is the comforter in all psychic suffering.
Indeed, bitterness and wisdom form a pair of alternatives:
where there is bitterness wisdom is lacking, and
where wisdom is there can be no bitterness.

—C. G. Jung

Learning Emotional Sobriety

I will make the mood I am in my responsibility rather than everyone else's. When my emotions become unbalanced, my thinking and behavior tend to follow and become unbalanced, too. Current research says my emotions impact my thinking more than my thinking impacts my emotions, because the limbic system sends so many more inputs to my thinking mind than the reverse. This is why my mood is so critical to how I function and why I need to do what's necessary to maintain a positive, upbeat outlook. The food I put in my mouth, the amount of exercise I get, my rest, relaxation, and relationships all impact the way I feel. Today I can use the tools of the program to teach myself to become emotionally sober rather than emotionally drunk. I can create new emotional grooves, new emotional wiring. I will begin to ask myself questions like *How important is it?* or *How much will this matter five years from now?* before I let my emotions and my behavior run away with me.

I experience my emotions in my body

I think that many oldsters who have put
our AA "booze cure" to severe but successful tests
still find they often lack emotional sobriety. Perhaps they
will be the spearhead for the next major development in AA,
the development of much more real maturity and balance
(which is to say, humility) in our relations with ourselves,
with our fellows, and with God. . . .

—*Bill Wilson*

Resolving My Past

I have such a thing as an unconscious in which I store the dark memories that feel too overwhelming to really bring into the light of day. I hear a lot about letting them go, about not dragging them into the present, but how do I do that? These are memories that were seared into place in the sheer heat of some hidden moment, memories I have driven down inside of me. I've given them different names, rewritten them a thousand times so that they are so layered with explanation, rationalization, and revision that even I cannot retrieve them from that baggage claim inside of me. They are almost unrecognizable. But then, in the clarity of some instance, in hearing another person's story, in getting triggered by who knows what, there they are. Stark, elemental, wearing the same old clothes they wore then. Fully breathing and alive, seemingly having no idea that they have been banished. There they are, shaking and furious, as if they are happening all over again.

My mind/body holds memory

I became what I am today at the age of twelve,
on a frigid overcast day in the winter of 1975. I remember
the precise moment, crouching behind a crumbling mud wall,
peeking into the alley near the frozen creek. That was a long
time ago, but it's wrong what they say about the past, I've learned,
about how you can bury it. Because the past claws its way out.
Looking back now, I realize I have been peeking into that
deserted alley for the last twenty-six years."

—*Khaled Hosseini,* The Kite Runner

Being Wrong

I cannot grow if I cannot be wrong. I cannot change if I cannot tolerate recognizing the error of my previous ways, my own smallness, my own ignorance. Holding onto an opinion or behavior, even a feeling, is foolish if reexamining it would be of benefit to me. I only hurt myself and frustrate those I am close to when I am unnecessarily stubborn. If I cannot occasionally shake my head at the fool I have been, how can I move into a greater and a better understanding? I can laugh at myself, I can have compassion for myself, I can feel a healthy amount of guilt and regret and then forgive myself and let it flow downstream. I can allow myself to be full of human error and still love and accept myself.

Being wrong does not compromise who I am

"If what you seek is Truth, there is one thing
you must have above all else."
"I know. An overwhelming passion for it."
"No. An unremitting readiness to admit you may be wrong."

—*Anthony de Mello*

Being Slowly Born

Each day I am born a little more, I learn things about myself that I didn't know. Each day I am a little stronger—a little more able to tolerate the intensity of truth, of seeing what is, of the pain of full awareness. The more aware I am, the more born I am. My own history lives inside of me, sometimes in a dormant state. As I grow in inner strength, I grow in my ability to feel what is frozen, and bits and pieces of me come clear within the window of my inner sight. Each time a numb part of me is felt, a dead part of me comes alive and I am born a little. Each time I touch wordless pain and convert it to words, I grow in emotional literacy. Each time I use those words to reflect on myself and gain insight, I grow in emotional intelligence.

Knowing myself allows me to be more fully alive

A single event can awaken within us
a stranger totally unknown to us.
To live is to be slowly born.

—Antoine de Saint-Exupéry

Lighting My Own Lamp

I will light my own lamp today rather than wait for someone else to do it for me. I will be willing to find inspiration. I will search out whatever it is that fills my heart and ignites a fire within me. Maybe it's music, reading, walking in nature, cooking, working, or being with someone I love. Whatever it is, I will allow it to fill my soul, to give my life meaning and a sense of purpose. If I wait for inspiration to drop down on my head from the heavens, I might wait forever. When here it is, right here, in my own mind's capacity to see the beauty and meaning that surrounds me all the time.

Life is a mystery and I am part of that mystery

No one and nothing outside of you
can give you salvation, or free you from the misery.
You have to light your own lamp.
You have to know the miniature universe
that you yourself are.

—*Banani Ray,* Awakening Inner Guru

FEBRUARY

Smoke Signals

The only survivor of a shipwreck washed up on a small, uninhabited island. He prayed feverishly for God to rescue him. Every day he scanned the horizon for help, but none seemed forthcoming.

Exhausted, he eventually managed to build a little hut out of driftwood to protect him from the elements and to store his few possessions.

But then one day after scavenging for food, he arrived home to find his little hut in flames, the smoke rolling up to the sky. The worst had happened; everything was lost. He was stung with grief and anger. "God, how could you do this to me!" he cried.

Early the next day, however,
vas awakened by the sound of a ship
that was approaching the island.
It had come to rescue him.
ow did you know I was here?" asked the
weary man of his rescuers.

We saw your smoke signal," they replied.

—Islamic story

My Moment to Change

This is my moment to transform my life. As things fall apart, that very disequilibrium makes way for the transformation of my spirit. The old ground is not holding, but new ground isn't in clear sight. I am somewhere in uncharted emotional and psychological territory trying to find my way. I will be humble today and open myself to learning what life is trying to teach me. I will grow on the inside. I will embrace rather than push away the insight, wisdom, and understanding that arise out of turmoil. I will be open to change.

I am a student of life

How privileged we are to understand so well
the divine paradox that strength rises from weakness,
that humiliation goes before resurrection;
that pain is not only the price but the very touchstone
of spiritual rebirth. Knowing its full worth and purpose,
we can no longer fear adversity, we have found prosperity
where there was poverty, peace and joy have
sprung out of the very midst of chaos.
Great indeed, our blessings!

—Bill Wilson

Humility

My grandiosity covered up my shame. My arrogance hid my insecurity. My unwillingness to learn from others covered up my chronic mistrust and suspicion. As long as I kept myself from knowing how shaky I felt inside by medicating, rather than feeling my insecure, anxious, or depressed feelings, I could remain in my head. I was the smartest dummy around. I had an answer for everything and a myriad of excuses and explanations that allowed me to keep a distance from what was really going on. I lived in my head because living in my heart hurt too much. Today I feel the freedom, strength and empowerment of humility. Without humility, I cannot learn. Without humility, I will not be able to open my eyes and heart to truly respect what life is saying to me, teaching me or giving to me.

I only have to be me

When I was young, I said to God, "God,
tell me the mystery of the universe."
But God answered, "That knowledge is for
me alone." So I said, "God, tell me the
mystery of the peanut." Then God said,
"Well, George, that's more nearly your size."

—George Washington Carver

Taking Care of What's Within My Reach

Today I realize that I have no right to complain about others being out of step if I, myself, am out of step. The best way that I can contribute to the world is by setting myself, my relationships, and my life right. I will not see myself as having a raw deal so that I can justify wallowing in self pity; instead I will have compassion for the part of me that is wounded and gently help and love it into a better place. I will not complain about what is going wrong without taking note of what is going right. Each day I will reach my arm out and resolve to be good to that corner of the world, my corner. I will not whine about the world today; I am part of the world. If each and every person cleaned up their own corner of the world, the world would transform.

I will set my corner of the world right

To put the world right in order, we must first
put the nation in order; to put the nation in order,
we must first put the family in order;
to put the family in order,
we must first cultivate our personal life;
we must first set our hearts right.

—*Confucius*

Ours Is a Disease of Attitudes

Today I will make the attitudes that I take toward life and relationships MY responsibility. If I don't change from within, change won't happen in my life. No one can get into my head and do my thinking for me; no one can get into my heart and do my feeling for me; no one can crawl into my skin and behave for me. The attitudes I carry around in my mind affect my life. The stinkin' thinkin' of the disease can make me look at life through a dark and distorted lens. My negative thinking about people, places, and things becomes a self-fulfilling prophecy. So does my positive thinking. How can I expect to change my life if I don't change my attitudes?

I will take a positive attitude toward my life

The basic thing is that everyone wants happiness,
no one wants suffering. And happiness mainly comes from
our own attitude, rather than from external factors.
If your own mental attitude is correct,
even if you remain in a hostile atmosphere,
you feel happy.

—H.H. the Dalai Lama

Detaching with Love to Free Myself

Today the reason that I detach with love is in order to free myself. Detaching with anger doesn't work: I remain preoccupied and live with a low level of distress. Detaching with the idea that eventually I'll be able to come back and fix, control, or change what I don't like isn't really letting go. But releasing, letting go, allowing something to truly take its rightful place in the scheme of things with or without me, allows me to be in my rightful place. When I live my life trying to fix, control, or manipulate events, people, and circumstances so that I can finally relax, I enter into an endless control battle. In life there will always be something to worry about, fodder for anxiety and struggle. How I handle this, whether I choose to enlarge worries and become consumed with them, or keep them in a healthy perspective, is my choice. Today I let go, so that I can spend more time being and less time obsessing and controlling. I let go and let God.

To fix is human, to let go divine

An appeaser is one who feeds a crocodile—
hoping it will eat him last.

—Sir Winston Churchill

FEBRUARY 6

Surrendering Isn't Giving Up

Today I surrender—I surrender my unrequited hopes and dreams into the care of my Higher Power, trusting that a power greater than me will restore them to sanity. I surrender my regrets from the past so that I can stop obsessing about what I might have done differently, and so that they don't leak into and contaminate my future. I will not let disappointment turn into despair. I will stop fighting life, trying to get it to fit into a narrow path that I imagine is the only path. I will instead surrender and trust that my life will unfold in good ways if I put the best that I have into it. I will love the life I have and value what is in it. I will surrender what I can do nothing about and focus on what I can change. Surrendering is not the same thing as giving up. Giving up grows out of a sense of helplessness, a feeling that nothing I can do will make a difference. Surrendering is a spiritual position of love and trust.

I surrender, I let go, I allow

All growth is a leap in the dark,
a spontaneous unpremeditated act without
benefit of experience.

—Henry Miller

Living in the Present

Today is the day that I will focus on. When I live in the future, I can get anxious and overwhelmed with fears of future failures. When I live in the past, I can become dogged by regret, resentment, or sadness. But somehow, when I stay in the present moment it all feels sort of okay. I am touched by the simple world that surrounds me; I am filled by a spiritual presence that is a part of the moment. When I stay right here and now, I feel held by an invisible force. It feels like enough just to get my cup of tea, look out the window, sit in nature, go grocery shopping, or go to a meeting. I can act responsibly today and have faith that today's sincere and responsible thoughts and actions are my best way of building a better tomorrow. I cannot live in tomorrow, or in yesterday, without losing today. And when I lose today, I lose the only soil on which I have to build my future.

My future grows out of my today

I just try to concentrate on concentrating.

—Martina Navratilova

My Limbic System and Emotional Sobriety

My emotions are processed by my limbic system, which governs and regulates mood, appetite, sleep cycles, libido, and motivation. Sadly, emotional stress and psychological trauma can dysregulate my limbic system and this dysregulation can actually undermine or even compromise my ability to manage my moods, my eating, sleep, sexual urges, and sense of motivation. I might get anxious, depressed, enervated, or moody and not find my way easily back to a comfort zone. It can also lead to using dysfunctional "mood managers" to achieve a false sense of balance or a "quick fix" to feel good. In recovery I learn balance. I learn to use natural mood regulators like exercise, journaling, rest, meditation, and sharing with others to achieve limbic balance rather than rely on dysfunctional mood medicators like drugs and alcohol or food and sex.

I will learn to naturally regulate my limbic system

Addiction, self medication and acting out
behaviors can be seen as a lack of ability to self regulate
and can stem from limbic dysregulation.

—*Tian Dayton, Ph.D.,* Emotional Sobriety

Smart Feet

Today I will have smart feet. I will know where meetings are and go to them, understanding that being in the presence of other people who are feeling their feelings is healing to my limbic system and strengthening to my own emotional wiring. It helps me to tolerate the power and intensity of my own emotions without acting out or self-medicating; then I can talk out rather than act out my emotions. Being in the presence of others who are in a balanced emotional state helps me to balance my emotional state, too. All mammals are wired to silently synchronize with each other. I am a mammal too, just like a horse, puppy, or cat—and my limbic system is soothed, calmed and brought naturally into balance when I am in the presence of others who are in a balanced state, whether those others are my dog or people. Meetings help me to attain limbic balance; I leave feeling more integrated, whole and refreshed.

I will get my soles in the room

For many, negative thinking is a habit,
which over time, becomes an addiction.
A lot of people suffer from this disease because
negative thinking is addictive to each of the Big Three—
the mind, the body, and the emotions.
If one doesn't get you, the others
are waiting in the wings.

—Peter McWilliams

Little Dreams

Today I will do some small thing to make my day more beautiful and positive. I only need to do a little better. I don't need to reach for the moon or become the perfect anything. Achieving little things will enhance my sense of self and move me a bit forward. Even cooking something wonderful, cleaning the house or ordering a closet or garage gives me a wonderful sense of accomplishment. Little good acts add up. They give me something positive to imagine. Little accomplishments are manageable, they don't overwhelm me and make me feel like I am constantly failing or running in place. They let me feel like I've achieved something real and purposeful. They give my day a positive focus. I will do a little deed or dream a little dream today. I will do something positive that gets me closer to a goal or makes a contribution to my day, to my world. Rather than complain about what isn't here that I want, I will take baby steps to create something that is. Dreams enliven my heart and stimulate my mind. Even my body feels uplifted by my positive thoughts. My energy and enthusiasm can help me move through blocks, and my commitment can show me that love and effort can be their own reward.

I love my little dreams

Please, do not visualize that we exist
above you such as in heaven. The concepts above
and below are products of your mind. The soul
does not swing upwards. It exists in the center
and orients itself in every direction.

—Hans Bender

Staying on the Path

My disease is not special. It looks a lot like everybody else's. What matters today is staying on my path. Life is going to feel intense for a while. That's okay. I have my supports and I will work them. I can go to a meeting, make a call, or do some uplifting reading. I am learning not to be unique. I'm learning to be a worker among workers. I will not discourage myself through wanting to be perfect all at once; I will be happy with small gains knowing that they are not small at all. I will take baby steps in the right direction. This way, I will move along at a manageable pace and absorb recovery slowly and well. When I want it all to happen today, I cheat myself out of my own growth and discovery. I frustrate myself and then I want to act out or pick up because I can't stand the feelings of despair that I am actually creating with my unrealistic and grandiose expectations.

I look for progress not perfection

I believe that unarmed truth and unconditional
love will have the final word in reality.
That is why right, temporarily defeated,
is stronger than evil triumphant.

—Martin Luther King Jr.

Allowing My Life to Evolve Naturally

I will allow my life to work out. My days of trying to push and shove people, places, and things into a shape that I imagine is right or good, are giving way to an increasing ability to let things happen. I will take an action and let go of the results knowing that my actions will bear fruit in God's time. My job is to take the appropriate and responsible actions to keep my life moving in a positive direction. The rest is up to my Higher Power. My job is to show up, to do the best I can one day at a time, and trust that unseen hands will guide me and help me along the way. My job is to keep my side of the street clean and let go of what isn't my business. Today, I am present in the now, understanding that in the now, the future and past are alive as well.

I am sick and tired of being sick and tired

According to Darwin's *Origin of Species,* it is not the most intellectual of the species that survives; it is not the strongest that survives; but the species that survives is the one that is able best to adapt and adjust to the changing environment in which it finds itself.

—Leon C. Megginson

Having Fun

Today, I will have fun. Living with addiction made me afraid of fun, I worried that it would give way to chaos. This fear made me mistrust the kind of letting go that having fun requires—it made me less spontaneous because I was holding onto my insides so tightly. But what's the point of all the work I do in recovery if my life doesn't become lighter and happier? Even though I am working through deep issues, there is no reason why I can't have fun and feel the delicious lightheartedness that comes with letting go of inner tension, old pain, and fear. Fun is when I relax and let things happen—when I can laugh at myself and other people—when I don't take everything in life so seriously. Fun is when it doesn't have to be all my way—when I can go with the flow, when I am idling at a normal rate, and I can be in the moment. Today I see that there is no good reason not to enjoy myself.

I can let go and have fun

On with the dance, let joy be unconfined is my motto, whether there's any dance to dance or any joy to unconfine.

—*Mark Twain*

FEBRUARY 14

The Intelligence of My Heart

I am what I think and feel all day. When I am calm, everything looks different, my thinking is less jagged, and my behavior more balanced. I can actually meet the little challenges of my day without exploding, imploding, or withdrawing. I have the emotional balance to be able to think through my feelings rather than leap into mindless action or medicate them. This way of living and relating leads to insight and connection rather than disconnection; it builds emotional muscle. I can actually hold more pain and more joy. I send calming messages throughout my body that influence how I think and act. My mind, in this way, becomes my servant rather than my master. What goes on in my heart affects my entire body. My heart's electromagnetic field far outpowers and outranges that of my brain or any other body system. Calming my heart calms my circulatory, nervous, and respiratory systems, and my digestive and excretory tracts. If I am calm in my mind and emotions, my overall level of physical functioning is enhanced and improved. If I'm frequently or chronically stressed or upset, my overall level of physical functioning is compromised. Today I see that just by calming my heart, I am taking care of my body.

I will breathe into my heart and imagine it calming

When you hear the word intelligence the first thing you probably think of isn't the heart. But research has shown that the heart is in fact smart. The brain in the head is dutifully obeying messages that are being sent from another brain, "the brain in the heart." The heart isn't just a throbbing mass of muscle, it's actually quite a sensitive instrument that is processing critical information, constantly communicating with the brain.

—*Kim Allen*, Heartmath

Threads

The Hopi Indians believed that every great religion contained one spiritual thread and that these threads are always seeking to connect themselves with each other. They felt that when these threads finally wove themselves together we would be pulled out of our darkness into a new spiritual light. I experience these threads in the rooms and once I see them there, I see them in many other places as well, all around the world, in fact. In the rooms we respect each person's path. Together we experience the presence of God through community, through surrender, through working the steps. We're on a path, not to perfection, but towards personal growth. We are there to occupy our chair as fully as we can, to grow in the presence of others, to listen, to share who we really are, not who we wish we were or think we should be. As these threads weave together, we are pulled out of darkness and toward the light.

I am part of the weaving of threads

Anything that's human is mentionable,
and anything that is mentionable can be more manageable.
When we can talk about our feelings, they become less
overwhelming, less upsetting, and less scary.
The people we trust with that important talk can
help us know that we are not alone.

—Fred Rogers

HALT

I will live a lifestyle, not a deathstyle. My recovery is my responsibility; if I don't take care of it no one else will, no one else can. If I feel myself slipping into negative thinking, lethargy, overtiredness, dark forecasting, or self pity, I will ask myself the questions that are important for me to answer. Am I too:

Hungry • Angry • Lonely • Tired

If the answer is "yes" to any of these, I will take care of business: I'll sit down and have a healthy meal, go to a meeting, pick up the phone, or take a rest. I will daily learn to ask myself if I have gotten enough exercise and rest. I will eat nutritious foods that give me the energy I need for my recovery and stay away from those foods that cause my blood sugar to spike then fall, leaving me depleted. I will seek out companionship and connection. I will make sure that I have kept time in my day for reflection and meditation.

I stay on the path through an exquisite blending of discipline and surrender

Each of us needs periods in which our minds can focus inwardly. Solitude is an essential experience for the mind to organize its own processes and create an internal state of resonance. In such a state, the self is able to alter its constraints by directly reducing the input from interactions with others.

—*Daniel J. Siegel,* The Developing Mind: How Relationships and the Brain Interact to Shape Who We Are

Past Anger and Resentment

I need to find a way to experience my old anger and resentment without living in it. When I live in it, I ruin my own day. When I deny it, I create a dark spot on my emotional lungs that keeps me from being able to breathe deeply and fully; I pretend that I don't have the anger that I have, and I miss the insights that my anger might offer into what hurts and upsets me. When I get lost or stuck in anger and resentment, I spend all my time justifying why I have a right to be angry. Or I project and disown it, making my painful or negative feelings about someone or something outside of me. Today, I will allow myself to feel my own anger and see what it has to tell me before I dump it, act it out, make it about someone or something else, or medicate it. I will sit with it and let it sit with me. I will witness my feelings without trying to control them.

I am capable of processing my anger

The conflict between the will to deny horrible events
and the will to proclaim them aloud is the central
dialectic of psychological trauma."

—*Judith Lewis Herman,* Trauma and Recovery

Out of My Pores, Please

I do not want this disease in my life anymore. I am willing to become conscious of its darkness in my psyche. For as long as I remember, this illness of addiction has surrounded me. It is everywhere in my family. The distorted and stinkin' thinkin', the grandiosity, the living on the edge, the inability to face reality, and the unwillingness to be humbled by our own powerlessness over the disease, tear at my heart and sicken my stomach. I see its poison enveloping generation after generation. I am disgusted, horrified, and deeply saddened by witnessing the wreckage of this illness.

The power of the disease is awesome

We carry our past with us . . . the primitive and inferior man with his desires and emotions, and it is only with an enormous effort that we can detach ourselves from this burden. If it comes to a neurosis, we invariably have to deal with a considerably intensified Shadow. And if such a person wants to be cured it is necessary to find a way in which his conscious personality and his Shadow can live together.

—*Carl Jung*

Projecting the Shadow

Today I will be mindful of my urge to project the feelings I do not wish to sit with onto someone else. When I make my negative feelings known about someone or something else, just because I can't allow them to be inside of me, I create relationship chaos for one thing, and for another, I don't heal my own pain. When I disown what I don't like about me and slather it all over another person, I disown a part of my healing as well.

I can live though and articulate my inner angst

We must be exceedingly careful not to project our own Shadows too shamelessly; we are still swamped with projected illusions. If you imagine someone who is brave enough to withdraw all his projections, then you get an individual who is conscious of a pretty thick Shadow. Such a man has saddled himself with new problems and conflicts. He has become a serious problem to himself, as he is now unable to say that *they* do this or that, *they* are wrong, and *they* must be fought against. He lives in the "House of the Gathering." Such a man knows that whatever is wrong in the world is in himself, and if he only learns to deal with his own Shadow he has done something real for the world.

—*Carl Jung*

Denial

Denying this disease does not make it go away. This disease wraps its tentacles around generation after generation. It slips seamlessly into the thinking, feeling, and behavior of all those around it, whether they use or not. I have watched each generation pretend that it wasn't all that bad, that it didn't do all that much damage; many felt that they didn't really need help. But they did. I have seen families not drink or drug, and imagine that this meant they had escaped the collateral damage of addiction. They couldn't see that many of their emotional and relational issues were related to this disease. This disease takes many forms because addiction can be traumatizing to all concerned, and trauma can create emotional and psychological complications that do not necessarily get better by themselves. Trauma can also create strength and resilience. Today, I recognize that dealing with damage does not mean that I am damaged goods, only that I want to know all of who I am. It is a sign of health to want more health.

I can get help

If Freud turns to literature to describe traumatic experience, it is because literature, like psychoanalysis, is interested in the complex relation between knowing and not knowing, and it is at this specific point at which knowing and not knowing intersect that the psychoanalytic theory of traumatic experience and the language of literature meet.

—*Cathy Caruth,*
Unclaimed Experience: Trauma, Narrative and History

Enmeshment

Today I recognize that enmeshment isn't closeness. Enmeshment is borne out of fear of separation, not desire to be intimate. It is a sort of hypervigilance, an over-closeness that comes from insecurity and a sense of self that isn't fully comfortable, or even fully developed. Intimacy requires that I allow you to be you and me to be me. It means that I am willing to learn how to hang onto a sense of self in another person's presence, and allow them to do the same. Intimacy isn't caving into someone else because I can't stand on my own. I can lean on another person, but I cannot hang on them without both of us falling down. I will do the work I need to do today, to be able to stand on my own and to be willing to allow someone I love to do the same. I can be separate and still be very much connected.

I want to feel good inside

As Louis Cozolino, PhD, observes, a consistent theme of adult psychotherapy clients is that they had parents who were not curious about who they were but, instead, told them who they should be. What happens, Cozolino explains, is that the child creates a "persona" for her parents but doesn't learn to know herself. What happens is that "the authentic self"—the part of us open to feelings, experiences, and intimacy—"remains undeveloped."

—*Peg Streep,*
Mean Mothers: Overcoming the Legacy of Hurt

FEBRUARY 22

Living in a World Beyond Me

Today I am stepping into the world on my own. Sometimes I feel like an orphan unmoored and alone. Sometimes I feel part of everything that is or ever was, part of something divine; not loose at all but firmly tethered to a world beyond myself. Deep love has allowed me to be with a piece of divinity, to touch the face of God. To peer across the common bounds of life into something eternal, something powerful, something deep and still and alive. Each step I take carries a strange new awareness of the temporary nature of life. In a way, I have no idea who I am or where I am going. In another way, I am more inwardly secure than ever. I feel strangely alive and in touch. I have looked at death and I see that it is not the final chapter. I now see life in death.

I am in touch with a deeper sense of life

We are not human beings having a spiritual experience;
We are spiritual beings having a human experience.

—Pierre Teilhard de Chardin

I Am Seen

I am seen for my magic. My gifts are recognized, acknowledged, and understood. I add value to my world; what I have learned has been hard won, and I have used it in the best way possible, to light the path for others. I am loved for who I am. What I give to the world is valued and held out in a space where healing happens. Who I am, what I have been through, and my unique vision of life inform what I do. My playful nature is mine to keep forever. It shimmers and sheds joy. I give pleasure to others just by being who I am. I have something of value to give the world. I am me, I am seen, I am alive.

I have a place held safe, secure, and beautiful on this earth

May the road rise to meet you,
May the wind be always at your back.
May the sun shine warm upon your face, the
rains fall soft upon your fields. And until we meet again,
May God hold you in the palm of his hand.
May God be with you and bless you:
May you see your children's children.
May you be poor in misfortune, rich in blessings.
May you know nothing but happiness from this day forward.
May the warm rays of sun fall upon your home.
And may the hand of a friend always be near.
May green be the grass you walk on,
May blue be the skies above you,
May pure be the joys that surround you,
May true be the hearts that love you.

—Traditional Irish Blessing

Low Self-Esteem

Today I will make friends with the part of me that has some low self-esteem. What's the big deal anyway? Everyone has a pocket of low self-esteem; in a way, it's a great point through which to connect with others. Trying to hide this pocket of me from others is silly—it leaks in odd ways and makes it seem like I have more of it than I actually have. Trying to hide it from myself keeps me from being creative. I need this uncertain, insecure edge to keep me honest and growing. Trying to eradicate it because I judge it as a bad thing to have, is dumb and short sighted. There's really nothing wrong with it; in fact it gives me a cozy, accessible, and unthreatening side. Low self-esteem is nothing to be afraid of and nothing that needs stamping out. I need to befriend this part of me, give it space, a voice now and then, and a soft pillow to rest its head on. Allowing this part of me to come out of hiding makes it less of a burden, gives it less power to disturb me, and shrinks its proportions in a natural way. I have the wisdom to know that I need all of me to feel fully alive, including my pocket of low self-esteem.

I embrace and include a pocket of low self esteem along with the rest of me

Manifest plainness, embrace simplicity,
reduce selfishness, have few desires.

—Lao Tzu

Serenity

There is nothing in my day that is more important than my serenity. Today, I will pay attention to the myriad of ways in which I am thrown off balance. When I feel myself losing my serenity, I'll take a moment to center myself, to breathe, to connect with that part of me that is eternal and unchanging. I will breathe. I will sit. There is peace within me that I can draw on each and every day. I will inhale and allow it to expand within me, and as I go about my day I will carry that lovely feeling of inner peace around inside. I'll remind myself that when I can calm my body, mind, and spirit, I interact differently with the people, places, and things of my day. I am here. My spirit is here. My serenity is at my fingertips. I am in charge of my deeper experience of living. I connect with my divine self and the divine energy that is ever present. I give myself the gift of inner peace.

I appreciate life

We who lived in concentration camps can remember
the men who walked through the huts comforting others,
giving away their last piece of bread. They may have
been few in number, but they offer sufficient proof that
everything can be taken from a man but one thing:
the last of the human freedoms—to choose one's
attitude in any given set of circumstances,
to choose one's own way.

—Viktor Frankl

Stepping into the Unknown

Today I step out into the open and trust that a bridge to the next thing, another stepping stone, my next step, will form beneath my feet. Every step I take is a step of faith. My faith is a blind faith—faith in what I cannot see, faith in something guiding my life, my steps, my being. I am held and sustained by a force that I am coming to understand more each day, a force that I can tap into, breathe into, lean into. I am held in a quivering stillness, rocked like a baby, cooed to by heavenly sounds, loved and touched by unseen hands. Something greater than me is breathing life into me.

I am surrounding myself with healing light. I am inviting a warm, yellow-white light to surround me. I breathe it in deeply into all parts of me and I breathe out any lingering fear or darkness. Healing energy is quietly pulsing in and around me, imbuing me with a feeling of well being. I allow this energy to fill each pore of my body. This healing energy has its own intelligence and I become one with it and direct it towards those parts of me that need healing. I rest in this vibrating yellow-white light and let it fill me, surround me and make me well. Even the act of allowing this lifts me up.

I breathe in, I lean in, I am here

Lean into me I will raise you up
Gather your faith and we'll walk on water
Hold out your hand when you can't go on
Let go and lean into me.

—Stefan Mitchell

Standing in Awe

I am the witness. I stand in awe. Today I understand that I am not God, I am not the master of the infinite, vast, and interwoven universe. I do not need to hang the moon, God will do that. It is not my job to make sure the sun comes up each morning. God will do that. I do not have to worry about dragging the tide in and back out to sea again. I can let go of a concern that it's my job to grow leaves on trees or flowers in the fields. God, or the unbelievable and incomprehensible natural world will see to all of this. Today my only job is to observe, to watch, to stand in awe at the mysteries of life, the wonders of the world. I am a wonder of the world, too. My heart beats by itself; I breathe in and out without even knowing how it happens. I have a body that carries me through life. When I can simply appreciate and admire the workings of the world, the mystery and majesty of being alive, that is enough.

I am part of a universal web of life and dynamic wisdom

When people say I am wise, or a sage,
I cannot accept it. A man once dipped a hatful of
water from a stream. What did that amount to?
I am not that stream. I am at the stream, but I do nothing.
Other people are at the same stream, but most of them
find they have to do something with it. I do nothing.
I never think that I am the one who must see to it that
cherries grow on stalks. I stand and behold,
admiring what nature can do.

—Carl Jung

Feeling Used and Manipulated

When I feel mistreated by anyone in my life I will remember to pull my heart back, breathe, and get some psychic space around me. If someone is intentionally playing games with my head, if they are playing payback or retaliation, or using distance and closeness, or acceptance and rejection in a mean or manipulative way, I will caution myself not to engage in the game. Even if my end of the game is only to be driven a little nuts by it, be excessively hurt by it, or want to play back at it to whatever degree, I will do something different. If I am feeling guilty and agitated because I am not doing the same old thing, because a new behavior is anxiety making, I will remind myself that same old thing just gets me the same old result. I will stay with a new behavior for one more day.

I will try something different, just to try something different

The healthy man does not torture others—
generally it is the tortured who
turn into torturers.

—Carl Jung

Witnessing My Own Reactions

When I am disappointed by another's actions, when I want to react just to get out of feeling the way I am feeling, I will try something different. I will observe. I will watch my urge to react; instead I will trace it back, allow awareness, fragments of memory, and feelings to emerge in my mind, and I will witness as they float past my inner eye. I will watch my emotions, even when I feel like I am experiencing a sort of emotional quicksand. I will breathe through it, stay with it, and witness what it offers up to me about my unconscious. I will never see myself, if I only act out my difficult feelings. I need to feel them, move through them, see them; and then, rise once again to the surface of my mind more whole and integrated for having explored my inner depths.

I witness what I am feeling on the inside

Be present as the watcher of your mind—
of your thoughts and emotions as well as your reactions
in various situations. Be at least as interested in your
reactions as in the situation or person that causes you to react.
Notice also how often your attention is in the past or future.
Don't judge or analyze what you observe. Watch the thought,
feel the emotion, observe the reaction. Don't make a
personal problem out of them. You will then feel something
more powerful than any of those things that you observe:
the still, observing presence itself behind the
content of your mind, the silent watcher.

—*Eckhart Tolle,* The Power of Now

MARCH

On Pain

And a woman spoke, saying, "Tell us of Pain."

And he said:

Your pain is the breaking of the shell that
encloses your understanding.

Even as the stone of the fruit must break,
that its heart may stand in the sun,
so must you know pain.

And could you keep your heart in wonder at
the daily miracles of your life, your pain would
not seem less wondrous than your joy;

And you would accept the seasons of your heart,
even as you have always accepted the
seasons that pass over your fields.

And you would watch with serenity through
the winters of your grief.

Much of your pain is self-chosen.

It is the bitter potion by which the physician
within you heals your sick self.

Therefore trust the physician, and drink his
remedy in silence and tranquillity:

For his hand, though heavy and hard, is guided
by the tender hand of the Unseen,

And the cup he brings, though it burn your lips,
has been fashioned of the clay which the Potter
has moistened with His own sacred tears.

—*Kahlil Gibran,* **The Prophet**

Necessary Losses

I need to honestly confront what I am carrying inside of me in order to grieve it. If there is a deadness within, I need to locate it, feel it, hold and grieve it. If I leave all of my wounds nebulous and unconscious, how will I translate them into words so that they can be thought about, understood, reframed, and reintegrated in a new light? There are many life losses that I go through because of this disease, which need grieving. There is the loss of time spent mired in disease rather than filled with health and happiness. There is the loss of self-respect, dignity, and inner contentment that the disease of addiction engenders. There may be the loss of my substance, of my dysfunctional or acting out behaviors. The more I learn and grow; the greater the distance between myself and those still mired in the disease may become. I may lose certain people, places, and things, or parts of them, as I move along my path of recovery. I may need to grieve the family that fell apart, the parts of myself that didn't get a chance to develop, or the family members I love but cannot be as close with as I may wish. All of these losses are real and need to be grieved so that I can move through them, learn, grow, and embrace the life that is now becoming more real and more my own each day.

I see that grief gives me back pieces of myself

It's hard enough to grieve, but when you don't know the truth, everything freezes and you can't move on. . . .

—*David Hare,* Page Eight

Mistrust

I can mistrust others; I expect the worst. If something about a person reflects qualities of someone who hurt me in childhood, whatever that person is doing today gets confused with all of my old hurt and pain, and I can get triggered. I can't see them as a separate person with their own qualities. I layer the shadow of the person who hurt me onto them, and I feel all of the feelings that are active, or even frozen, inside of me. I transfer old pain onto a new relationship. Once this energy gets going inside of me, working anything out is fairly hopeless. I just see that other person in a dark light, whatever I am feeling towards them is magnified by unresolved, even unfelt pain and resentment from another time in my life. My judgment gets cloudy and I get lost in a negative spin that I have trouble coming out of. Old ghosts dance through the relationship almost as if they were part of it. Yesterday and today get completely mixed up. Today I will step back when I am lost in transference, and see if I am projecting unfelt pain from yesterday onto a relationship today.

I can separate the past from the present

But the memories that hang heaviest are the
easiest to recall. They hold in their creases the ability
to change one's life, organically, forever. Even when
you shake them out, they've left permanent
wrinkles in the fabric of your soul.

—*Julie Gregory,* Sickened: The Memoir of a Munchausen by Proxy Childhood

A Deeper Experience of Being Alive

Today I am open. The morning and I meet and greet each other like old friends. I am alive and in this world for another day by the grace of God. I am in charge of my body, mind, and soul, and it feels right and good. I belong to this world and this world belongs to me; I am meant to be here. I understand that a spiritual awakening, one that is quickened by the challenges life has dealt me, is my path to healing. My life looks different. I am learning to allow it to unfold a day at a time. I am becoming aware of the deeper experience of being alive. I am learning to let life work out rather than forcing it into place. I am living simply and enjoying simple pleasures. I am awake and alive for one more day.

I am grateful

Responsibility does not only lie with the leaders of our countries or with those who have been appointed or elected to do a particular job. It lies with each of us individually. Peace, for example, starts within each one of us. When we have inner peace, we can be at peace with those around us.

—H.H. the Dalai Lama

Becoming Real

All I need to be today, is who I am. My job is to actualize the gifts that are in me. I am better off discovering and mining my own unique talents and working to bring them forward, than trying to imitate someone else's talents. I will live each day as it comes. I will allow my authentic self to emerge into the moment and manage my responses to life in an emotionally sober and conscious way. Recovery is a process of facing and removing those obstacles that are in the way of my becoming more of me. It has been my willingness to risk and trust that my Higher Power will hold me, which has brought me to life again, and has turned the long and lonesome road back to myself into a spiritual challenge and adventure. I recognize today that I am more alive when I stop trying to be whatever it is that I think I should be in order to be okay, and I allow myself to refine and attend to who I am.

I am open to life and all it holds.

How many cares one loses when one decides not
to be something but to be someone.

—*Coco Chanel*

Sticking With It

I am allowing myself to take a clear direction today, one that will enable me to build a foundation and a structure, within which I can live a clean and wholesome life. Commitment to a path is really commitment to myself. When I procrastinate, put things off, and hesitate to do what I know I need to, I slide sideways. I get foggy, motionless, and even depressed. Half-commitments produce half-results. Today I will walk the walk, not just talk the talk. It will not be good for me to half-commit myself; to work my recovery with one hand tied behind my back, to get to a meeting or incorporate the principles of the program into my life only when I feel I have an extra moment. I will give recovery my all, I will give it my best shot. Today I will recognize that one small, good action leads to another. I will get up out of my chair and do something that is positive, trusting that it will lead me in a Good Orderly Direction. I will choose a path.

I put first things first

Somebody should tell us, right at the start
of our lives, that we are dying. Then we might live
life to the limit, every minute of every day.
Do it! I say. Whatever you want to do, do it now!
There are only so many tomorrows."

—Pope Paul VI

The Gift of Illness

I see today that illness of all kinds can be my path towards inner expansion. When I am shocked by circumstances that feel out of control, a door opens within me. That door can plunge me into darkness or be a shaft of light. Or both. When I am thrown into a place where nothing makes sense, I look for a new order to give my life meaning. In that new order, I can change spiritually. I can grow. If I am forced by circumstances to rethink my life, I can experience my life differently. When my life feels reduced, I can see life itself more starkly. What is of value shines more brightly and what is superfluous appears suddenly less important. Today I value just being alive and on a spiritual journey for one more day. What I do with it, what I see in the time I have been given, is up to me.

I look for the lessons

Most people have come to prefer certain of life's experiences and deny and reject others, unaware of the value of the hidden things that may come wrapped in plain and even ugly paper. In avoiding all pain and seeking comfort at all costs, we may be left without intimacy or compassion; in rejecting change and risk we often cheat ourselves of the quest; in denying our suffering we may never know our strength or our greatness.

—Rachel Naomi Remen, MD

We're as Sick as Our Secrets

What I hide, hides me. When I'm more invested in keeping something hidden than in unearthing and exploring it, I need to wonder why I am doing that. Is it shame at what others will think that keeps me silent? Is it that I cannot imagine being forgiven or that I cannot forgive myself, for someone I was or something I did? Is it loyalty to a family system that believed that family business always belonged behind closed doors? Whatever it is, I need to take a good look at it today and see if keeping something hidden and secret is affecting my recovery. I need to get honest with myself and feel the feelings I don't want to feel when I think of coming out of hiding. The energy it takes me to keep something hidden is energy that is not freed up for my recovery. I need to process what I am hiding so it has less of a hold on me. I need to release it for my sake and for the sake of those I love, who sense what is hidden in the unspoken, emotional atmosphere, but feel crazy because I don't fess up and own what I am carrying and leaking all over the relational atmosphere.

I am responsible for what I am hiding and I am willing to look

We dance round in a ring and suppose,
But the secret sits in the middle and knows.

—Robert Frost

Dark Narcissism

Constant self-deprecation is not necessarily humility. Feeling less than, undeserving of attention, or bad about myself is not humility. In fact, being stuck in negative self-concepts can be a sort of dark narcissism: it puts me at the center of the universe and allows me to be endlessly self-preoccupied. Making myself smaller than everyone else is not humble. God means me to be a beloved creature of the universe. To take my place in the scheme of things, to be part of the mystery of life and enjoy all that the world has to offer, including myself. God made me along with everyone else, I am no better or worse than anyone. Excessive preoccupation with how small I am compared to others is just the reverse of excessive preoccupation with being bigger than others. Neither are right-sized.

I am ready to participate in life

There is, in every event, whether lived or told, always a hole or a gap, often more than one. If we allow ourselves to get caught in it, we find it opening onto a void that, once we have slipped into it, we can never escape.

—*Brian Evenson,* Fugue State

Courage

I cannot possibly meet the challenges of my life without courage. Today I understand that courage is something I develop. Each time I go through an experience that stretches me, each time I hold my own feet to the fire, each time I discipline myself and hold myself to a slightly higher standard than before, I grow inside, I get a little bit stronger, I strengthen my own courage and resolve to meet the next challenge. I see life as it is today. I do not ask that the world conform to my idea of perfection in order to love it. Today I will not ask life to be something I am not willing to be. I won't ask the world to shower blessings onto me that I am not willing to deserve by my own right action. I see beauty and perfection in things as they are, not as I wish them to be. I forgive life for being imperfect, I forgive people for being imperfect, I forgive myself for being imperfect.

I can live life on life's terms

Once the soul awakens, the search begins and you can never go back. From then on, you are inflamed with a special longing that will never again let you linger in the lowlands of complacency and partial fulfillment. The eternal makes you urgent. You are loath to let compromise or the threat of danger hold you back from striving toward the summit of fulfillment.

—*John O'Donohue,* Anam Cara: A Book of Celtic Wisdom

Secondary Gains

Victimhood can have hidden agendas. It can allow me to be insensitive to others as I "meet my needs" in recovery or allow me to feel justified in being selfish with my time and resources. It can keep me from growing up and taking responsibility for my own life. Nursing a grudge can be very seductive and feel secretly gratifying. It can give me a dysfunctional kind of entitlement that is just as powerful as any other form of entitlement—or let me to curl up in a corner and not try when the going gets tough. The moment I slip into using victim thinking to justify my own selfishness or hold others hostage to my "low self-esteem or hurt self," I am misusing it. This kind of victim thinking will only keep me stuck, and others along with me. I may have been a victim at many points in my life, but just for today I recognize that victim thinking is healthy only if it allows me to recognize and honor my own hurt, anger, or pain so that I can feel it and move through it, and thereby learn to be gentle with myself.

I loosen my attachment to my own victim thinking

How resilient was the body, to return to its prior form so quickly! Yet the mind was formed of a less pliable substance. The emptiness in her thoughts would not be so easily filled. Instead there was a hollowness among them—a place she had reserved for future joys which now would never arrive."

—*Galen Beckett,* The Master of Heathcrest Hall

Fixing

When we see those we love sink further and further into this disease, it is painful to witness. We watch those we love steeped in denial, coming up with a new set of rationalizations for each manifestation of the disease—and we feel deep frustration, and sometimes despair, at their unwillingness to see the reality that is growing like yeast within them and before their eyes. It hurts to hear them use rationalizations to let themselves off the hook. But those rationalizations, that denial is part of their disease. It is infuriating to watch them go about their day seemingly free of the kinds of anxieties and worries that we experience because their denial, at least temporarily, seems to be working for them. It leaves us feeling helpless, frustrated and alone. It makes us want to scream or to fix them.

When I try to fix to make my own pain go away, it doesn't work. The "help" I give is too loaded down with my own pain and anger, and the messages get muffled. I feel torn: I am thrilled to be changing and growing, horrified that it took me this long, guilty that I seem to be getting better if others I love are not, and anxious that I could wake up one morning and find that this recovery has all been a dream.

I can detach with love

Unrealistic expectations often lead to disappointment,
while simple unbiased attention and detachment to
outcome often lead to pleasant surprises.

—*Gary Hopkins*

Distorted Reasoning

This disease can distort everyone's reasoning, because we use our thinking to twist and bend the truth into a more acceptable shape. We rationalize and deny what is right in front of us, make excuses, and sometimes lie, because it makes us feel better than to admit the truth. The alcoholic lies to hide his or her uses and abuses; the family members lie to hide the extent to which addiction has taken hold of their loved one, and to conceal their own fear, pain, and confusion from themselves and the world. Pretty soon, our thinking becomes so filled with denial and rationalization that we lose our own sense of what is normal. Eventually our sense of reality becomes distorted.

Today, I am willing to live life on life's terms, not mine. I am able to tolerate the truth because I know that I have a program; I have accepted the things I cannot change and changed the things I can.

I am willing to live with the truth rather than lies

Do you remember the story of Philomel who is raped and then has her tongue ripped out by the rapist so that she can never tell? I believe in fiction and the power of stories because that way we speak in tongues. We are not silenced. All of us, when in deep trauma, find we hesitate, we stammer; there are long pauses in our speech. The thing is stuck. We get our language back through the language of others. We can turn to the poem. We can open the book. Somebody has been there for us and deep-dived the words. I needed words because unhappy families are conspiracies of silence. The one who breaks the silence is never forgiven. He or she has to learn to forgive him- or herself.

—*Jeanette Winterson,* Why Be Happy When You Could Be Normal?

Hypervigilance

My fear apparatus got very much overused in my family. I was constantly geared up for fight or flight. And when I couldn't do either of those, I froze in my tracks; I went numb inside or tried to become invisible till the feeling of danger passed. But all of the pain that I shut down stayed inside of me. It gets triggered, and I overreact to situations and relationship dynamics that I might otherwise handle more calmly. Even though I am not still living under the same kind of stress as I once did when I was surrounded by active addiction, my body and mind carry the imprint of that trauma and overreact. I live as if the stressor is still present. My old pain and anger are surfacing after the fact in a post-traumatic stress reaction. When I overreact to circumstances in life, when I get too angry, hurt, stressed or withdrawn, when I go from zero to ten, or ten to zero, and have trouble regulating my emotional responses, I will stop, look, and listen. I will go inside and observe whether or not my overreaction is fueled by my unresolved pain.

I need to heal from emotional and psychological trauma

If it's hysterical, it's historical.

—Twelve-Step program slogan

Empowering My Own Day

There are no victims, only volunteers. If there is something I don't like in the way things are going for me, I will see what subtle but significant changes I can make.

- I can change the subject, if someone goes on and on about things that I don't want to talk about.
- I can quietly remove myself from a situation that's triggering me.
- I can change my routines, if I am getting bored or depressed with the way things are; I can change the way I get to where I am going.
- I can set boundaries with my time, if I am feeling overscheduled.
- I can give myself 20 minutes of daily quiet to nourish my spirit.

My time and what I do with it is precious to me—it is all I have to call my very own. I won't throw it away and then blame someone else for gobbling it up. I have a right to protect the quiet and enjoyment of my day, to do more of those things that give me pleasure and fewer of those things that run me down. If I am living up to my responsibilities, that is enough.

I won't throw my time away with both hands

You have brains in your head. You have feet in your shoes.
You can steer yourself in any direction you choose.
You're on your own. And you know what you know.
You are the guy who'll decide where to go.

—Dr. Seuss

Saving Myself

Today I resolve to save the only life I can—mine. I will step into life, into the now and see what is here for me. I will let the past be in the past—I can do nothing about it, and spending my life trying to change what has already happened will only make it continue to manifest and come alive in my present and future. When I resist the moment, the here and now, I disconnect myself from the source of all life and energy. When I embrace the moment, I am part of its creative power; I join in its transformation into the next moment and the next and the next. I enter the now. When I love just where I am, I imbue it with a kind of magic, I see in it a certain perfection. Then I release it so something else can follow. When I live in the past or in the future I live in my head—I am not in my own skin. When I'm able to be in the moment, my life feels somehow more grounded and manageable, I realize that I can only do something about where I am right now. I become available for the aliveness, spontaneity, and spirituality of the here and now. If my outer world feels limited, I can enter my inner world, which has no limits; I can go places on the inside that make life feel alive and generous and abundant.

I go from here

When you are present, when your attention is fully and intensely in the Now, Being can be felt, but it can never be understood mentally. To regain awareness of Being and to abide in that state of "feeling realization" is enlightenment.

—*Eckhart Tolle,* The Power of Now

Hanging In There

I will hang in there. I am in it for the long haul. I am committed to a path of healing, today, tomorrow and for the rest of my life. Life is a constant process of injury and healing. When I let wounds fester, when I have them and don't treat them, they turn into serious illness. And they manufacture more illness. Then I have to do a kind of emotional surgery to drain the wound, remove the toxic material and get better. Today I will resolve to develop the kinds of life habits that create lifelong health, wellness and recovery. I will take an integrated and intelligent approach, I will leave no part of me behind, wounded and abandoned.This means that I stop self-harming and self-medicating behaviors for good; when I slip into one, I back up and slip out the moment I am aware of it or it is pointed out to me. I will eat a balanced, healthy diet for the rest of my life; treats will be just that, treats, not daily fare. I will exercise daily, I need mood managing chemicals to be part of my life and I want my body to be as beautiful as it can be. I will get the rest I need. I will keep good, wholesome, fun and loving company, and I will engage in constructive activity. Recovery just kicked the door of healthy living open. I am in this for life.

I am committed to lifelong healing and optimal living

Diamonds are nothing more than
hunks of coal that stuck to their jobs

—Malcomb Forbes

Fear of Change

Today, I am able to live with my fear that I will not like myself or those close to me if I change, or if they change. Change can be threatening as well as exciting. Recovery includes many transformations and new choices. It doesn't seem to matter to my fearful self if the change is for the better or worse; in fact, change for the better can sometimes feel even more threatening. Some of the changes I am undergoing make me feel lonely because I am seeing things I didn't see before. My family and friends don't necessarily change with me, and sometimes they even feel alienated by some of the changes I'm making. It is hard for me to let them grow at their own pace when I am changing so fast. I will remind myself today that I can only grow for me, that I do not need to amputate relationships with those I love because they aren't changing in the ways I want them to. They have their own Higher Power, and it's not me. I can still love who I want or need to love *and* have my new life and sense of self. I can let me be me and you be you.

I can forgive people for not being who I want them to be

A successful person is one who can lay a firm foundation with the bricks that others throw at him or her.

—*David Brinkley*

Amends

I am willing for healing to take place in ruptured relationships. I have been doing the best that I can. So my acknowledgment that I may have hurt someone else need not diminish me. I have also been hurt; I can extend the same understanding to myself that I do to others. We have all been doing the best that we knew how with the awareness we have to work with. My willingness to make amends speaks to my spiritual growth and desire for honesty. Today I understand that it is for me that I forgive, for my own inner peace; I cannot control the outcome or another person. I'll take the action and let go of the results. Making amends to others sets things straight with me. I can't do anything about another person's behavior but I can keep my side of the street clean.

I am determined to feel clean inside

Just because you think that hate and non-forgiveness
are justified in a certain case, wake up and realize
that you are still poisoning your own system and
you are doing more damage to yourself.

—Doc Childre

Surrender

Today I will place the problems I cannot solve into the loving hands of my Higher Power. I will surrender. I will stop straining for a solution that is not readily coming. Problems get solved in God's time, not mine. If I wait for each and every problem to be solved before I feel good, I will walk right by my own life. I have to learn to live in between the solutions, to live the day that has been given to me rather than the day I don't have. When I live the day that I am in, when I stay in the present, I find, mysteriously, that is where God lives, too. There is no better time to be with God, to live close to spirit, than right now. Today I will give myself the gift of living in the moment.

God lives in each tiny moment

I may not have the life I want, but I am
learning to live the life I have.

—Lois W.

The Seed of Faith

Faith is my friend, my lamp in the darkness, my breath. When I have faith I know that I am sending something positive out into the universe, something that is whole and good and creative. My faith has the power to enter the ether and bring forth, to mend what was broken and restore what was lost. Faith as small as a mustard seed can grow, it has potential to become bigger every day. I will breathe into this moment and have faith that good things are coming my way, that situations that give me pain or thoughts that bring anxiety can become quiet, that life is working itself out through divine guidance, and I can align myself with that force. When I forget to have faith, I forfeit a lot of peace of mind and carry an unnecessary burden of pain. When I remember to, I can leave the problems of my day in the loving hands of my Higher Power, then I can go about my day doing, being and giving my best. I am relieved of the burden of being master of the universe.

I am willing to have faith today

The smallest seed of faith is better
than the largest fruit of *happiness.*

— Henry David Thoreau

Spiritual Transformation

Today, I see that to change my life I have to change myself. When I say that I would like world peace, first I will understand that without inner peace there will be no world peace. One of the ways in which I can serve the cause of humanity is to be, within myself, a genuinely spiritual person—respecting all sects and creeds, but standing on my own as a conduit of higher truth, recognizing that each person has equal access to that knowledge. I will look for truth today within myself, rather than outside. I will not wait for peace to be handed to me as some sort of prize for good behavior, but will do the inner work needed to achieve it. Today I give and receive the gift of peace.

I seek truth within myself

As human beings, our greatness lies not
so much in being able to remake the world—that
is the myth of the "atomic age"—as in
being able to remake ourselves.

—Gandhi

I Am A Leader

My family may have a disease—and it's not me. My family may drink poison and serve poison up to each other, but I don't have to. My family may choose to deny the impact of addiction and the trauma that follows it, but I don't have to. My family may defend their right to stay sick, but I want to get well. My family, for whatever reason, may seem determined to not identify the family illness that has made us all sick. But the illness stands out to me in Technicolor. I see it and I trust my own eyes. I do not need to pass on the pain that I have experienced, nor do I need to internalize the trauma and experience it as mine. Today I have the tools to gain some distance from my own pain. As I process it, I realize that my "internalized oppression" is not all of me, it is something I can face, understand, work through, and release. I can learn new ways of being and treat my own children differently from the way I was treated. I can be loyal to the parts that were good and pass them on, and release my my fixation on the parts that were dysfunctional.

This disease is real

Do not follow where the path may lead.
Go instead where there is no
path and leave a trail.

—Harold R. McAlindon

Creating a False Self

Growing up with parents who were lost in their own dysfunction was scary. I adopted a false self that didn't rock the boat; I placated and behaved in such a way as to please, so that I could ward off my fears of rejection, criticism, and having the family problems projected at me. The lesson I learned was that I had to work hard for the love and acceptance I wanted to receive. I have lived this out by feeling that if I didn't work harder than the next guy, I wouldn't be loved or accepted; eventually this became the only way that I could receive it, through this constant overdoing and overfunctioning. Today I see that this way of staying "connected" is not in my best interests or those of anyone I am close to. When I overdo in order to feel safe and deserving, I create anxiety and a shadow of mistrust in my intimate relationships.

I do not need to overfunction in order to deserve or receive love

This ability to grieve—that is, to give up the illusion of his "happy" childhood, to feel and recognize the full extent of the hurt he has endured—can restore the depressive's vitality and creativity and free the grandiose person. He will be very deeply shaken, but one day he will feel the desire to end these efforts. He will discover in himself a need to live according to his true self and no longer be forced to earn "love" that always leaves him empty-handed, since it is given to his false self—something he has begun to identify and relinquish.

—*Alice Miller,* Drama of the Gifted Child: The Search for the True Self

Arrogance and Grandiosity

I will let myself slowly become right-sized. Grandiosity and arrogance are part and parcel of this disease, defenses against feelings of shame, helplessness, hopelessness, and invisibility. I compensate for what I feel is missing from my life, from myself, by having fantasies of who I think I am. These compensatory fantasies are sad, really—they are a signal of where I feel lacking. When I feel small inside, I try to be big on the outside in order to make myself feel better. Just for today I will let myself feel big on the inside recognizing that no one is small in God's eyes, and I needn't be small in my own eyes. Today I can tolerate my own feelings of insecurity and smallness knowing that they are feelings, not facts. I can breathe, witness, and allow them to pass. I am fine as I am; I live in the presence of God, and with God's help, hand in hand, I will walk through this day.

I find my right size in each and every feeling, thought and action

When you please others in hopes of being accepted,
you lose your self-worth in the process.

—David Pelzer

Shifting Helplessness to Powerlessness

Today I will allow my irrational feelings of helplessness over the disease to shift to a chosen state of powerlessness. Powerlessness is a conscious act of surrender and recognizes that I cannot control people, places, and things. Helplessness is part of the trauma response, part of the collapse that any human or animal goes into when they feel that there is nothing they can do to help change things for the better. When I allow myself to shift into a chosen state of powerlessness, I make a profound move inward and upward. I shift from victimhood to empowerment. I may be powerless over this disease, but I am empowered in my life. My life is full of choices that I can make minute by minute, day by day, decade by decade. I can stop being Sisyphus pushing the same rock up the same mountain. I can let go of my wish to control: I didn't cause it, I can't control it, and I can't cure it. I find safety and comfort in my Higher Power. I let go and let God.

I am powerless but not helpless

When you get into a tight place and everything goes against you, till it seems as though you could not hold on a minute longer, never give up then, for that is just the place and time that the tide will turn.

—Harriet Beecher Stowe

Letting Myself Feel My Feelings

Sometimes I want to over intellectualize my emotions rather than feel them. I want to stay in my head because entering my heart hurts and makes me feel vulnerable. I want to come up with quick answers, to "figure things out" in order to make my uncomfortable feelings stop. But today I will get out of my own way and recognize that the answers I seek are not only intellectual but embedded in experiencing where I really am. My solutions will arise naturally as I allow myself to sit quietly, feel what I feel, and experience where I am. When I can't allow myself to do this simple, but not so easy thing, I get stuck in my head, invested in being right and lost in my own intellectualizations and rationalizations. I cannot heal what I cannot feel. Until I can allow myself to sit and quietly feel what I sometimes ward off, I will not have access to those parts of me, I will not understand what drives me to self-medicate or act out, I will not fully heal.

I will quietly breathe and feel and breathe and feel

It is only with the heart that one can see rightly;
what is essential is invisible to the eye.

—*Antoine de Saint-Exupéry,* The Little Prince

Easily Triggered

Events in the present can trigger pain from the past. But the problem is, I don't know that past pain is making the situation in the present feel overwhelming. I have denied my own pain so often that I don't even know how to identify, own, or articulate it. I don't know how to separate yesterday's pain from what's getting triggered today. And when I get into that place I become a powder keg waiting to explode when ignited. I want to say all the things I never got a chance to say then, feel the feelings I shut down as a kid, cry the tears that have been locked inside. I make yesterday's pain about today's circumstance. But I have been down that road before, many times, and it gets me nowhere and does no one else any good. Today, I will humble myself before the power of this disease to destroy lives. I will recognize my own powerlessness. I will invite God and time and prayer in.

I do not need to pass on the pain

When you're born a light is switched on, a light which shines up through your life. As you get older the light still reaches you, sparkling as it comes up through your memories. And if you're lucky as you travel forward through time, you'll bring the whole of yourself along with you, gathering your skirts and leaving nothing behind, nothing to obscure the light. But if a Bad Thing happens part of you is seared into place, and trapped for ever at that time. The rest of you moves onward, dealing with all the todays and tomorrows, but something, some part of you, is left behind. That part blocks the light, colours the rest of your life, but worse than that, it's alive. Trapped forever at that moment, and alone in the dark, that part of you is still alive.

—*Michael Marshall Smith,* Only Forward

Loving My Family and Hating the Disease

I can love my family and hate the disease. I can love myself and hate the disease. I can love life and hate the disease. I will not let this disease poison everything I care about, all that is and should be mine to love. Addiction has a life of its own that can be more powerful than the body's and psyche's ability to fight it off. It enters the human body and makes it craving and desperate. It floods the mind and makes thinking distorted, depressed, and disturbed. It wraps itself around the human heart and makes us feel hopeless, paranoid, and mistrustful. This disease has invaded and degraded my family system. When I reach for healing, my heart is pulled toward the people I may be leaving behind—at least that is how it feels. But today I know that the only person I can heal is myself. If anyone else chooses recovery, it will be in their time, not mine. Just because I am healing today, does not mean they won't heal tomorrow. Today I see that the best thing that I can do for me, for future generations, and even for my family of origin, is to heal, to light a path in a better direction. Addiction drew me down a dark path, recovery lights a path towards life.

Healing myself is the best thing I can do for the world

We are not mad, we are human, we want to love,
and someone must forgive us for the paths we take
to love, for the paths are many and dark, and
we are ardent and cruel in our journey.

—Leonard Cohen

The Next Right Action

All I need to do today is to take the next right action. I cannot see into the future, I only see what surrounds me at this moment. All I need to do is the task at hand, as well and sincerely as I can. When I do this earnestly and daily, the rest takes care of itself. I cannot solve my life in a day. I cannot erase my past in a week nor do I want to. When I get stuck in regretting or ruminating about the past, or become preoccupied with living in the future, I get overwhelmed and life feels like an out-of-body experience. My fears of the future immobilize me and my pain from the past pulls me down. Just for today, I will not obsess about tomorrow. The only day I am in is today, and the only moment I can do anything about is now. I see the wisdom in being here and now, in putting one foot in front of the other, in living this moment as well as I can and letting God take care of the rest. I put my cares and worries into the loving arms of my Higher Power as I take my next step into my day, the only step that is mine to take.

I will take the next, right action.

We can't go from zero to sixty in a day or even a week when it comes to shifting our food-habit gears. We have to take baby steps, starting with an increasing awareness of our habits and a willingness to chip away at the ones that aren't doing us any good. Slowly, with time and commitment, we move away from the rat-race, multitasking mentality to a place where we want to give our meals and ourselves the time and attention we deserve."

—*Mary DeTurris Poust,* Cravings: A Catholic Wrestles with Food, Self-Image, and God

I Let Go

Today I release my old self a thousand times; I release the moment that just passed. I allow my body to lead me through space as my senses collect data and I process the sights, sounds, smells, and feel of the world with my mind. I observe, I interact, I move through. Each moment is alive and each moment passes. I am a part of it: I move through it but I am not the mover; something much larger than me is moving me through my life. I give in to this amazing, all-powerful, and all-wise force. I am led and I follow, I lead and I am followed, I move tandem. I just move through my life, unknowing and known, wise and a fool, dragging along parts of me that are slowly waking up and learning to feel alive, and letting go of parts of me that are dying off naturally.

I allow myself just to be a trusting part of a beautiful universe

Awakening is not a thing. It is not a goal, not a concept.
It is not something to be attained. It is a metamorphosis.
If the caterpillar thinks about what the butterfly it is to become,
saying 'And then I shall have wings and antennae,' there
will never be a butterfly. The caterpillar must accept
its own disappearance in its transformation.
When the marvelous butterfly takes wing,
nothing of the caterpillar remains.

—Alejandro Jodorowsky

Letting Life Take Its Own Course

I will have faith today that life is taking the course it is meant to take. I will have faith that the situations that are crawling around my insides, giving me agita, making my breath short and my throat tight when I think about them, will somehow unravel themselves in a way that will make me think: Why did I cause myself all of that unnecessary pain? Why didn't I have a little more faith that this was going to work out? Why didn't I let go and let God? When I forget the power of faith in my life, I forget one of my best and most trustworthy tools of recovery. Faith. I will have faith, right now, that a situation that is baffling me is turning out, at this very moment, in a way that is right for all; I just don't see it yet. I will breathe, back up, and allow my mind to go to a higher place where it can observe more clearly.

I have faith that my life is working out

As your faith is strengthened you will find
that there is no longer the need to have a sense
of control, that things will flow as they will,
and that you will flow with them, to your
great delight and benefit.

— Emmanuel Teney

APRIL

Life Lessons

I've learned that you cannot make someone love you.
All you can do is be someone who can be loved.
The rest is up to them.

I've learned that no matter how much I care
some people just don't care back.

I've learned that just because someone doesn't
love you the way you want them to doesn't mean
they don't love you with all they have.

I've learned that it takes years to build up trust,
and only seconds to destroy it.

I've learned that it's not what you have in your life,
but whom you have in your life that counts.

I've learned that our background and circumstances
may have influenced who we are, but we are
responsible for who we become.

I've learned that we are responsible for what we do,
no matter how we feel.

I've learned that either you control your attitude or it controls you.

I've learned that sometimes when I'm angry I have the right to
be angry, but that doesn't give me the right to be cruel.

I've learned that maturity has more to do with what types of
experiences you've had and what you've learned from them and
less to do with how many birthdays you've celebrated.

I've learned that two people can look at the exact
same thing and see something totally different.

I've learned that no matter how good a friend is, they're going to
hurt you every once in a while and you must forgive them for that.

I've learned that it isn't always enough to be forgiven by others.
Sometimes you have to learn to forgive yourself.

I've learned that just because two people argue,
it doesn't mean they don't love each other.
And, just because they don't argue, it doesn't mean they do.

I've learned that no matter how bad your heart is
broken the world doesn't stop for your grief.

I've learned that no matter how you try to protect your children,
they will eventually get hurt, and you will hurt in the process.

I've learned that you should never tell a child their dreams
are unlikely or outlandish. Few things are more humiliating,
and what a tragedy it would be if they believed it.

I've learned that heroes are people who do what has to be done
when it needs to be done, regardless of the consequences.

I've learned that you can keep going long after you think you can't.

—Kaye Cunningham

Finding a Passion

I will find a passion. Whether cooking, painting, writing, cleaning, golf, scrap booking, volunteering, or something with gardening or animals, I will find something I truly enjoy doing and I will do it. When I engage in an activity that I feel at one with, I soothe, challenge, and nourish myself. It gives shape to my day and meaning and purpose to my life. I am fortunate enough to live in an age where there are many possibilities for things that I can learn to do, and much access to information on how to do them. I know that I enter a kind of quiet and energized inner space when I do things I enjoy. And I emerge feeling more integrated and whole. I will give myself the space in my life to do what ignites my spirit. I see finding a pleasing activity as part of my recovery.

Whatever my passion, I will do it and enjoy it

Certain passions—say, for painting, writing, sports, cooking, teaching or whatever activity we're truly engaged in—can also allow us to enter what Mihaly Csikszentmihalyi of the University of Chicago calls the "flow state." In his extensive research in this area, he has found that people are most likely to enter this state when their skill level and the difficulty of the task itself are properly matched. Too little skill leads to frustration, and too little challenge leads to boredom. In the flow state, time tends to disappear, we engage in a deep, effortless involvement where ordinary cares are out of consciousness. We're receiving immediate feedback and we're goal-oriented. While in this flow state, our concern for self disappears; however, when we emerge, our self feels stronger.

—Tian Dayton, PhD,
Emotional Sobriety

Keeping My Soles in the Room

I will get myself to a meeting today. I won't go to hear anything life-altering or to say something brilliant. I will just go to keep my soles in the room, knowing that my soul will somehow follow, even if I cannot fully see it. I will go to gather my senses, to hear what I hear, to get the emotional or limbic balance that comes when I sit with others like me in a room that is dedicated to telling the truth in a calm way. My limbic or emotional system is balanced by other humans (read: mammals) like me through a phenomenon called limbic resonance. When I sit with a room of calm people my nervous system calms, too. I actually repattern my neurological wiring in this way, I develop pathways for experiencing my emotions calmly by being around others who are in that same zone. I will trust that good actions today are my best way of creating a good tomorrow.

I will go to a meeting

I believe God is managing affairs and that
He doesn't need any advice from me. With God in charge,
I believe everything will work out for the best in the end.
So what is there to worry about.

—Henry Ford

Secrets

The secrets that we keep actually keep us. I can live my life in a web of lies without ever uttering a falsehood. The web of lies is composed not just of what I say, but also of the vast amount of honesty that I withhold. There is a difference between considerate honesty and aggressive frankness. Honesty recognizes the personhood of both people and is an act of trust; but too much ill motivated frankness in the name of truth telling, can border on mean. I can know the truth and then make choices about what to do with it. Keeping secrets is a foolish attempt to stay safe from the truth. We tell ourselves we are sparing another person or protecting ourselves, but what I need from me and what other people need in order to make sense of me is the truth. When I withhold that truth, whether from myself or others, I withhold myself. I am creating distance that no one can cross because the real way across the divide is the way of honesty. Today I can know the truth, sit with it, and share it appropriately, choose to share it at some other moment, or know it within myself.

I am as sick as my secrets

The weakness of a soul is proportionate to the
number of truths that must be kept from it.

—Eric Hoffer

Softer and Stronger

I can let my guard down today because I have faith in my ability to feel pain and come out of it. Each time I dip into my own inner depths, I come out with more of me, with another piece of understanding of my own inner world and what's in it. As I develop the ability to tolerate the power of my own intense emotions without acting out, and I learn to translate those emotions into words so that I can both reflect on them and share them with others, I build emotional strength, resilience, emotional intelligence, and sobriety. I also become softer and more accessible. My recovery is making me softer and stronger. Softer because I am willing to experience my real feelings, the ones beneath my brittle defenses; stronger because I am developing the ability to talk out rather than act out my emotions. I am becoming a friend to myself; I am learning the value of calm and sane reflection.

Inner strength allows me to feel my feelings

Emotions such as tension, frustration, and sadness can trigger a drop in the blood supply to the heart. When we're under stress, the body assumes its survival is threatened so it releases adrenaline into the bloodstream which in turn activates the body's fight or flight response. When this emergency response becomes chronic, that is if our stress response gets revved up too often throughout the day, the actual beating rhythm of our heart, that is our "heart rate variability" can become deregulated and chaotic which then throws off all of the body systems that the heart impacts.

—Doc Childre and Howard Martin,
The Heartmath Solution

Loving My Parents

It is my right to love my parents. My love for them is not personal, it is a powerful bonding need of mine built into me through nature. When my parents used or misused my love, they were misunderstanding their role. They were taking my love for them personally and making it about being good or bad, doling love out like a reward or a punishment. But this is against nature. Nature meant for parents and children to bond unconditionally for survival. That is why I need to honor my parents. Not because they deserve it, but because I deserve it. I deserve to feel whole inside and connected to God's plan. It's not personal. When I hate my parents, I hate a part of myself because my parents are literally wired into me. Today, my victory over the disease is to love my parents even if I hate their disease. Whether we choose to spend a lot of time together is not the issue; loving my parents is about freeing my own heart to feel fully, to trust in life and relationships, and to move beyond hate, hurt, and resentment.

Today I love in order to heal my self

Faith makes all things possible.
Love makes them easy.

—D. L. Moody

Siblings

My siblings and I grew up with a terrible disease. That disease became part of how we related to each other each and every day. That disease became much bigger than us and infiltrated our interactions and burdened our relationships. When our parents dropped the ball, we stepped into that void by trying to take over responsibilities our parents were ignoring. We grew to have way too much power over each other. We took advantage of each other's vulnerability as often as we helped each other through, and that made our relationships very confusing. We formed traumatic bonds living in the trenches with active addiction. We weren't really young together. We couldn't really move through our developmental stages freely, trusting our parents to keep us safe. As I get healthier, I can see this more clearly, and that hurts; but it also liberates me from feeling beholden to anxious and ambivalent bonds. Today I can learn new styles of bonding; I can take what I learned that was healthy and carry it forward as I release the unhealthy parts

I release myself and my siblings,
I let go and let God, I bless them and me

You can't necessarily trust your eyes
if your mind is out of focus.

—*Mark Twain*

ACoA: Passing On the Pain

Today I take responsibility for the disease that is within me. One of the pitfalls of growing up with addiction is that I learned to point the finger at another person, to say that the disease was within them and not me. To think that if they changed, things would finally be all right; I would finally be all right. Today I recognize that whether or not I drink, the fallout of trauma is mine to deal with, it is my disease. Some ACoAs self-medicate with food, sex, overfunctioning, or even alcohol or drugs. Some pass on twisted forms of thinking or relating with no awareness that they are doing it; this is one of the most insidious forms that passing down pain can take. It forces our children to absorb our disowned pain. Because they don't know what else to do with it, they make it somehow about themselves. So the numbed pain passes seamlessly down through another generation and all the while, I do not see it as belonging to me, but to my parents. Today I recognize that I am the swing generation, the passer-on-er. If I don't clean up my own pain, my children will have to live it out as their fate.

I take responsibility for my own dysfunction

Some people's lives seem to flow in a narrative;
mine had many stops and starts. That's what trauma does.
It interrupts the plot. You can't process it because it
doesn't fit with what came before or what comes afterward.
A friend of mine, a soldier, put it this way. In most of our lives,
most of the time, you have a sense of what is to come.
There is a steady narrative, a feeling of "lights, camera, action"
when big events are imminent. But trauma isn't like that. It just
happens, and then life goes on. No one prepares you for it.

—*Jessica Stern,* Denial: A Memoir of Terror

Inner Newness

I am new inside. I feel pink and tender, as if young tissue were growing within me. I have been willing to take an ultimate risk by looking at the state of my life and my own insides, not as I wish they were, but as they actually are. I have experienced an inner death. I have walked through spaces inside my mind and heart that felt life-threatening, and I have felt the terror of full honesty. What I did not expect was this sense of birth and newness. Somehow, life feels full of possibility for new experiences. I thought that I would be stuck in anger and blame forever, but I see today that I did not need to feel so down on myself for feeling those feelings. They are just a part of the process. Like all things in nature, I am part of a constantly evolving process; I move and shift and change and move and shift and change.

I move through, I am constantly evolving and adapting

Growth is the only evidence of life.

—John Henry Newman

Faith in a Providential God

Today, I know that there is nothing to be afraid of because my Higher Power and the energy of love underpin all that is. At the very core of me is not darkness and fear, but light and love. Love can be frightening to let in—it brings up both fears of disappointment and of responsibility. I can be hurt if I open my heart, but that is just part of being alive. Hate lets me off the hook; though it is a natural human emotion, I can easily dismiss and distance what I hate. But I don't have to fear love as I do, it no longer has to mean enmeshment and sick obligation—because love can allow me a new kind of distance, through space and ease and acceptance. Love can allow me to let people, places, and things be. When I allow myself to recognize love as a fundamental mystery of creation, I sense that no matter what happens I will be all right; I am where I am meant to be, and I can surrender my wish to control people, places, and things.

I allow love to be the basis of my life

You must love all that God has created, both his
entire world and each single tiny sand grain of it.
Love each tiny leaf, each beam of sunshine.
You must love the animals, love every plant.
If you love all things, you will also attain the divine
mystery that is in all things. For then your ability to
perceive the truth will grow every day, and your mind
will open itself to an all-embracing love.

—Fyodor Dostoyevsky

APRIL 10

Bearing Witness

When I have an undesirable thought today, like jealousy, anger or self-doubt I will just observe it in my mind. I will allow the thought to really be there. I won't try to deny it or eradicate it. I will simply give it space and witness it. As I do this, the thought transforms. As I see it for what it is and accept it as a part of me, I give it the breathing room it needs to play itself through, to change it into something else. I cannot hide from me, nor do I wish to. I can be my own best friend by allowing myself the space to think what I am really thinking and feel what I am really feeling, knowing that it doesn't have to lead to blind action. There is another more powerful and fruitful action that I can take. It is in simply witnessing, allowing and trusting that this process will lead to awareness, transformation, and a more permanent change than is possible through denial. Today I will give myself the gift of self-reflection.

I can change my inner being through the simple but powerful act of witnessing

. . . you start paying attention to yourself. You become a witness to your own being. You start watching your thoughts, desires, dreams, motives, greeds and jealousies. You create a new kind of awareness within you. You become a center, a silent center which goes on watching whatsoever is happening. You are angry, and you watch it. You are not just angry, a new element is introduced into it: you are watching it. And the miracle is that if you can watch anger, the anger disappears without being repressed.

—*Osho*

Trust and Faith

I will have faith today, faith in the unseen, faith that my sincere actions will produce good results, faith that the heart and goodness that I put into my life and relationships will bear fruit. I will take an action and let go of the results, knowing that the energy of that action will be carried by unseen hands. Faith is a gift. When I have faith, I can let worry go and use my energy to be constructive, to build, to create, and to enjoy my life. Each and every moment God is waiting to hear from me; there is nothing too small to ask for God's help in, nothing too trivial to take to prayer. Today, I ask for God's help in all my affairs. Nothing will shake my faith. The only real faith is blind faith. If I am only willing to have faith in what life has already proved to me, that is not faith. That is simply believing what I see. I will have faith in what I cannot see, faith in what I see in my mind's eye as a possibility, faith in the voice I hear with my inward ear and the song I sing inside my heart. The world will not beat me, this disease will not write the last chapter of my life. If what surrounds me is discouraging and disheartening, I will have faith in what I cannot see. I will nourish a knowing in my heart that life is good, that I am good, that being alive is a gift, a gift that it is up to me to accept, embrace and value. Nothing will shake my faith.

I have faith in what I cannot yet see with my eyes

I still believe people are really good at heart.

—Anne Frank

APRIL 12

Being in the Moment

Today, I see that the only real point of power is in the present. Life cannot be lived backwards or forwards, but only in the context of today. If I truly let myself have this moment and all that it contains, I will be in quiet possession of great eternal wealth. All that is, is in this moment. It is where all the waters meet and all the wisdom of the ages lies; it is the now that calls me to it with open arms, that lets me sink into it like a child leaning into his mother's lap. I work out my issues and preoccupations, not because it is right or good or proper, but because it allows me to be in fuller possession of my present. I can act in this moment only, past actions are over and I cannot reach my arms into the future no matter how hard I try. Today I will release those parts of me that remain tied up in endless preoccupations, so that I can be more fully in the now.

I allow myself this moment

A human being is a part of the whole, called by us "Universe," a part limited in time and space. He experiences himself, his thoughts and feelings as something separated from the rest—a kind of optical delusion of his consciousness. This delusion is a kind of prison for us, restricting us to our personal desires and to affection for a few persons nearest to us. Our task must be to free ourselves from this prison by widening our circle of compassion to embrace all living creatures and the whole of nature in its beauty. Nobody is able to achieve this completely, but the striving for such achievement is in itself a part of the liberation and a foundation for inner security.

—Albert Einstein

Living in Emotional Extremes

Cycling back and forth between behavioral extremes mirrors my own cycling back and forth between emotional extremes. Overeating and undereating, overspending and underspending, overdoing and underdoing, reflect my own lack of ability to self-regulate; they are part of the seesawing from agitation to numbness, from overwhelm to underwhelm, that is part of the stress/trauma response. I used to rely on medicators for my mood management, to keep me from falling into a dark hole inside, like drugs, alcohol, food, sex, debting, and spending. But they only get me into trouble and keep me locked in a cycle of bingeing and purging. In recovery, I have learned healthy ways of managing my moods and I am going to use them. I can exercise, share my feelings, journal, take a walk, have lunch out doors, rest, meditate, or enjoy some uplifting reading. All of these activities elevate my mood. I have an inbuilt capacity for self-regulation that I can nourish, use, and grow. My contribution to society is the best version of me that I can be.

The universe can self-regulate and so can I

I have absolutely no pleasure in the stimulants
in which I sometimes so madly indulge. It has not been in
the pursuit of pleasure that I have periled life and
reputation and reason. It has been the desperate attempt
to escape from torturing memories, from a sense of
insupportable loneliness and a dread of
some strange impending doom.

—Edgar Allan Poe

Prayer and Miracles

Today, I will pray for a miracle in a situation that seems too much for me to handle or understand. There are times when I just don't have what it takes to work out a situation. I'm too loaded up with fears and anxieties. What could it hurt to pray for a little divine guidance or intervention? At the very least, it will help ease my burden and make me less anxious and fearful; and at best, it will aid in a genuine shift in perception that might truly help my situation. When I feel stuck and as if I've explored every option and am still nowhere, I will pray for a miracle. I will be open.

Nothing can change if I stay locked in the same old thoughts cascading downward. Praying for a miracle will jimmy open a stuck door inside of me so that a shaft of light can shine. I want to see the challenges of my life as opportunities to undo inner knots that keep me tied to a time and place within myself that repeats and repeats itself without awareness. I want the tough moments, if I face them and process them, to be the keys that unlock my own inner wounds and turn them into wisdom, insight, and understanding.

I allow my consciousness to reach out into the unknown and ask for help

A miracle is a shift in perception and prayer
is the medium of miracles.

—A Course in Miracles

Keeping My Eye on the Ball

Just for today I won't give every little thing that grabs my energy and attention more importance than it deserves. This hanging onto inner turmoil that is part of my trauma legacy keeps my own wounds fresh. In the scheme of things, all of my petty annoyances aren't all that important. I don't have to take them so seriously that they disturb my inner peace. When I let myself get annoyed over little things, I create a negative frame of mind that builds on itself. I repeat my past in my present. When I am constantly preoccupied with all that's wrong, I forget to remember all that's right. Recovery gives me some tools to get my mind off of the treadmill. I will hold my tongue, zip my lip, and think before I act. That way, I'll have a moment to experience what feelings might be driving my picking and criticism, and I will focus on processing and calming my emotions rather than giving them outlets that will only feed the beast and make it even more hungry. Today I can tell the difference between emotions that require processing and attention and petty gripes and discharges that just make problems get bigger.

I will get out of my own way today

We don't see things as they are.
We see things as we are.

—Anaïs Nin

Acts of Kindness

Today I will open to acts of kindness from either the giving or receiving end. When I demonstrate kindness, whether to a person or an animal, I experience a shift in my own mind and body, a change in me. When I receive an act of kindness, the same thing happens; something in me grows soft and my level of contentment increases. Both giving gracefully and receiving gracefully are important—giving creates good feeling and good karma, and receiving humbles me and teaches me to show gratitude. I feel somehow better on the inside, which makes the world feel like a brighter place. Even witnessing someone showing goodness, kindness, or appreciation creates a wonderful awareness or feeling inside of me. Kindness changes the quality of the moment, the quality of my day, the peace and serenity I experience within and around me.

I am open to random acts of kindness

According to research, anyone who is on the receiving end of an act of kindness, or any person who performs an act of kindness, experiences an increase in levels of serotonin and their immune system is elevated. And not only are those directly involved in acts of kindness benefited, the observer of an act of kindness also experiences the same benefits, an increase of serotonin and *their* immune system is elevated. In each case it's like "a dose of an anti-depressant" because anti-depressants are designed to enhance serotonin levels.

—Tian Dayton, PhD,
The Magic of Forgiveness

The Power of Anger

Today I am learning that I can tolerate the strength of my angry feelings without acting out or collapsing under their weight. I can be angry and listen to another point of view. I can be angry and sad or hurt. I can be angry and forgive. I can listen to my anger for what it's trying to tell me about my own reactions to people, places, and things. I can reflect on whether or not current anger is being fueled by unresolved historical anger. I can use it to motivate me towards a necessary change. Some of the anger I feel today is what I was unable to express, or for that matter even feel, as a child, adolescent, or adult trapped in a dysfunctional system. I sucked up any feelings that were too threatening to the system and jammed them into my body, into my unconscious. Today I am able to experience my anger and put it into words so that I can talk it out, rather than act it out or medicate it. I can "hold" it without exploding or cutting off. I can talk with someone about it rather making another person into an unwitting victim, the same way I was an unwitting victim. Knowing that I have the strength to experience and articulate my own feelings builds confidence and strength within me. Each time I handle my anger well, I build resilience and an ability to handle it even better the next time.

I am capable of experiencing the power of my anger and learning from it

I am no longer afraid of anger. I find it to be a creative, transforming force; anger is a stage I must go through if I am ever going to get to what lies beyond it.

—Mary Kaye Medinger

Feelings Journal

I will journal whenever I feel the need to, in order to work out my powerful feelings and thoughts. If I can work through my thoughts and feelings by writing them out, I can get the ones that create problems for me out of my way. When I write things out, I get a kind of clarity about what's going on with me. My feelings pour out onto the paper and as they do, naturally glean insights. I see something new, I find a new piece of me, a new awareness, a new order, context, or perception of events. I feel creative as I bring my less-than-conscious emotions into an expressed state; I let the child in me, the adolescent, wounded person, bright being, victim, or artist find a voice. It is such a simple solution, so available and immediate. I need a place to allow my private thoughts, my innermost self to emerge and be held out in a transforming, alive space. When I journal today, I will simply put my pen on the paper and free-write. I will let my thoughts and emotions flow freely onto the paper without any thought or editing. I will let the contents of my mind and heart spill all over the page. Later, I will notice how I have made sense of what's inside me—how my thoughts and feelings have become more integrated.

I put pen to paper and let my inner world flow

The reason for evil in the world is that people
are not able to tell their stories.

—Carl Jung

Fixation, Forgiveness, and Release

I will do what I need to do today to fully process the issues in my life that remain unresolved; to examine, understand, and bring to light my mental fixations on trauma, knowing that the resentment and pain that I continue to possess against another person possess me and can hold future generations hostage to my pain. Today I recognize that forgiveness is a gift that that benefits not only me and perhaps the person I am forgiving, but the generations that follow as well. It is a gift that releases my own spirit, that restores my own inner peace, and gives my children and grandchildren a chance to write their own stories. Just because I forgive something, it doesn't mean I am condoning it. It only means that I value my own inner peace, and that of those I love, more than carrying resentment.

I forgive to set generations free

I was doing a show on victims confronting their criminals. A 17-year-old girl was on the air speaking to the man who, four years earlier, had beaten her beyond recognition and left her for dead. She'd had 17 surgeries and complete facial reconstruction. She said to him, "I don't hate you. I hate what you did to me. And I have had to learn to forgive you so I could go on with my own life." To this day it is the most powerful thing I've ever seen. In that moment, she expressed why we're here—to learn to love in spite of the human condition, to transcend the human condition of being fearful. We get so bogged down in worldly things we don't understand that we're here for a spiritual quest. Understanding that this is a journey is the most exciting part of being human. It has revolutionized my life.

—Oprah Winfrey

Wounds to the Self

There are parts of me that are being held in silence that long to speak, places within me that want to be felt and understood. Though my sorrow may make me feel like I am falling apart, I know I will not. I am capable of tolerating emotional pain and coming out the other end with a deeper connection to my authentic self. I am capable of tolerating my own rage and helplessness without acting out or self-medicating. I trust in myself and a power greater than me to hold me through my pain. With the help of prayer and community, I can survive my own feelings of pain, fear, frustration, and anger. The yearning inside of me for what I may have lost, or for what never got a chance to happen, is natural and a part of the grief process. I am willing to feel it and to get past it. If I shut it down, minimize it, or rewrite it into some cover-up story, I am only hurting myself in the long run. I need to feel whatever pain or hurt I may be forgiving, whether it's myself I'm forgiving or another person. Hidden wounds have great power to disrupt my relationships. They burst out when they are pressed on, and make the moment feel dangerous. They leak into future generations who will have to ferret out which piece of old family pain they are carrying and, without a map to follow, try to discern how it has strangely morphed into an unrecognizable shape and how this new shape carries old wounds.

I can tolerate the strength of my own pain

There are wounds that never show on the body that are deeper and more hurtful than anything that bleeds.

—*Laurell K. Hamilton,*
Mistral's Kiss

Passing On the Pain

I need not be loyal to trauma today. Recovery gives me choices that the generations above me may not have had. I can walk into a twelve step room, I can learn the tools of the program, I can educate myself about trauma, addiction, and self medication. I can take classes on parenting; I can do things differently. If I am willing to face my past, work through it with the help of others, and transform my relationship to it, I can live a new kind of life. I want a lifestyle, not a deathstyle. I want my children to have a chance at a healthy life; I will not wait for the world to change so that I can change. I will change, and in this way, I will help to change the world.

I take responsibility for the patch I stand on

Preoccupation with death, death identity, and loyalty
to the ancestral suffering and to the deceased are other features
[of trauma]. That loyalty will cause you to create suffering
in your own life. It is not a conscious process.
We pass this trauma on because parents have been
traumatized and the children often pass trauma
response patterns to their children. We all parent the way we were
parented unless something happens to enlighten us in a different
way or help us to learn a different way of being with our kids.
I was a better mother when I was working on writing a
parenting curriculum because it kept me on my toes.
I liked to do that work because it kept me on
track much better with my daughter.

—Maria Yellow Horse Braveheart, Ph.D.,
Keynote Speech at Fifth Annual White
Bison Wellbriety Conference

Filling in the Emptiness

Growing up with parents who dropped the ball made me an overfunctioner. I learned to scan the family to see what was missing, needed, or expected; then I scrambled to fill it. There were so many empty spots, dead spots, black holes. So much was missing. So much didn't happen. So much couldn't happen. I tried to fill in gaps without having to be asked—there was no one really in charge anyway, no one to say "Please could you . . ." or "Thank you for . . ." just endless stuff left undone, unattended to, empty. The downside of this was that I learned to, live under the radar, and work harder than anyone else, whether or not it was appreciated. The upside was sort of the same. I don't need to be asked; I see what needs to be done and I do it. These have been great strengths in my life—I am useful, self-motivated, and a valuable part of a team. I don't wait to be handed a task or a life, I go out and find it. The part I need to get over is the feeling that I am only lovable or acceptable when I overfunction and ask for little back.

Today I can tolerate not overfunctioning

All mankind is of one author, and is one volume;
when one man dies, one chapter is not torn out of the book, but translated into a better language; and every chapter must be so translated. . . . As therefore the bell that rings to a sermon, calls not upon the preacher only, but upon the congregation to come: so this bell calls us all: but how much more me, who am brought so near the door by this sickness. . . . No man is an island, entire of itself . . . any man's death diminishes me, because I am involved in mankind; and therefore never send to know for whom the bell tolls; it tolls for thee.

—John Donne

Giving Myself Presents

I will take extra good care of myself today. Only I know what really, really pleases me. Part of my recovery is to recover my ability to feel good inside, to enjoy what is mine to enjoy without pushing away pleasure. Letting something feel good without mistrusting that feeling is a joyful experience. Nothing lasts forever. I can draw strength from the impermanence of life rather than weakness. I will take care of myself today knowing that the good feelings I have are also carried in the atmosphere around me and affect my close relationships. If I wear myself out unnecessarily, withhold tiny pleasures that would be just as easy to let myself have, I create a backlog of need. Then I want something big to make me feel better. But even when I get it, the pleasure doesn't last. Today I will give to myself as if I were a deserving and smiling little child, love myself as if love were the most natural thing to share, and soothe and hold myself when I need soothing and holding. I will allow myself those quiet pleasures in my day that please me, knowing that when I nourish and care for myself in little ways, it has big reverberations inside of me and in my relationships. My good feelings about life and love rest more on a thousand tiny moments that one or two big ones.

Life is in this moment; pleasure is in this moment

We are always getting ready to
live but never living.

—Ralph Waldo Emerson

APRIL 24

Forgiveness and Becoming Whole

Forgiveness is what enables a person to become whole again rather than to live broken. It is perhaps a moment when we choose, or by seeming coincidence, meet choice along life's path between neurotic preoccupation with the pain of life and spiritual growth; a moment when the spirit guides the flesh. When our wish to lead a happy and purposeful life outweighs our need for revenge.

Forgiveness is an act of great courage and self love

A middle-aged man came to place his child in one of my classes, but I realized I had no room at all. I looked at this man and immediately knew. This was the guard who had beaten me nine years before. A spirit caught me. I understood that I had to find space for his boy. I could not repeat the harm that had been done to me. I asked him, "Do you know me?" He said, "No." I asked him if he remembered a night in July of 1956. Just then, the man looked at my face and started crying. He began to walk away, but I stopped him, saying, "Wait, I'll take the child. I have carried scars for years, but I have forgiven you all those things." That man might have left me permanently disabled, but in allowing me to help his boy, he made me feel fulfilled in what I wanted to do for young people.

—*Joel Kinagwi,* The Meaning of Life

Preoccupation with Pain

My preoccupation with processing pain may be trauma-based, I may be trying to right a wrong that my young mind could never fully understand. I have spent my life thinking that the pain in my home was somehow my fault, mine to fix, mine to carry until I got everyone better. And I have spent my life trying to get my family into treatment, help them to get involved in the things that have helped me. I reasoned somehow, in some corner of my undifferentiated, child mind, that if I kept less for myself, there would be more for others. I didn't see that life is not some circle, some quantity, some literal pie in the sky with portions cut out of air. We all have to find our own recovery, to fix what is in us and let someone else fix what's in them. It's not that I don't want to help or to take responsibility; it's just that if someone doesn't manage their own life, their own thoughts, their own body, mind, and actions, no one else can do it for them. I keep thinking that if I work hardest and longest, somehow other people will get better. Today I will take care of myself.

I will get and keep myself well

. . . We kind of sacrifice ourselves and live our lives in ways that we think might undo this trauma that is not ours to undo. We can't undo it—it happened. We can heal from it. It is interesting to look at how you are living out your own life and whether you are sort of fixated to the trauma and stuck in it and just trying to make up for it somehow.

—*Maria Yellow Horse Braveheart, Ph.D.,*
Keynote Speech at Fifth Annual White Bison Wellbriety Conference

Easy Does It

Just for today, I will take my day a few hours at a time. If I can set a positive intention for the next few hours that is all I will ask of myself for now. Then, I will set a positive intention for the few hours that follow. I will lean on the wisdom of the rooms, and I will work the tools of my program. In this way, I can strengthen my recovery and grow in emotional sobriety. I will take baby steps knowing that each step I take builds a better me. No rush. I have time. I want the tools of my program to become a part of me so that I can draw on them when I need to; so that when I am shaky inside, feeling up against more than I can handle, or wanting to isolate or give up, I have somewhere to turn. I will breathe when I feel tense, take a break when I need to, and simplify my day before I get overwhelmed. I won't generalize and catastrophize problems so much that they take over my day. By breaking my day down into manageable segments and meeting each segment as it arises, I will stay in the moment. I will allow my day to unfold, to work itself out, to be pleasant. I will take it easy. I will not layer a simple day with too many complicated thoughts. I will put one foot in front of the other.

I have all the time in the world to grow

If the ladder is not leaning against the right wall,
every step we take just gets us to
the wrong place faster.

—Stephen R. Covey

Internalized Oppression

I have lived with chaos and stress for so long that I have internalized it as my own, and then I play it out in so many ways. I overstress on the inside, I blow things up because that somehow feels like the right size to me, too big is my norm. But what I do with stress within myself creates much more inner chaos than a situation today may merit; it gives me more trouble than the situation itself. How I react on an emotional and mental level to something that someone else has done or said, or to a circumstance in my life, compounds the stress reaction inside me. It's a way that I drag my past into my present. My biggest problem, when it comes to feeling stressed out, is my own reverberation. I obsess in a way that is hard on my body. I hurt myself physically by getting stress hormones to course through my body that affect my health and vitality. I blow things up in my head make them worse than they are. I undermine myself, I take away my own spontaneity and creativity, I lose touch with the fact that I have choices, and I see things in black and white terms. Today I will be honest with myself about the ways in which I exaggerate stress, obsess unnecessarily, and create more inner pressure than necessary.

I will obsess less and relax, breathe and step back more

Experience has taught us that we have only one enduring weapon in our struggle against mental illness: the emotional discovery of the truth in the individual and unique history of our childhood.

—*Alice Miller,* The Drama of the Gifted Child: The Search for the True Self

Creating My Own Rituals

Rituals ground me in my own day. My morning tea, my walk through the park, dinner with my family; these are the daily rituals that give my life a sense of continuity and solidity. They hold me, they bond me with those I love. Recovery is full of rituals. Meetings, daily reading, sharing with friends and quiet moments of self-reflection; these are sustaining and healing rituals that deepen my sense of life and remind me of what's really important. They are part of what gives my life its symmetry. I need these rituals to help me remember what to value. And they join me with life, with the feeling of what we're all really made of under the skin. Rituals speak in their own voice, and today, I am listening.

I respect the importance of rituals in my life

The holiest of holidays are those
Kept by ourselves in silence and apart;
The secret anniversaries of the heart.

—Henry Wadsworth Longfellow

Waiting for My Life to Happen

Today I will not wait for my life to happen to me as if I had nothing to do with creating it. I won't simply wait for my ship to come in, or good fortune to figure out my address and knock on my door. I will find good fortune and knock at its door. I will do this by becoming willing to shift my awareness in a direction that is life-affirming and enhancing. I will be up for seeing myself as a lucky person, as someone for whom life just works out. I will fan myself with the breezes of positivity rather than the flames of negativity. I will enter my day with an open, confident attitude. I will trust the day to hold enough good in it. I will place my hand in the hand of my Higher Power, my angel, and be guided by unseen hands. I will have an open, willing, and joyful attitude that allows the good in the day to find me. I will identify with the source of all that is and invite good into my day.

I trust life, I trust good energy, I trust me

When you arise in the morning, think of
what a precious privilege it is to be alive—
to breathe, to think, to enjoy, to love—
then make that day count!

—Steve Maraboli

APRIL 30

The Unmanifested

I live in a world behind the world, in a world of silence and song, sweet aliveness, peace, and pleasure. I sit and float in that world happily and without agenda. When I am in this state, I cease comparing my insides to everyone else's outsides. I feel that there is plenty of room for me and plenty of room for others. I have a kind of peace, a kind of knowing that sets me free on the inside. I cease to matter so very much in my smaller form and matter more as a carrier of life, someone stepping into this day with an open attitude and a free mind. I feel that the world is waiting to greet me, just because I am a part of it. I trust that the world wants good for me, that life wishes to fulfill me, that I am God's child held, rocked, and loved. I can draw on this reservoir of inner peace throughout my day: as I make room for it, it will be all the more accessible.

There is more to the world than what I see with my eyes

When your consciousness is directed outward,
mind and world arise. When it is directed inward,
it realizes its own Source and returns
home into the Unmanifested.

—*Eckhart Tolle*

MAY

Kuan Yin's Prayer for the Abuser

To those who withhold refuge,

I cradle you in safety at the core of my Being.

To those that cause a child to cry out,

I grant you the freedom to express your own choked agony.

To those that inflict terror,

I remind you that you shine with the
purity of a thousand suns.

To those who would confine, suppress, or deny,

I offer the limitless expanse of sky.

To those who need to cut, slash, or burn,

I remind you of the invincibility of Spring.

To those who cling and grasp,

I promise more abundance than you could ever hold onto.

To those who vent their rage on small children,

I return to you your deepest innocence.

To those who must frighten into submission,

I hold you in the bosom of your original mother.

To those who cause agony to others,

I give the gift of free flowing tears.

To those that deny another's right to be,

I remind you that the angels sang in celebration
of you on the day of your birth.

To those who see only division and separateness,

I remind you that a part is born only by dissecting a whole.

For those who have forgotten the tender mercy
of a mother's embrace,

I send a gentle breeze to caress your brow.

To those who still somehow feel incomplete,

I offer the perfect sanctity of this very moment.

Being Where I Am

Wherever I am I will take as where I am meant to be. Whatever is happening, I will accept as my path. I have what I have, I am where I am, and that's what I have to work with. I will move forward exactly from this spot knowing that it is exactly the spot I am meant to move from. Within where I am are all of the forces of the universe with me and ready to guide me. I can't build myself on someone else, I have to build on who I am. I can't be someone else, I have to be who I am. If I am dissatisfied, I can change. When I disown or undermine who I am at this moment, I use my discouragement as a reason not to try, not to put one foot in front of the other and take the next right action. I will appreciate the gift of recovery in my life and I will be grateful for God at work in all my affairs.

I trust where I am

Take the result as the path.

—Zen koan

Comparing and Despairing

Comparing and despairing is just another form of self-sabotage; it's another way of not taking responsibility for my own life, for who I am, for my day. I need to remember that emotions run high during recovery. My joys are higher, I feel my sorrows more keenly as I heal them, and my longings are stronger. The world is more intense than it usually is. When I forget this, I get afraid of what I'm experiencing if it doesn't fit my image of what I'm supposed to be experiencing. I start to feel out of step if I'm not where I think I should be. I see others as more able to manage their lives or having a better experience than I am having. Then I engage in a cover-up, only the person I am covering up is me. When I do that, I am only half there. I will let myself have my full range of feelings, knowing that they may, at times, be a bit of a roller coaster, but knowing also, that I will land comfortably at the end of the ride. Peace begins with me.

I accept the emotional intensity of healing

False happiness is like false money;
it passes for a long time as well as the true,
and serves some ordinary occasions; but when it is
brought to the touch, we find the lightness
and alloy, and feel the loss.

—Alexander Pope

The Experience of Pleasure

Today I recognize that it is the simple pleasures that bring me the greatest joy. What good is earning a living if I don't enjoy my life? What good is recovery if I don't become grateful for the life I am saving, namely mine? I will consciously build my capacity for experiencing joy and serenity. Waking up and feeling good; enjoying the weather, a friend, a cup of tea. I will bank this feeling of goodness and pleasure and draw on it throughout the day; I will expand my inner reservoir of peace. When I allow myself simply to be with life, rather than chase after what I think my life should be, a mysterious thing happens. Life is enough.

Being present in the now is my counter to anxiety, if nothing is wrong now, then I can let go and breathe and relax. I can be in my skin and in my body. Being in the now also allows me to take in beauty and experience pleasure which is part of my healing. I can resolve the pain I carry so that I can experience the pleasure that surrounds me.

There is nothing like the present

Having access to that formless realm is truly liberating. It frees you from bondage to form and identification with form. It is life in its undifferentiated state prior to its fragmentation into multiplicity. We may call it the Unmanifested, the invisible Source of all things, the Being within all beings. It is a realm of deep stillness and peace, but also of joy and intense aliveness. Whenever you are present, you become "transparent" to some extent to the light, the pure consciousness that emanates from this Source. You also realize that the light is not separate from who you are but constitutes your very essence.

Eckhart Tolle

MAY 4

Opening the Gifts of My Life

I will actualize that gifts that are in me today. I will be less preoccupied with who I'm not and more occupied with who I am. God has placed gifts within me that I am meant to develop and share. My responsibility is to come to know what my gifts are, then to cultivate and strengthen them as I share them with the world. Today I will not walk right past myself looking for who I think I should be. Each day is a new day, a gift. Today I will open the day slowly, like a present that's wrapped in hours. I will be open to what my world offers me. The world comes to greet me like an old friend each morning. My daily habits comfort and ground me. The thought of moving into my day pleases me. I am part of the mystery, part of the magic of being alive, part of this world I have been born into, part of the rhythm of life. Life unfolds one second at a time and today I will be present to witness it. How much of my life do I let pass by unnoticed? How many of my feelings go unfelt? Today I will recognize that my time on earth is limited. I choose to value my life a day at a time and embrace it while I have it.

I am open to life's gifts

The clock is running. Make the most of today.
Time waits for no man. Yesterday is history.
Tomorrow is a mystery. Today is a gift.
That's why it is called the present.

—Alice Morse Earle

Giving of Myself

I will not give things instead of love. I will recognize that the people who need and depend on me for that sustaining kind of love and attention will be hurt and confused if I ignore their real need for me. I need to give those who are close to me real love. They have cast their fate with mine and I owe them this. They depend on me and I need to understand that and step up to the plate and do what's necessary and right. When I let others commit themselves to me, through marriage or having children, I need to be responsible to them. If I don't follow through and take care of their hearts, I leave an important role in their lives gaping and unfullfilled. Today I will love those who depend on me for love and I will also be appropriately grateful, when those I need and depend upon, give me the caring and concern that nourishes my heart.

I love simply and through actions

I wonder if the snow loves the trees and fields, that it kisses
them so gently? And then it covers them up snug,
you know, with a white quilt; and perhaps it says "Go to sleep,
darlings, till the summer comes again."

—*Lewis Carroll,* Alice's Adventures in Wonderland & Through the Looking-Glass

Joy

Today I will embrace the experience of joy. I am being continually reborn. Each day life repairs and renews itself, I witness, as all that's in this world transforms from one state to another, whether it's the daily weather or me. Flowers bloom and then their petals drop to the ground and become fertilizer for new growth. Seasons change. The sun comes up and at the end of each day it disappears for the night only to reappear bright, strong, and warm the next morning. I am part of this natural and daily renewal of life. The real purpose of life isn't to grab and get, to preen and try to outdo the next guy. The real purpose of life is to deepen my ability to experience joy. Joy is the gift. Joy is the endgame. Joy is the accomplishment. Joy is what fills me up. When I am able to feel joy, I don't need to chase around trying to get the world to admire and envy me on the outside because I feel hollow on the inside. When I feel joy, I am happy in my own life, because I understand that it is the only one that is actually mine to live, the only one through which I can connect with spirit.

Joy is its own reward

Identification with your mind creates an opaque screen of concepts, labels, images, words, judgments, and definitions that block all true relationship. It comes between you and yourself, between you and your fellow man and woman, between you and nature, between you and God. It is this screen of thought that creates the illusion of separateness, the illusion that there is you and a totally separate "other." You then forget the essential fact that, underneath the level of physical appearances and separate forms, you are one with all that is.

—Eckhart Tolle

Pumping Adrenaline

Today I recognize my hypervigilance. I sucked it up too many times as a kid; I held my breath and waited for scary moments to pass. But I am still holding my breath. When I encounter the flicker of fear, I tense up just the way I did as a kid and expect the worst to happen. This makes me act edgy, reactive, and weird. I am primed for overreaction; my nerves are kindled and ready to jump. I see this now as something I need to work with on a body/mind level. There are alternative forms of treatment, health-enhancing activities, and tools and techniques that can help me to have a calmer body and mind. I do not want to import my past into my present through overreacting to situations that do not require a large reaction, I will only make extra trouble for myself and others that will create old pain in new relationships.

I pay attention to my triggers

Hypervigilance is talked about in Adult Children of Alcoholics meetings. It's basically staying on guard and waiting for the other shoe to drop. The best example is a kid coming into an alcoholic home after school trying to size up whether they are going to be safe or not or how they are going to keep themselves safe and what they are going to do. So the adrenaline starts going and the cortisol is released. They start having racing thoughts trying to figure out what they need to do to be safe—who is going to be there, who is going to be drunk, who is not, who is going to hit them, where should they go, and so forth. That's a good example of hypervigilance. When you are chronically traumatized, you start reacting to everything in that way. You start staying on guard in all kinds of situations.

—Maria Yellow Horse Braveheart, Ph.D.,
Keynote speech at Fifth Annual White Bison Wellbriety Conference

Inner Beauty

If I do not trust me, who can I trust? If I do not have faith in me, who will, who can? This is my job and no one else's. To love myself; to encourage myself, to recognize that my life is a gift from God, no more, no less than anyone else's. It is my charge in life to find the path that God and I lay out for me and walk it with love in my heart as something only I can do. I have a beauty in my soul that is mine alone, it shines if I let it, it is there when I see it. I hold the light switch in my hand. It is my life and no one can live it for me, or as me. If I do not live it, it will not get lived. My trauma history taught me to mistrust others. Today I learn that the only person I can change is me. I will learn to trust myself and then I will naturally have healthier interactions because I will more easily be able to tell if others are trustworthy or not.

I will make sure my actions are trustworthy

Trust yourself. Create the kind of self that you will be happy to live with all your life. Make the most of yourself by fanning the tiny, inner sparks of possibility into flames of achievement.

—Foster C. McCellan

Silver Linings

Life is my teacher if I can learn to read the subtle messages that reveal themselves to me a day at a time. I will look for the lesson. When life offers up its inevitable challenges, I will try to understand what I am meant to see that I am not seeing, what I am meant to hear that I am not hearing, what I am meant to know that I am not knowing. When I can see a higher meaning in what is manifesting in my life, suddenly I feel that I am on a journey of self discovery, suddenly the situations in my life feel like lessons sent by God. As this happens, the circumstances of my life become a kind of spiritual clay in my hands—they feel fluid, malleable, and as if they are becoming something wonderful before my eyes. My creativity kicks in and I feel back in the saddle, as if I am co-creating my life with the universe rather than being handed a day. There is always a silver lining if I look for it. There is always an open window if I glance in a new direction. Even if I don't see it readily, I trust that it is there and that it will reveal itself to me over time.

I can see this in its best light, there is always a silver lining

Man's main task in life is to give birth to himself,
to become what he potentially is.

—Erich Fromm

My Contribution

I am whole, and intact, and as such I have a positive contribution to make to this world. My work needs me. Whatever my gifts are, I will share them. I will not hold back, telling myself I am not ready, not smart enough, nor good enough. Today is the day. This is as good a place to begin as any. I will do the task that's before me, accomplish something and move on to the next. I will produce good works and I will share those openly with others. As I expand my own consciousness, it becomes my responsibility to share what I learn with the collective. I will do what needs to be done cheerfully. I will give myself the gift of feeling purposeful, today.

I have a contribution to make to this world

Nothing that is worth doing can be achieved in a lifetime; therefore we must be saved by hope. Nothing we do, however virtuous, can be accomplished alone; therefore we are saved by love. Nothing which is true or beautiful or good makes complete sense in any immediate context of history; therefore we must be saved by faith.

—Reinhold Niebuhr

Fixing Others

When I try to fix others, I will remember that all of my good intentions can easily be outpowered by the disease's propensity to remain in place and get progressively worse. When I get frustrated because others don't seem to "get it" the way I am getting it, I will remember that one day I stood in their shoes, and that by the grace of God I am no longer there. Others will heal in God's time, not mine. Others will see in God's time, not mine. Just for today, the only recovery I am truly responsible for is my own. When I want others to hear what I am saying, I will remember my own previous problems with hearing. I will remember that I can only really teach by example and that I lead and share by who I am, not by what I say.

I will not forget that this disease is more powerful than me

Before healing others, heal yourself.

—Lao Tzu

Opportunity

I can start over each day. I can start over each hour of each day. I tell the world what I want more of, by what I am thinking and feeling right now, right this minute. Like attracts like. Today, every hour on the hour, I'll let myself send out an order by my pleasant thoughts and feelings for more of the same. I will allow myself to see something positive. If I feel myself cascading down a path of negative thinking and moody emotions, I'll stop and consciously observe what is going through my mind. If I'm jumping on a treadmill of negative, critical, or resentful thinking, I will watch my thoughts and feelings, learn what I can about the kind of thinking that heads me on a downward spiral, and then gently move in a more positive direction. I will upgrade a negative thought for a less negative one; I will trade a downcast feeling for a less downcast feeling. I needn't pressure myself to leap from negativity into being fully upbeat, but I will take baby steps toward thoughts and feelings that create a more peaceful, pleasant climate inside of me. Life is full of chances and so is my day. I can start it over any time I want to.

I shift my life one thought at a time

As a matter of fact I had a terribly traumatic childhood.
But afterward I sort of reraised myself.

—*Michael Gruber,* The Good Son

Hope

Hope is on my horizon. I feel it in my bones, I sense it in my being; I know it to be part of who I am. I will never give up hope. Hope for a better world, a better life, a better me. Hope is that feeling that led explorers to cross dangerous oceans in search of a new world. Hope is what keeps people who are imprisoned from giving up. Hope is what allows those who have all they hold dear taken from them to begin again. Hope is natural. It is a gift that I will allow myself to have. It is my mind's way of bringing itself into a better place and my heart's way of lightening. When I have hope inside, the world looks brighter and happiness seems more possible. This elevation of my spirit is actually, in itself, a way of feeling better right now.

Today I hold hope in my heart

Hope is important because it can make the
present moment less difficult to bear.
If we believe that tomorrow will be better,
we can bear a hardship today.

—Thich Nhat Hanh

Optimism

Today I take optimism seriously. I recognize the power of my thoughts to impact my body, my life, and my relationships. When I think positive thoughts, I elevate my immune system. Optimism helps me to live longer. I attract other positive thinkers into my life when I am optimistic, and those who dwell on the negative tend to fall away. I draw experiences to myself that help to move my life toward where I want it to be, and help to shape my day in ways that feel good, when I take responsibility for what's going through my own mind.

I am responsible for what I think

Optimists, according to research, tend to do better in coping with life's stresses than pessimists. They are more likely to use problem-solving strategies to tackle difficulties as they arise, to put a positive spin on stressors, and to look for ways to make the best of a bad situation. Optimism has also been linked with longevity. In a thirty-year study published in Mayo Clinic, it was found that those classified as pessimists had a 19 percent higher risk of mortality than those who were optimists. Seeing the glass as half full, it turns out, might just be creating a glass that is half full.

—*Tian Dayton, PhD,*
Emotional Sobriety

Putting In the Elbow Grease

I will be willing to do the daily work that is required to have the life I want to have. A good life is brought forth through many doors. The door of visualization, the door of allowing good to enter my life, and the door of work to sustain and maintain what manifests. As I progress along my path I will learn how to "work smarter"; how to use my energies more efficiently and waste less time needlessly. I'll learn how to get out of my own way and let my energies flow more freely. I'll learn how to listen to others, take in what they say, and then make my own decisions—how to have boundaries that are porous and flexible rather than rigid or brittle. I will find my sense of self and be able to sustain it even in the presence of others. I'll develop strength, wisdom, patience, and compassion. I will develop my own unique gifts and strengths.

I am willing to work

Character cannot be developed in ease and quiet.
Only through experience of trial and suffering can the
soul be strengthened, vision cleared, ambition
inspired and success achieved.

—*Helen Keller*

MAY 16

The Creative Power of My Mind

I can do so much to influence and create my own life. What I do today becomes who I am tomorrow. Every action I take, every thought I think, and the feelings I experience throughout my day are creating both my present and my future. The beautiful part about this is that it is so empowering; the scary part is letting myself know how much my life is affected by my own attitudes and actions. Life wants to fulfill me. I block my own experience of life's radiance by trimming it around the edges, by saying no to that full and serene feeling that I get when I rest in my own spiritual center. When I am present to the here and now, to the magic of the moment, I am saying "yes" to life, I am inviting goodness to surround me, I am allowing the feelings I like experiencing to be present, to be mine.

I value the life that is mine

Now is the only time.
How we relate to it creates the future.
In other words, if we're going to be more cheerful
in the future, it's because of our aspiration and
exertion to be cheerful in the present.
What we do accumulates; the future is the
result of what we do right now.

—Pema Chödrön

Living Truly

Today I will live the life I wish to have. If I want not be manipulative or deceitful in my relationships, I will be an honest person. If I want goodness and decency surrounding me, I will be good and decent. If I want to feel love coming towards me, I will love others. Today I won't ask life to be something I'm not willing to be. Today, I accept that what I put out, comes back to me. Today I recognize that we are all, each of us engaged in a constant human struggle against our own, personal demons. We each of us have our story to tell, we all have pain, angst, dashed dreams and unfulfilled promises. Life is part beautiful, part struggle for all of us. No one sails through unscathed. We are all here for only as long as we are here for and it's up to each of us to play the hand we're dealt with as much poise, dignity and decency that we are capable of.

I see past the surface

Any time you are with anyone or think of anyone
you must say to yourself: I am dying and this person
too is dying, attempting the while to experience the truth
of the words you are saying. If every one of you agrees
to practice this, bitterness will die out, harmony will arise."

—Anthony de Mello

Blessings

I can lose my blessings. If I don't appreciate them, they can disappear. If I feel overly entitled, if I take what is mine for granted, if I behave as if life's blessings are simply owed me and I don't need to notice or appreciate them, I am literally telling them to shrink. I am throwing them away with both hands. I am saying "no" to life's blessings. There is a divine wisdom to gratitude, because what I focus on with appreciation has a way of expanding in my life. If I erase my blessings, I don't feed them with the grace of gratitude. If I am aware of them, if I appreciate them, I show the creative force that brings forth all good things that I am awake enough to see and value what has been so generously given to me. I invite good to grow in my life.

I know enough to say thank you

Hem your blessings with thankfulness
so they don't unravel.

—Author unknown

Dark Forecasting

I will take a vacation from my myriad of little self doubts. Those stories I am ever making up about what is going on in someone else's mind, about me, that I then respond to as if they are real. I am not living in chaos today—I don't need to constantly protect myself from small assaults to my well-being. Everything that happens in a room is not about me, unless I choose to make it about me. What other people are feeling is generally about them until I jump into its path. I will keep myself out of that path, I will stop personalizing other people's feelings and thinking they are about me. I will leave their negativity, anger, and pain with them; it's not my job to fix it, it never was. No one can take my peace of mind away from me if I don't let them. Who will be the wiser if I am nice to myself on the inside today? Whose rules will I be violating if I give myself a break from the cascading thoughts that get me nowhere fast? Why shouldn't I just let myself be happy inside? It can be my little secret. I will just feel good about myself. I will just let myself not go to places on the inside that only get me lost in more places on the inside. I will enjoy a peaceful mind today.

How I feel is my own business.

Our doubts are traitors
And make us lose the good we oft might win
By fearing to attempt.

—*Shakespeare,* Measure for Measure

Hidden Pain

Today I recognize the nature of trauma memories. When I was a child, confronted with huge, out of control parents, or ignored so much that I questioned if I were even there, I went numb. I just hurt too much to process the pain I was in, but my senses stayed busy absorbing bits and pieces of information that it stuffed into random parts of my mind and body. A patch of blue sky, the smell of something cooking, cut grass, booze, perfume, a slap, hurtful tones, angry eyes . . . all a part of my unconscious memory bank. I don't remember them as a coherent story, my thinking was just too muddled to do anything but let these images drift wordlessly into the lake of my unconscious.It's not that I mean to hide them, just that I don't really know where or how to find them. That's why when these memories get triggered, they feel so confusing.

When memories get triggered, I will accept and process them

Equally as powerful as the desire to deny atrocities is the conviction that denial does not work. Folk wisdom is filled with ghosts who refuse to rest in their graves until their stories are told. Murder will out. Remembering and telling the truth about terrible events are prerequisites both for the restoration of the social order and for the healing of individual victims. The conflict between the will to deny horrible events and the will to proclaim them aloud is the central dialectic of psychological trauma. People who have survived atrocities often tell their stories in a highly emotional, contradictory, and fragmented manner that undermines their credibility and thereby serves the twin imperatives of truth-telling and secrecy. When the truth is finally recognized, survivors can begin their recovery. But far too often secrecy prevails, and the story of the traumatic event surfaces not as a verbal narrative but as a symptom.

Judith Lewis Hermann, Trauma and Recovery

Keeping the Focus on Myself

Today, I see that having my own life begins inside of me. It is not just a function of what I do, but the attitude with which I move through my day. Having my own life is about checking in with myself to see how I'm doing. It's wearing a sweater if I'm cold and taking a break if I'm tired. It's making sure that I'm having enough fun in my life, paying attention to what I enjoy doing and doing more of that, and finding ways of reducing what doesn't feel good. Having a life is letting myself have my own unique likes and dislikes, and acting on them in constructive ways. It is not organizing my life so that it is good enough for everyone else, forgetting that it needs to be good enough for me as well. In recovery, I learn to keep the focus on myself in healthy rather than narcissistic ways. I recognize that taking care of my relationships has to include taking care of my relationship with myself. I occupy the center of my own life.

I am with myself on the inside

Your time is limited, so don't waste it living
someone else's life. Don't be trapped by dogma—which is
living with the results of other people's thinking.
Don't let the noise of others' opinions drown out your own
inner voice. And most importantly, have the courage to
follow your heart and intuition. They somehow already
know what you truly want to become.
Everything else is secondary.

—*Steve Jobs,*
Stanford Commencement Speech, 2005

Repeating Patterns

The relationship dynamics that I recreate and reenact over and over again send up a red flag marking the spot of where my unconscious pain lies. When I see a dysfunctional relationship pattern in my life repeat and repeat itself, when the relationships are different but the pattern is the same, I will stop, look, and listen. This is where I will dig for water, where I will mine for gold. When I can feel and process the unfelt pain, fear, anger, or sadness that holds patterns in place, the well will open and the waters of my unconscious will flow freely again. I will gain insights into parts of me that have been frozen and out of my conscious awareness. When I cannot feel those difficult feelings, I act them out through blindly recreating the same sorts of situations and dynamics that I am most afraid of. Or I avoid situations or relationships that I fear might trigger pain that I am afraid to feel. I stop taking the risk to go for what I want in life because I unconsciously fear the loss of it, or being hurt all over again.

I will allow myself to see and feel what drives me from underneath

Repetition compulsion is a psychological phenomenon in which a person repeats a traumatic event or its circumstances over and over again. This includes reenacting the event or putting oneself in situations that have a high probability of the event occurring again. This "re-living" can also take the form of dreams, repeating the story of what happened, and even hallucination.

—Wikipedia

Unprocessed Abuse

Whenever I am heading for extreme reactions, I will look within. When I go from no feeling to intense feeling, from numbness to supercharge, from zero to ten, I will check in with myself to see what I might have stored in my unconscious that is fueling an extreme overreaction. It's the stuff from my past that can trigger this kind of unconscious reaction—the humiliation, anger, shame, rejection, rage, or sadness that I blocked out of my consciousness then, because it was just too scary to feel. I didn't necessarily have anyone as a kid to help me right-size my feelings of fear and helplessness, and too much of the time, the people I'd have gone to for comfort were the ones hurting me. So I just pretended nothing was happening.

I can face and feel hidden pain and bring it back to consciousness

The psychological distress symptoms of traumatized people simultaneously call attention to the existence of an unspeakable secret and deflect attention from it. This is most apparent in the way traumatized people alternate between feeling numb and reliving the event. The dialectic of trauma gives rise to complicated, sometimes uncanny alterations of consciousness, which George Orwell, one of the committed truth-tellers of our century, called "doublethink," and which mental health professionals, searching for calm, precise language, call "dissociation." It results in protean, dramatic, and often bizarre symptoms of hysteria which Freud recognized a century ago as disguised communications about sexual abuse in childhood. . . .

—*Judith Lewis Herman, M.D.,* Trauma and Recovery

Feeling Good

I am the one who ultimately needs to sustain my own state of mind. If I don't keep my spirits strong, no one else will, no one else can. My state of mind and my mood are my responsibility. I will set the intention of feeling good, knowing that that is a way of increasing good entering my day. My breath connects my body with my spirit so breath awareness is a time honored way to elevate my mood. Today I will take moments throughout my day to consciously breathe out the negativity and anxiety that are in me, and breathe in peace and serenity. Through breathing easily and deeply, I invite spirit in. This is a simple form of meditation that I can do when I am sitting still, lying down, or walking. I can let my mood lighten as I repeat this gentle process over and over again, until I experience a subtle shift. Meditating in this way is accessible and easy. It gives me a way of calming my mind and body and restoring good feeling whenever I want to.

I make this simple breathing meditation a part of my daily life

It's really important that you feel good,
because this feeling good is what sends out a signal
to the universe and starts to attract more of itself onto you.
So the more you can feel good, the more you will attract
the things that help you feel good and are able to
keep bringing you up higher and higher.

—Dr. Joe Vitale

Lighting One Candle

Today, I will light one candle and that candle is myself. I will keep my own flame burning. I turn my sight to light and love and goodness. For today, there is no need to be discouraged. So what if I see and identify all the ills of society and diagnose it as sick—what good will that do me or anyone else? I heal society by healing myself. Who I am impacts all that is around me and shapes my corner of the world. I am responsible for my impact. Just as life is lived one day at a time, the world will heal one person at a time. Each time I think a positive, loving thought, it goes into the ether and vibrates. My prayers will not go unanswered because they are the prayers of so many. There are so many good people from all walks of life, all corners of the world. We have something very profound in common, our love of life, our love of our world, our respect for the life that has been given to us and to others.

I have a contribution to make

At times our own light goes out and is rekindled
by a spark from another person. Each of us has cause
to think with deep gratitude of those
who have lighted the flame within us.

—Albert Schweitzer

A Spiritual Awakening

This is a journey without a goal. Recovery has opened my heart and soul to spirituality. Where before I thought I had to have all the answers, today I learn to live in the question, to be open to learning and letting something new and vital in. Where before I thought I had to be unbending and stand firm whether or not I knew why, today I learn to surrender, I allow life to happen rather than trying to force it into place. I see that I need not have all the answers, and I understand that my ego and self-will often blind me to the wisdom that is present in the moment. Today I value the experience of being alive more than being right. I understand that there is strength in bending and freedom in letting go and letting God.

I accept that I will never fully understand—
I embrace the mystery

All the greatest and most important problems of life
are fundamentally insolvable. . . . they can never be solved,
but only outgrown. This "outgrowth" proved on further
investigation to require a new level of consciousness.
Some higher or wider interest appeared on the
person's horizon, and through this broadening of his
or her outlook the unsolvable problem lost its urgency.
It was not solved logically in its own terms but
faded when confronted with a new
and stronger life urge.

—Carl Jung

Embracing the Void

There is emptiness as well as fullness to life. Today I will embrace them both. I will see the emptiness as a spiritual void that is actually full in a completely different sort of way. A God-shaped hole. When I allow myself to embrace my own inner emptiness rather than run from it, a paradox happens. What was unknown becomes known, what was frightening becomes tolerable, and what was empty becomes full. The void I feel inside of me is really a spiritual wilderness. When I enter it, barren trees flower and bear fruit. It is alive and vibrating. It soothes and sustains me and I feel tingly and alive on the inside.

There is a world within me waiting to be born

The void is that which stands right in the middle
of this and that. The void is all inclusive; having no opposite,
there is nothing which it excludes or opposes. . . .
It is living void, because all forms come out of it,
and whoever realizes the void is filled with life
and power and the love of all things.

—*Bruce Lee,* Striking Thoughts:
Bruce Lee's Wisdom for Daily Living

How Important Is It?

I have much more choice about what I feel than I realize. If I'm feeling stressed out, I will even out my breath and relax. If I'm obsessing about something, I will ask myself how important this thing will be in five years; I will remind myself that stressing only makes things worse. It clouds my judgment and makes everything bigger than it needs to be. If I set my mind toward being in a relaxed mood, I will find a way to get there. My day will feel more pleasant if I consciously head it in that direction. The events of my day will run more smoothly. Today I want to enhance my experience of peace, ease, and a feeling that life is working out as it is meant to.

I give my feelings space as I allow them to shift upwards

. . . The body initially defends itself against adverse circumstances by activating the sympathetic nervous system. This has been called the alarm reaction. It mobilizes the body for the "fight or flight" response, which can be seen phylogenetically as an adaptive short-term reaction to emergency situations. In many cases, the stress episode is mastered during the alarm reaction stage. Often, however, stress is a longer encounter, and the organism moves on to the resistance stage, in which it adapts more or less successfully to the stressor. Although the person does not make the impression of being under stress, the organism does not function well and becomes ill. According to Selye, the immune system is compromised, and some typical "diseases of adaptation" develop under persistent stress, such as ulcers and cardiovascular diseases. Finally, in the exhaustion stage the organism's adaptation resources are depleted, and a breakdown occurs. This is associated with parasympathetic activation that leads to illness, burnout, depression, or even death.

—Ralf Schwarzer, Ph.D., "The Role of Stressful Life Events," September 20, 2001.

Living Beyond My Capacity

I will not live beyond my capacity. When I overschedule myself, I become stressed. When I become stressed, my nerves get frayed. When my nerves get frayed, my thinking gets rigid or fuzzy—I am not calm and clear. When my thinking and feeling are pressured, my behavior gets short; I do and say things that I regret. When I am stressed over a long period of time, my adrenal glands stop functioning properly. I burn them out. I become vulnerable to sickness in a way that I am not normally vulnerable. Or I grab at ways of feeling better fast that have sent me down a slippery road. Maybe I eat junk food because it momentarily smoothes out my rough edges by releasing dopamine into my blood stream; just like alcohol and drugs it acts as a mood alterer, giving me a feeling of being high, relaxed, easy with everything. Or I spend money to alter my mood . . . I grab stuff I don't need and my income gets eaten up. But eventually I crash—I get logy and sluggish from the food, hung over from alcohol, jagged from drugs, or spend money I could actually use constructively to reduce stress and make my life more carefree and comfortable.

I will watch how stressed out I allow myself to get

Pain is a relatively objective, physical phenomenon;
suffering is our psychological resistance to what happens.
Events may create physical pain, but they do not in
themselves create suffering. Resistance creates suffering.
Stress happens when your mind resists what is. . . .
The only problem in your life is your mind's
resistance to life as it unfolds.

—Dan Millman,
Everyday Enlightenment

Projection

Today, I understand that when I project my feelings outward and see them as belonging to other people and not to me, I postpone my own self-awareness and growth. Sitting with anxiety, anger, rage, or jealousy may not be pleasant, but actually experiencing my own feelings is the only way to get through them. When I project my feelings to get rid of them, when I make my feelings and reactions about someone else, I weaken myself. I learn nothing about what makes me tick; I get temporary relief or satisfaction, but not that aha! insight that springs me loose from my own stuck place. Generally, the feelings that I have the hardest time sitting with say something about me. I might project anger, for example, because it's easier for me to live with the idea that someone else is angry at me than to let myself know how furious I am with them. The only way I can deal with difficult feelings is first to claim them as my own.

I am willing to sit with my reactions and mine them for gold

The images of the unconscious place a great responsibility upon a man. Failure to understand them, or a shirking of ethical responsibility, deprives him of his wholeness and imposes a painful fragmentariness on his life.

—*Carl Jung,*
Memories, Dreams, Reflections

What I Could Not See

My family disease of addiction took something away from me. It stole the life that was supposed to be mine. All of our carefully laid plans, the simple and orderly world that was set out in front of me by loving hands and hearts, blew up in my face, was torn away from me—and I bled inside. I still bleed sometimes; the wound, it seems, never completely heals. Today, I am grateful that this happened, not because I relish pain but because I see that there was a better life waiting for me that I would not have embraced without pain. There was a life of the spirit that grew inside of me because I had no choice, I had to choose life: the pathway became so narrow that I had to step onto it or just tumble into an awful darkness.

I am aware of the gift that being surrounded by addiction and mental illness gave me

We must be willing to let go of the life we planned
so as to have the life that is waiting for us.

—Joseph Campbell

JUNE

Footprints in the Sand

One night I dreamed I was walking along the beach with the Lord.
Many scenes from my life flashed across the sky.
In each scene I noticed footprints in the sand.
Sometimes there were one set of footprints.
other times there were one set of footprints.
This bothered me because I noticed
that during the low periods of my life
when I was suffering from
anguish, sorrow or defeat,
I could see only one set of footprints.

So I said to the Lord,
"You promised me Lord,
that if I followed you,
you would walk with me always.
But I have noticed that during
the most trying periods of my life
there have only been one
set of footprints in the sand.
Why, when I needed you most,
have you not been there for me?"

The Lord replied,
"The times when you have
seen only one set of footprints,
is when I carried you."

—Mary Stevenson

Home

I will value my home today. I will take time for those I love. I will take time for myself. I know that my time is the most valuable thing I have to give or to have for myself. Our world runs at a fast pace; we are all on a track to get somewhere, but at the end of the day, where are we all going in such a rush? What am I looking for so hard in the future that makes it worth running right by my present? I need time for refueling, for rest, refreshment, and renewal, and I need it each and every day, each and every week. I need time for those I love. I need time to nourish love with those with whom I am deeply connected. Their mere presence in my life is stabilizing and sustaining. I will not take time, myself, or others for granted.

I do not need perfection as much as connection with myself and others

Would that there were an award for people
who come to understand the concept of enough.
Good enough. Successful enough. Thin enough.
Rich enough. Socially responsible enough.
When you have self-respect,
you have enough.

—*Gail Sheehy*

My Actions

Who I am speaks louder that what I say. My actions are worth more than words, they have a meaning that resonates throughout my life and the lives of those with whom I am related. When I use words of love but don't back them with actions of love, I send out a false and confusing message. I confuse and wound others by giving them the hope of something good then disappointing them. When my actions are consistent with what I say and feel, I am easier to relate to, and others can find me and connect with me more readily. I have a calming rather than a complicating influence. My actions count, they send powerful messages to those around me. They lead somewhere. They are my imprint on my world.

I act with an awareness that my actions have an impact

I feel that the essence of spiritual practice is
your attitude toward others. When you have a pure,
sincere motivation, then you have right attitude
toward others based on kindness,
compassion, love and respect.

—H.H. the Dalai Lama

Dissociation Versus Psychic Freedom

Sometimes I can feel envious of someone for whom denial works. They seem to go through life oblivious to the collateral damage their addiction or their dysfunctional behavior or their narcissism causes the rest of us. I feel cheated; why can't I just deny something, push it out of consciousness, pretend it isn't there, and walk around with that same kind of smile? It doesn't seem fair. But at the same time, their smile feels false, their behavior feels disconnected, and they don't appear to have real relationships. It's hard to resist wanting to deny, but it just doesn't work for me. While I don't want to be married to my pain, still, denying it isn't strength, I see that. Denial is just postponing enlightenment. All that stuff is still there, unnamed, unfelt, and ready to burst forward and rock the boat.

I want to be real with myself, free but real

People who are dissociated do not suffer.
But this is only because they have abandoned their
healing process and numbed their pain. Enlightenment grows
from the fertilized soil of suffering. People who are dissociated
call themselves enlightened. But this is only because they
have they have no conception of what enlightenment is.
Enlightenment is the polar opposite of dissociation.
People who are dissociated feel they have mastered forgiveness.
But this is only because they completely deny the harm
done to them—and the damage remaining. The enlightened
forgive spontaneously and without effort because they
have fully embraced their damaged parts and grieved
every honest ounce of their misery.

—Daniel Mackler

Childhood Stress

Stress affects my body and my mind. When I am under stress, I tend to do the same thing more intensely, but less efficiently. Stress undermines my state of health and makes me feel stuck in nonproductive, compulsive routines. I lose my spontaneity, my ability to make easy, good choices. Stress chemicals do everything from locking in the storage of fat cells to making my hair and nails brittle. Stress is contagious, growing up around stress and chaos affected my body. With nowhere to go, I plowed them into my own physiology where they affected my health and well-being. I hid them everywhere in my body. Right-sizing and understanding my emotions affected my health—my head, stomach, and back ached, my legs held it, my shoulders, my chest. I held my breath and made it shallow. I just had more stress than I could process, no one to help me make sense of it, and I didn't know what else to do. I just froze it up anywhere and everywhere it would fit.

Today I understand that my body paid a big price for too much stress

As her analyst had told her: the deeper buried the distress, the further into the body it went. The digestive system was about as far as it could go to hide.

—*Richard Matheson,*
What Dreams May Come

I Can Manage Me

Today when I feel stressed I will use my stress busters. I will take a walk or exercise, use my breathing to calm and quiet my nervous system, listen to music, take a warm bath, or sit quietly by myself and meditate. I know what works best for me to get back into a relaxed space. Sometimes it's just collapsing in front of my favorite funny show. These activities release serotonin or dopamine or both into my bloodstream. These are nature's mood stabilizers, my body's built-in antidepressant. When I learn how to trigger my relaxation response naturally, I can manage my moods through pleasant activity, and I can build these mood managers into my daily life. Just when I am giving up dysfunctional mood managers, I am adding functional and fun ones, the kind that enhance my health, beauty and good feeling about myself. But the key is, I will notice when I am stressed and do something to counter it before it spins out of control, and I will make these activities part of my daily life! Today, I will take responsibility for my own state of calm.

I know what calms me

Being in control of your life and having realistic expectations about your day-to-day challenges are the keys to stress management, which is perhaps the most important ingredient to living a happy, healthy and rewarding life.

—Marilu Henner

A Wish

Today I will make a wish. I will make a wish and trust that it will find wings. I will see it flying through the air, blown from a loving hand toward eternity. Like a child in the morning sunlight, I will feel the potential magic of the moment. Like a child, I will think that mornings are for wishing; wishing with excitement, with an innocent faith that what I wish for, can come forth. I will see my wish as already fulfilled, I will experience it as if it is happening right now, as if it is real. I am making my wish right NOW. I will rely on unseen hands to carry my wish lovingly and tenderly and scatter it into the firmament so that it can be seeds that grow. I will see it being fertilized with all that is alive, nourishing and needed. I will trust this moment to communicate itself to more moments.

My wishes have wings

Wish on everything. Pink cars are good, especially old ones. And stars of course, first stars and shooting stars. Planes will do if they are the first light in the sky and look like stars. Wish in tunnels, holding your breath and lifting your feet off the ground. Birthday candles. Baby teeth."

—Francesca Lia Block

Meditation

I have a part of me that quietly observes the rest of me. Today, right now in fact, I will rest quietly in my "observer mind" and simply witness inner workings. I will breathe in and out as I do this and feel my body relax and let go of stress. I'll do this several times throughout my day today. I will not tell my mind to do or be anything. It will be as if I am sitting on the banks of a river watching the water flow by. My thoughts are like that water. I will watch my thoughts with no more thought of getting involved in them or changing their course than I would the river. I will simply witness and allow myself to observe my thoughts flow by just as I would observe the river rippling, sparking with light, thick and dark with mud, rough, calm, wavy or serene . . . flowing, flowing, flowing by.

I strengthen my own "inner witness"

Meditation brings wisdom; lack of mediation
leaves ignorance. Know well what leads you forward
and what holds you back, and choose
the path that leads to wisdom.

—Buddha

Cutoff

When I am angry I will explore my feelings rather than act out in rage or withdraw into stony silence. What do those strategies accomplish other than prolonging the pain? Cutoff is a relationship dynamic. When there is pain the solution is seen as withdrawing or cutting off contact, leaving another person feeling out in the cold. Rage is a self-indulgent dump at another person's expense. These are the sorts of strategies that pass through generations. The mother who cuts off the daughter teaches the daughter that this is the way to deal with emotional pain. Years of being shut out create a barrier of defense in the daughter that she carries into her relationships with her spouse and children. The father who rages models raging for the children. Both of these strategies depersonalize the other person. Refusing decent communication causes great pain to both sides and literally cuts off any possibility for resolution. Cutoff and rage are temporary gratifications, an acting out of a jumbled mass of feelings of fear, hurt, rage, and a wish to hurt another. But they only lead to more alienation and hurt.

I can deal with anger without raging or withdrawing

To think justly, we must understand what others mean;
to know the value of our thoughts, we must
try their effect on other minds.

—William Hazlitt

Just for Today

Just for today, I will make a resolution that I actually have a shot at keeping. A day at a time, I will move towards my goal, celebrating each small gain in good feeling about myself and my life. I will keep my resolution for another 24 hours, for one more day, and congratulate myself for doing so. I will understand that if I slip in my resolve on one day, I will not waste my valuable time beating myself up. I will simply climb right back on the moment I become aware of it, and have that good feeling of knowing that I can make mistakes, lots of them, and they won't stop me or discourage me. Just for today I will approach my resolution with an attitude of gratitude, happy that I have the wisdom, purpose, and inner strength to have it at all; feeling grateful that I have the clarity and will to take that very crucial next step. Because just for today, I know that it's the next step that really counts.

I walk through my year one grateful step at a time

Always bear in mind that your own resolution to
succeed is more important than any other.

—*Abraham Lincoln*

A Longing of the Soul

I open my heart in prayer, I become one with God. I ask freely knowing that God wishes me to feel an inner pressure, a longing to unite with life and fulfill my destiny. I yearn openly and unselfconsciously like a baby looking into its parent's face. I allow my soul to be seen, I give myself away and throw myself into the arms of God with the same abandon that a child throws himself into his parent's arms, knowing that he will be caught, knowing that my only job is to heave myself toward God and trust. When I pray, I see a deeper purpose in my life, and I am able to picture myself happy and whole. Meaning is more transparent. Things make sense, somehow. The events of my life seem to have a natural order to them and I can glimpse their pattern, flow and meaning. I am less bothered by what others think and expect, and more aware of my own being, my own needs, my own path. I will see my life as good, full, happy and purposeful. I reach out.

I pray with all of me

Knock, And He'll open the door
Vanish, And He'll make you shine like the sun
Fall, And He'll raise you to the heavens
Become nothing, And He'll turn you into everything.

—*Rumi*

Telling the Truth

I will not lie because it's easy or gives me a free pass, one that I will pay for later. I will tell the truth today, to those I am close to and whom I deal with in my daily affairs. Mostly I will not tell lies to me. This doesn't mean that I have to blast anyone around me, insult others, or be hurtful or rude. It simply means that I recognize the power of inner honesty. I will neither beat myself up with brutal honesty, nor slip into victimhood because I use "honesty" as a way to blame others. I will recognize the value in my life of a simple sort of truthfulness that is balanced, a truthfulness that allows me to be comfortable within my own skin, that gives me pride in myself. An honesty that is born out of my own need to live in integrity and wholeness.

I will not rip myself or others up with a thousand little lies

For every good reason there is to lie, there is
a better reason to tell the truth.

—Bo Bennett

Grooves

I really want to change patterns that get me the same old thing over and over and over again. But it feels like a tall order. It requires so much discipline just at that moment when I am about to slide comfortably back into acting in the same old dysfunctional ways. There is something so delicious about staying stuck in an old groove, wallowing in the same old place. Today I will see that pattern, that stuckness, that unwillingness to let go as part of an unhealthy pattern that gets and keeps me stuck. I am aware of this pattern, I can accept that it is in me and I can soon, in a minute, an hour, a day, or a week, take a small action to change it. Each small change causes a shift in the whole pattern, if a butterfly flapping its wings on one continent can affect weather on another, a small change in my pattern can cause a shift that is unpredictably resonant.

I make a small change knowing that it might make a big difference

Insanity is doing the same thing,
over and over again, but expecting
different results."

—*Narcotics Anonymous*

Eating Well

Food is medicine. Everything that I put into my body becomes part of me, affects my mood, my health, and my state of fitness. Food is fuel, it's what I run on. Food becomes the quality of my skin, organs, muscles, blood, and bone. I cannot lie to my body about what I put into it. It is what I will use for energy and what I'll wear around each and every moment. If I try to trick my body, it won't really work. My body is infinitely intelligent, more than any machine; it will adapt to what I put into it. But what it can't make use of, will get stored as fat, or will drain my vitality, or overtax my organs. My body will try to get rid of what it finds toxic at great expense to my health. If I fill it with too many unhealthy things, it will eventually rebel, it will get sick, it will tell me that I have pushed it too far. I cannot lie to my body. I will not try. I will pay attention to what I eat.

I am responsible for what I put into my body

South Central Los Angeles [is the] home
of the drive-thru and the drive-by. Funny thing is,
the drive-thrus are killing more people
than the drive-bys.

—Ron Finley

Standing in Awe

Today I will appreciate the miracles that surround me on a daily basis. A blue patch of sky, leaves rustling in the wind, someone's warm smile. The very fact that I am breathing and alive connects me to the deepest mysteries of the universe. My life is full of these daily wonders if I am available to see them, if I take a moment to stand in awe. The mystery of this life is ever unfolding in front of both my inner and outer eye. I will not walk right past what makes me feel alive today, in order to chase my shadow or get someplace sixty seconds sooner. I will build a little time for wonder and beauty into my day. I will walk to or from work, go outdoors for lunch, or take time to listen to the birds. I will not rob myself of the experience of my own day trying to get to the day that I think I should have.

The real miracle surrounds me all the time, I just need to see it

In the end, it's not going to matter
how many breaths you took, but how many
moments took your breath away

—Shing Xiong

JUNE 15

Choosing My Attitude

I have the power to choose my own attitude no matter what my circumstances. Today I understand the innate power of this subtle shift. My ability to choose the attitude I will take puts something into my hands that can change the way I experience my own life beginning right this moment. If I use the circumstances of my life to define who I am on the inside, I am ignoring the fullness of my being, I am crushing my inner world and bending it into the shape of whatever is happening in the moment. Who I am on the inside, how I choose to experience myself and the life I have is up to me. Life may, in some ways, happen to me but I have infinite choice as to how I see, think about, and experience my day, and that also shapes my day.

Today I take responsibility for my own attitude

When we are no longer able to change a situation—
we are challenged to change ourselves.

—Viktor E. Frankl

I Thank You, God

Today I will say, "Thank you, God", each time something happens that feels nice. If I enjoy my cup of tea in the morning, I will say "Thank you, God." If I see a quarter on the sidewalk, I will pick it up and thank God. If someone smiles at me in a way that feels good, if the sun feels warm on my back, if my car starts, my dinner is there, or someone in my life is with me for another day, I will say "thank you," recognizing that these are all blessings. By the end of the day, I will have thanked God for a lot of things. I will have remembered what makes my life worth living. I will have increased my conscious contact with the source of all good.

I am aware of a divine presence in all things

You've gotta dance like there's nobody watching,
Love like you'll never be hurt,
Sing like there's nobody listening,
And live like it's heaven on earth.

—William W. Purkey

Prayer

I will pray today. I will not try to do anything without God's help, whether it's finding something in a cupboard, figuring out what to have for breakfast, or changing my life. I will allow God into each and every intimate detail in my life trusting that God's love is all-pervasive, all-knowing, and cannot be used up. It is not about being deserving; God and I are meant to be one in the same. It is not about being good enough; God is with me always. It is I who stray from God, not God who strays from me. I understand that God's reach extends as far as I extend. I will allow God's presence to imbue my life with a sense of being alive and in constant, constant contact. I will allow God's presence to fill me and guide and hold my life. There is no such thing as poverty or lack when I live in God's eternal love and presence.

I invite God into my heart

Love is a fruit in season at all times,
and within reach of every hand. Anyone may
gather it and no limit is set. Everyone can reach this
love through meditation, spirit of prayer, and
sacrifice, by an intense inner life.

—Mother Teresa

It's a Process

Today, I let go and become real. I know that by holding on too tightly, I squeeze the life out of myself and those around me. Recovery has taught me to value being authentic above being something or someone. Recovery is a process of facing and removing those obstacles that have been in the way on my road back to myself. It has been my willingness to risk and trust that my Higher Power that has brought me this far will hold me and bring me to life again. I will live each day as it comes and give some of what I have received. So many people have helped me along the way—it is also part of my recovery to share what I have learned, in case it might help someone else. As I give, I also receive.

I am open to life and all it holds

I am spinning the silk threads of my story,
weaving the fabric of my world. . . . I spun out of control.
Eating was hard. Breathing was hard. Living was hardest.
I wanted to swallow the bitter seeds of forgetfulness. . . .
Somehow, I dragged myself out of the dark and asked for help.
I spin and weave and knit my words and visions
until a life starts to take shape.
There is no magic cure, no making it all go away forever.
There are only small steps upward; an easier day,
an unexpected laugh, a mirror that
doesn't matter anymore.
I am thawing.

—*Laurie Halse Anderson,* Wintergirls

Calming Down

Sometimes when I am upset with someone I love, I lose sight of all feelings except my feelings of resentment, worry, and anxiety. I forget that this is a person I generally love and trust. I completely lose touch with all of the other more benign feelings I have toward them the rest of the time. I get black and white: they are all good or all bad, I cannot find an in-between. I get lost in one feeling only. Anger is blind. When I am lost in it, I can't see or feel anything clearly. Sometimes I think this kind of anger has a component of fear in it. Fear that I won't get my point across, fear I will be blamed for something. When I can't get past my anger and fear, all healthy communication stops. At these times I will allow myself to calm down inside before I try to negotiate anything. I'll try to use the moment to grow rather than make things worse, I'll try something different.

I give myself time to get calm

Opposition is a natural part of life.
Just as we develop our physical muscles through
overcoming opposition—such as lifting weights—
we develop our character muscles by
overcoming challenges
and adversity.

—Stephen R. Covey

Inner Cleansing

Recovery uncovers parts of me that I have held in storage. Thoughts arise, thoughts I have blocked out during normal waking hours. They scare me, sometimes. But as I allow them to come forward they become less threatening. They only really have power when I fear them and push them away. If I welcome them into the sunlit rooms of my mind, they sort of spread out and relax. Today I understand that I cannot really keep secrets from myself because they pollute me from within. Today I let these thoughts and feelings have room to breathe, and as they do, they dissipate. I am in a process of healing. I am taking the time to allow my body, mind, and spirit to become clean and whole.

I awaken to my inner life

Over the years, I have come to realize that the greatest trap in our life is not success, popularity, or power, but self-rejection. Success, popularity, and power can indeed present a great temptation, but their seductive quality often comes from the way they are part of the much larger temptation to self-rejection. When we have come to believe in the voices that call us worthless and unlovable, then success, popularity, and power are easily perceived as attractive solutions. The real trap, however, is self-rejection. As soon as someone accuses me or criticizes me, as soon as I am rejected, left alone, or abandoned, I find myself thinking, "Well, that proves once again that I am a nobody." . . . [My dark side says,] I am no good . . . I deserve to be pushed aside, forgotten, rejected, and abandoned. Self-rejection is the greatest enemy of the spiritual life because it contradicts the sacred voice that calls us the "Beloved." Being the Beloved constitutes the core truth of our existence.

—Henri J. M. Nouwen

Other People's Stuff

I give another person so much power over me when I overreact to things they do that I don't like. But when I don't pick up the tossed gauntlet, when I let the comment, feeling, or zinger simply drop at their feet, one of a few things might happen: Their negative energy will dissipate, it will be directed elsewhere, or it will boomerang somewhere along the line in their own lives. But it will no longer surround me. I cannot necessarily keep their negative blast away initially, but I have a choice about whether or not I load their energy with my own negative thoughts. Feeling all sorts of resentful feelings or creating bad attitudes in my head that then become mine, is really a choice that I am making, not a foregone conclusion. Today, if someone behaves in a way that I don't like, I will let it lie, I will leave their controlling and negative energy with them, knowing that if I engage it, I will simply be falling into a pattern that feels dysfunctional to me. And if I don't engage it, if I don't have a lot of other thoughts about it, if I don't dwell on it, I will not make their negativity my negativity.

I leave other people's stuff with them

I do not claim to have attained optimum emotional well-being. Actually, I think that may be a lifetime goal. For me it's an ongoing process that requires awareness, knowledge, and practice. I do know what good emotional health feels like, and that motivates me to keep at the practice.

—*Andrew Weil, M.D.,* Spontaneous Healing

Staying Calm

Peace begins with me. I need to remember that emotions can run high when I am growing and changing inside, when I am challenging myself to stretch. My joys are higher and my longings are stronger. The world is more intense than it usually is. When I forget this, I start to feel out of step if I'm not where I think I should be. I compare my insides with everybody else's outsides and use that to make myself wrong. I want to push away my inner world and I get a little afraid of what I'm experiencing if it doesn't fit my image of what I think I'm supposed to be experiencing. Then I engage in a cover-up. But when all is said and done, the only person I am covering up is me, and I am only half there. Today I will let myself have my full range of feelings, knowing that they may, at times, be a bit of a roller coaster, but knowing also that I will land comfortably at the end of the ride.

I am willing to see more of me

Dissimulation, secretiveness, appear a necessity
to the melancholic. He has complex, often veiled relations
with others. These feelings of superiority, of inadequacy,
of baffled feeling, of not being able to get what one wants,
or even name it properly (or consistently) to oneself—
these can be, it is felt they ought to be,
masked by friendliness, or the most
scrupulous manipulation.

—*Susan Sontag,*
Under the Sign of Saturn: Essays

Being Realistic

My post-trauma personality traits will not necessarily get better on their own. In fact, they are likely to get worse. I carry the residue of relationship trauma, or I may have grown up trapped for years, if not decades, in a home that was trauma inducing. I had little access to outside support and had to make maladaptations to those who held authority and power so that I would not be abandoned psychologically, emotionally, or physically. Dysfunctional relationship dynamics wove themselves into my development and I carry wounds that need attending. I have modeled problematic behaviors. Today I need to make a real commitment to getting the kind of help I need to work out my unresolved pain; to move from numbness to aliveness, from dissociation to integration. It is my responsibility to do what I need to do to get better so that I don't pass on pain to the next generation.

I will do what it takes to heal

Many abused children cling to the hope that growing up will bring escape and freedom. But the personality formed in the environment of coercive control is not well adapted to adult life. The survivor is left with fundamental problems in basic trust, autonomy, and initiative. She approaches the task of early adulthood—establishing independence and intimacy—burdened by major impairments in self-care, in cognition and in memory, in identity, and in the capacity to form stable relationships. She is still a prisoner of her childhood; attempting to create a new life, she reencounters the trauma.

—*Judith Lewis Herman*, Trauma and Recovery

Remembering to Take Care of Myself

Today is a day to be reborn into the life I already have. To see and value it differently. To cherish it knowing that it is mine only for a while. I am God's gift to me. God has lovingly placed my life into my own hands to care for. God means for me to cherish and care for my own life in each and every way. I am responsible for what I do with me and what I do with my life. In caring for me, I am loving God's world. I am showing love and respect for what God has put into my hands until I rest once again in God's arms for all of eternity.

God has given me to me to love and care for

I didn't expect to recover from my second operation
but since I did, I consider that I'm living on borrowed time.
Every day that dawns is a gift to me and I take it in that way.
I accept it gratefully without looking beyond it.
I completely forget my physical suffering and all the
unpleasantness of my present condition and I think only
of the joy of seeing the sun rise once more and
of being able to work a little bit, even
under difficult conditions.

—Henri Matisse

JUNE 25

Releasing of Perfectionism

Today, I will not demand that my life be perfect in order for me to love it, nor will I demand that all my relationships be perfect for me to value and respect them. If I try to make my life and relationships perfect, I will be constantly engaged in a neurotic battle with my endless pictures of perfection. There is no such thing as an ideal, and to insist that life be ideal is to miss the forest for the trees. I will not condemn myself to the constant feeling that I have drawn the short straw. Perfection is in the eyes of the beholder—it is subjective. I will not ask the moment to be more than the moment—I will not be conditional in my love. I have wisdom today to see that the happy person is the one who has found a way to love the life they have, and then mysteriously, life seems to give them more to love. Today, I will be this person, too.

I see perfection in what is

Perfectionism is the voice of the oppressor,
the enemy of the people. It will keep you cramped and
insane your whole life, and it is the main obstacle between
you and a shitty first draft. I think perfectionism is
based on the obsessive belief that if you run carefully enough,
hitting each stepping-stone just right, you won't have to die.
The truth is that you will die anyway and that a lot of
people who aren't even looking at their feet are going to
do a whole lot better than you, and have a
lot more fun while they're doing it.

—*Anne Lamott,* Bird by Bird: Some Instructions on Writing and Life

I Can Have the Life I Want

The first step toward having something new enter my life is to see it in my mind's eye. I will allow my mind to see myself in a wonderful life. I will be specific, I will live in this life, breathe in it, talk to those in it with me, smell it, sense it, and embrace it as entirely possible. And I will see this and let it go over and over again in my mind. I'll taste it, smell it, live it, and move in it. I will not stop here. I will take meaningful steps towards it; I will take the actions that will take me along the path. And each day, I will allow the good feeling of loving what I already have to seep into my bones. I will not see it as up to someone else to actualize my life. I will not have dreams that are impossible and use those as an excuse to say nothing good happens to me. I will have real dreams and take real steps.

I can see, feel and sense my life, it is here

You can achieve anything you want in life
if you have the courage to dream it, the intelligence
to make a realistic plan, and the will to
see that plan through to the end.

—Sidney A. Friedman

Holding On

I will have faith. I will know, in the deepest part of me, that tomorrow will be brighter. I will not give up. There are more days to be lived, more hours to be enjoyed, more life ahead of me—and I don't want to miss it. I believe in miracles for others, so why not for me? My life will continue to unfold and I want to be there to see it, to feel it, to enjoy it. All faith is blind faith, faith in what I cannot see. Today I will have this kind of faith—I will have faith that I will find my way, faith that I can heal, faith that I can move past self-destructive behaviors one by one, faith that I can find and sustain love. I open my heart to receive, I have faith.

My faith makes my day feel better, more grounded, and more purposeful

You can have faith with or without religious affiliation—
faith is a state of being. Faith is putting hope and
power into that which we cannot see now . . .
but know we will see in the future. Faith is the art
of holding on to things your reason has
once accepted in spite of your
changing moods.

—*C. S. Lewis*

Gratitude

I see the dynamic power of gratitude at work in my life. My life is like a garden that I water with appreciation, and what I appreciate quietly and steadily grows in my life. It flowers, expands, and gives off a kind of fragrance that makes my life sweeter. Everything responds to praise, why not life? I live in an alive, creative universe in which everything is constantly growing. My gratitude and appreciation nourish the soil of my day, they supply necessary nutrients that allow my life to be fertile and bountiful. Gratitude can act as an antidote for anger and resentment. It is an organizing and motivating emotion, much like anger, but it heads me in a much better direction. It reframes and helps me to focus on what is right in my life, rather than what's wrong. And it attracts more of itself, because it puts out a good feeling into the atmosphere. When it is the real thing, it's catchy, it's contagious, it makes a situation more pleasant for everyone.

I am grateful for my day

Being and appearing grateful is not only the greatest
of virtues, but the parent of all others.

—*Cicero*

Nothing Dies

I can never lose what I love because the feeling of love will live inside me always. Sometimes I am afraid of love because I fear that if it goes away, I will feel lost. But today I see that this cannot be because, love itself is its own reward. Anything I have loved has become a part of me; it lives on good terms with my inner world and provides me a source of sustenance and strength that I can draw on in my quiet reverie. I cannot really lose what I have truly loved, because the trace and fragrance of love lingers in my heart.

What's alive and well in my mind and heart has great power for me

Learn to get in touch with the silence within yourself and know that everything in this life has a purpose. There are no mistakes, no coincidences, all events are blessings given to us to learn from.

—Elisabeth Kübler-Ross, M.D.

Charting My Own Course

Today I will chart my own course. My course may have many pieces of others woven into it, modeling journeys others have taken, traits and ideas that I have made mine over the years, reshaped and applied to my own needs, my own journey. But my course is a sort of push from within as well, one that I need to listen to and allow to guide me in a direction that feels right. I will use my intelligence as my map and my intuition and presence of mind as my compass. I will steer toward what I think and feel makes sense for me. I may never get to the North Star, but I will use it to guide me through the dark night, to lead me in the right direction, in the direction of my choosing. My life is spent on the waves, navigating storms, tacking through calm seas, and catching the right wind so as to make best use of it to carry me great distances. Each day, each week, each month, and each year have their changes in weather, and learning to navigate them well is what allows me to make best use of them. When I navigate my life thoughtfully, when I deal with the storms, enjoy the calm, and set sail on favorable winds, I am working intelligently with the forces that are part of life.

I play the hand that I am dealt as well as I can

Ideals are like stars; you will not succeed in
touching them with your hands. But like the seafaring
man on the desert of waters, you choose them as your guides,
and following them you will reach your destiny.

—*Carl Schurz*

JULY

If I Had My Life to Live Over

If I had my life to live over, I would have talked less and listened more. I would have invited friends over to dinner even if the carpet was stained and the sofa faded. I would have eaten the popcorn in the"good" living room and worried much less about the dirt when someone wanted to light a fire in the fireplace. I would have taken the time to listen to my grandfather ramble about his youth. I would never have insisted the car windows be rolled up on a summer day because my hair had just been teased and sprayed. I would have burned the pink candle sculpted like a rose before it melted in storage. I would have sat on the lawn with my children and not worried about grass stains. I would have cried and laughed less while watching television—and more while watching life. I would have shared more of the responsibility carried by my husband. I would have gone to bed when I was sick instead of pretending the earth would go into a holding pattern if I weren't there for the day. I would never have bought anything just because it was practical, wouldn't show soil or was guaranteed to last a lifetime.

Instead of wishing away nine months of pregnancy, I'd have cherished every moment and realized that the wonderment growing inside me was the only chance in life to assist God in a miracle. When my kids kissed me impetuously, I would never have said, "Later. Now go get washed up for dinner." There would have been more "I love you's" . . . More "I'm sorrys" . . . But mostly, given another shot at life, I would seize every minute . . . look at it and really see it . . . live it . . . and never give it back.

—Erma Bombeck

Half Measures Avail Us Nothing

I understand today that half measures get me nowhere. I frustrate myself and those around me when I refuse to make a commitment to myself, and I don't put my full intent behind my desire to make a change that needs making, nor do I pull my full weight. When I just sort of do something, I ask for a just sort of result. And I don't even experience the good feeling of giving something my best shot. I set myself up for a kind of disappointment and failure when I make half efforts, when I drag my own feet and get in my own way. I disappoint myself and I disappoint others. I confuse myself as to whether or not I dare to try; I use *not trying* to protect myself from fear of failing. And I keep myself stuck. A small change taken on sincerely is worth more than a large change done half-heartedly.

I will do something with enthusiasm

Do, or do not. There is no try.

—*Yoda,* The Empire Strikes Back

Giving

Today I will try giving for its own sake, with no particular motive, recognizing that giving and receiving are somehow the same channel. When the pipe is open, things flow in both directions simultaneously. Giving with an open heart is its own reward. But why is it so hard? First of all, I often give because I want something back, I give in order to get. Then I feel used and ripped off when I don't get it. Second, I sometimes give for approval or closeness; then I feel rejected and let down if my giving doesn't achieve that. And third, I sometimes give from an empty place, I give when I don't want to. Perhaps then I should just step back and preserve my energy, understanding that it's okay to "give" because it's part of what needs to happen that day—but I won't confuse that with open handed giving.

I will give openly and happily or not call it giving

No person was ever honored for what he received.
Honor has been the reward for what he gave.

—Calvin Coolidge

Reversing Roles

I will consciously reverse roles with another person today. I will stand in their shoes and look through their eyes. I will think, imagine, and place myself sincerely in another person's place as much as is possible, seeing things, for a moment, from their perspective. When I do this I am much better able to understand how to act toward and with someone. Reversing roles consciously is not the same as getting lost in someone else's head. I know that I am momentarily leaving the safe and familiar confines of my own mind in order to gain a deeper understanding of another person. And then I come back to me, with a greater understanding of them, myself, and the dynamic between us.

I can see things from another person's point of view

If there is any great secret of success in life,
it lies in the ability to put yourself in the other person's
place and to see things from his point of view—
as well as your own.

—Henry Ford

JULY 4

Loving Myself through Action

Today I will not hold myself to back-breaking standards. I will be generous with self-praise, self-support, and self-affirmation. Giving to others and withholding from myself doesn't work. I tend to treat other people the way that I treat myself. If I am stingy with me, I will, somewhere along the line, act that out with other people. If I am hard on myself, I will tend to be hard on others. I am the only person who is with me all hours of the day, and I know what feels good and warm to me. I know what makes me feel sustained from within. Today, I will encourage, support, and congratulate myself. Each time I do something that pleases me I'll say "thank you" to myself. Each time I do something well, I'll tell myself "good job." I will be my own best cheerleader.

I am my own best friend

Perfectionism doesn't believe in practice shots. It doesn't believe in improvement. Perfectionism has never heard that anything worth doing is worth doing badly—and that if we allow ourselves to do something badly we might in time become quite good at it. Perfectionism measures our beginner's work against the finished work of masters. Perfectionism thrives on comparison and competition. It doesn't know how to say, "Good try," or "Job well done." The critic does not believe in creative glee—or any glee at all, for that matter. No, perfectionism is a serious matter.

—*Julia Cameron,*
Finding Water: The Art of Perseverance

Making My Own Luck

I will not wait for luck to find me today; I will make my own luck. Life is an endless stream of doors opening and closing. If I wait for doors to slam shut on me, or if when they begin to close I just get anxious, defensive, and defeated, I will send out an energy that further closes them. If, on the other hand, I access my options, decide what I have that I can parlay into the next situation, or what dreams this might be a good time to investigate and fulfill, I will be choosing me. I will be making my own opportunity. When I do this I not only feel energized, I also refine my ability to hone my own interests and talents and actualize them. I become more of me rather than stagnate or spin my wheels. I see a door of opportunity that might be ajar, then I kick it further open. And I walk thought it.

I see opportunity, I create opportunity,
I choose me and luck follows me

Life's under no obligation to give
us what we expect.

—Margaret Mitchell

It's the Small Stuff

I will pay attention to the details of life. I will wash my face and smile at myself each morning and take an extra moment to choose something to wear that pleases me. I'll make myself something delicious to eat each morning and I'll take my time in eating it. I will walk to work or to do my errand if possible, take a stroll at lunch or after work so that I can spend some time outdoors. When I am on my way home I will pay attention to transition kinds of thoughts. I'll leave work behind and warm myself up to walking in the door of my home. I will muse on pleasant ways to spend my evening and I will have a cozy and self nurturing routine before bed. I will relax and enjoy a good night's sleep, allowing myself all the time I need to unwind and relax beforehand.

I will nurture myself throughout my day

Be faithful in small things because it is
in them that your strength lies.

—Mother Teresa

Blaming

Sometimes when something feels like it's wrong with me, I want to blame someone else for how it got that way. I want to make sense of it, get the pieces to hang together or create some sort of story that makes someone else the culprit so that I'll feel less baffled and alone in my pain. But blame is a never-ending cycle that becomes preoccupying and actually sends my energy outward. If I could accept with some level of simplicity that this is just where I am, perhaps I could marshal my own inner resources to get better or make small, positive changes. When I blame I get into a habit of mind that just isn't self-nourishing. I feed myself with resentment rather than encouragement. I drain my strength and throw it outward just at that moment when I need it to sustain me on the inside.

I will watch my tendency to blame

All blame is a waste of time.
No matter how much fault you find with another,
and regardless of how much you blame him,
it will not change you.

—*Wayne Dyer*

Personal Change

My impulses for change come from within. As I move down the path of self-discovery and self-awareness, certain ways of being no longer make sense to me. I have an urge to live differently, to see the situations of my life in a different light. To change the way I think, the way I feel, and the things I do. I see the same old things in a new way. When I change on the inside, my outer world subtly reflects those changes. As I remove the mental and emotional blocks that kept me stuck in repeated, less-than-satisfactory behaviors, the way I feel, think, and behave evolves. As I learn new things and try out new behaviors, I get different feedback from the world around me. Then I respond to this new feedback and act in new ways, which in turns gets me more new feedback. I have a new loop with my world that builds upon itself, a positive, slow spiral upward.

I am constantly changing the more self aware I become

The changes in our life must come from
the impossibility to live otherwise than according to
the demands of our conscience not from our
mental resolution to try a
new form of life.

—Leo Tolstoy

Making Plans, Changing Plans

Living with addiction and dysfunction left me with an anxious relationship with plans. Our family polarized along two extremes: some of us could not make plans and had to "hang loose" to such an extent that no one could stick to much of a schedule; and some of us could not change plans, we made them and clung to them. Each of these is a result of feeling disturbed by plans that were constantly falling apart, and by extension, by lives that were falling apart. What we had thought we could count on was no longer holding. Plans were constantly collapsing in midair. As a defense against feeling the anxiety that not being able to count on a plan engendered, or the chaos and disappointment of plans exploding or disappearing into nowhere, some of us pretended plans didn't matter—we adopted laissez-faire attitudes designed to disguise pain. Others held onto plans so tightly in an effort to get something to happen in a normal way that we couldn't roll with changes. Today, I am somewhere in the middle, I can make a plan and I can thoughtfully change a plan.

I can make, break, and remake plans in a thoughtful manner

If you don't know where you're going,
you'll wind up someplace else.

—Yogi Berra

Personal Truth

Today, I know that no one from my past needs to see things the way I do for me to get better and move on. Trying to convince others of what I have learned through my own journey can be an exercise in futility and delay my progress. First of all, each of us has our own truth that is unique unto itself. Second, each of us is at a different level of understanding and acceptance of who and where we are in life. Each member in my family had different experiences. That I thought we somehow matched up was an illusion. We each experienced our childhoods in our own way, and we have a right to our own perceptions. I do not have to get anyone to see it my way in order for me to feel comfortable. My truth is my truth, theirs is theirs. When I have truth inside, I need not live falsely. I tell the truth to others; this enables me to build trusting relationships. I increase my own self esteem because I am not hiding things or bending reality. I'm not behaving like I have something bad inside of me that I don't want others to see.

I just tell the truth; it's easier that way

If you tell the truth you don't have to remember anything.

—Mark Twain

Individuation

Today, I see that some of my anger toward my parents or their generation is about my need to separate from them and seek an individual identity. Even if my parents were wonderful, it would be natural to want to become my own person. Healthy parents have an easier time allowing this process because they have their own identity and intuitively understand what their children are doing. They know they did a good job and so have less shame, less guilt, and less need to outsource their pain. And likewise, fulfilled kids have an easier time letting go of the past; they are less anxious and ambivalent about moving into their own lives because they know they have a home to return to. Less healthy parents take separation as a personal indictment. This can make them want to hold on even tighter, or to reject and push away the relationship when there is conflict. Less healthy kids hold onto their past waiting for it to correct itself somehow. It is difficult to separate under these circumstances because each conflict gets loaded up with fears of abandonment. It is difficult to establish an individual identity without fearing the threat of either loss or engulfment.

I have the courage to individuate

To find out what is truly individual in ourselves,
profound reflection is needed; and suddenly we realize
how uncommonly difficult the discovery
of individuality in fact is.

—*Carl Jung*

Dealing with My Stressing, Stressed Out Reactions

Oftentimes it isn't the actual events, situations, and people in my life that are my biggest problem when it comes to feeling stressed out. Rather it's what I do with a stressful situation within myself that gives me trouble. If I overreact on an emotional and mental level to something that someone else has done or said, or to a circumstance in my life, my stress gets compounded. I obsess in a way that can make feelings seem overwhelming and unmanageable, and I pound that stress straight into my body. I undermine myself—I take away my own voice and vitality. Today, I will be honest with myself about the ways in which I make my own stressors worse because of what I do with them in my mind.

I will obsess less and relax, breathe, and step back more

Not all addictions are rooted in abuse or trauma,
but I do believe they can all be traced to painful experience.
A hurt is at the centre of all addictive behaviours.
It is present in the gambler, the Internet addict, the compulsive
shopper and the workaholic. The wound may not be as deep
and the ache not as excruciating, and it may even be entirely
hidden—but it's there. The effects of early stress or adverse
experiences directly shape both the psychology
and the neurobiology of addiction in the brain.

—*Gabor Maté,* In the Realm of Hungry Ghosts: Close Encounters with Addiction

Learning from Life

There are no "buts" today. I am what I am, others are what they are, life is what it is. I will not parenthesize my growth with a "but," or hold back my forward-moving spirit with second-guesses. For today, I am living with things as they are. I am exactly where I am meant to be, learning what I need to learn. All I need to do is move through situations with willingness to learn and openness to feel. When feelings are brought up, I can accept them as what is happening within me—no need to resist and analyze them. Transformation will happen in the moving through and the acceptance of what's happening right now. I trust that my life is unfolding in such a way that what I need to become aware of, will reveal itself to me. I am willing to learn.

I see meaning in my day to day life

Every true man, sir, who is a little above the level of
the beasts and plants, does not live for the sake of living
without knowing how to live: but he lives so as to
give a meaning and a value to his own life.

—Luigi Pirandello

The Purpose of Amends

When I make a true amends or accept a true amends from someone else, I am able to hold what is still of value of a relationship. We are both saying, "This thing we have is worth keeping." When someone makes an amends to me they are giving me what I need to keep the good alive. Without an amends, without this taking of responsibility, I am left with a mistrust, wondering if they realize the power of their own behavior. I can't right the relationship inside of me. They deprive me of something I am owed, a recognition. They are not valuing the relationship enough to humble themselves and ask for my forgiveness. When I don't make an amends that I owe, this is what I do to someone else. I do not give them back the part of my heart, the part of my goodness that I took away by my hurtful behavior. I don't give them a reason to trust my love. I don't give either of us another chance.

Amends keep the goodness of a relationship alive

Saying sorry doesn't always
mean you admit that you're wrong,
it only means that you value
your relationship
more than your pride.

—Nishan Panwar

I'll Do My Part

I will not ask life to give me more than I give it. If I want my life to be generous to me, I will need to be generous to my life. Daily I am surrounded by opportunities to make more of me, more of my day, more of my life. If I treat them like old clothes dropped on a floor, they will just lie there. It's up to me to pick them up and try them on. I can wear them for a day and discard them, or I can add to them, trim and tailor them to suit me. Today I will try on life. When I put my toe in the water and give something new a try, one thing inevitably leads to another, one opportunity leads to another and another and another. So as I get good at trying things on, I get better at moving along in life.

Opportunities are mine if and when I make them mine

A wise man will make more opportunities than he finds.

—Francis Bacon

Seeing Things in a Right Light

Life isn't simple. One of the ways that I can grow from life's adversities is to see what is positive about a difficult situation, to look for the deeper meaning. Pain can be the fire that clears the field for new and tender growth. Some seeds germinate only at very high temperatures. My soul has high temperatures, too—an inner blaze that allows the very center of a seed to come to life, to take root and to grow into what it is meant to be. I will look at a situation in its highest light today. I will turn it and turn it in the kaleidoscope of my mind, seeing it slightly anew each time, finding a way to view it that allows me to see it in a light that leaves room for acceptance, growth, and movement, while still remaining connected to my authentic self.

I help myself by reframing

Once all struggle is grasped, miracles are possible.

—Mao Tse-tung

I Will Be Me

I will be me, today. One thing I never seem to do well at is trying to be someone else. I can imitate and learn from others, but I cannot be them. Only they know how to do that—it's a natural outgrowth of all that they have experienced in life, of all they are. That's the bad news. The good news is no one can be me as well as me. Being me builds on who I already am. It uses and optimizes my own human and cultural capital. It's exercise for my personality and my spirit. If I allow myself to actualize my own unique gifts and visions they will have originality to them, a freshness.

I am worth optimizing, I have my own unique gifts and talents

God didn't make a mistake when He made you.
You need to see yourself as God sees you.

—Joel Osteen

A Garden in My Soul

Today, I realize that if I am to stand centered and strong within my life and self, I will need to plant a garden within my own soul. A garden for me to nurture and to nurture me. A haven of beauty. I will find my own voice and sing my song because if I don't sing it, it will not be sung. It is all I have and it is enough. I do not need to prove anything to anyone anymore. I have come home—to me. The truth is, I was here all along, only I forgot to look for myself. Instead, I searched for me in other people's meaning and became lost in their stories. I am not lost today. I know that there is nowhere to look for me but within myself, and no one to lead me there but me.

I am my own temple

This is my simple religion. There is no need
for temples; no need for complicated philosophy.
Our own brain, our own heart is our temple;
the philosophy is kindness.

—H.H. the Dalai Lama

Blaming Myself

When someone is angry at me, I can't get it out of my mind. I worry that they have seen something awful about me—something dark is showing that I want to hide. Secretly, I am ashamed. I plug into a place inside of me where I feel bad about myself. I don't know how to let go. Immediately, their anger towards me becomes my anger towards myself, or my litany of self-justifications or defenses all designed to keep me from feeling down on myself. But in this way, their anger becomes my problem because somewhere inside of me I accept what they say as true, more real than my own interpretation. I defend myself because I think I need defending. I accept their idea that I am in the wrong. Today I will pull myself out of the dark hole one foot at a time until I am in the light. Today I will imagine that all may not be my fault—I will let a window open in my assumption that I am in the wrong.

I accept my life experiences as making me who I am today

There is no man . . . however wise, who has not at some period of his youth said things, or lived a life, the memory of which is so unpleasant to him that he would gladly expunge it. And yet he ought not entirely to regret it, because he cannot be certain that he has indeed become a wise man—so far as it is possible for any of us to be wise—unless he has passed through all the fatuous or unwholesome incarnations by which that ultimate stage must be preceded.

—Marcel Proust

The Art of Living

I believe in the basic goodness of the experience of being alive. This feeling of inner zest for living, this spiritual awareness that my life is meant for me, and this gratitude that I feel in my heart for the life I have been given blow past any inner doubt; they cancel out all the rest. I am connected to the grand play, to the mystery, to the simple yet profound awareness that I am alive for another day. I am here to be all of who I am, I am a co-creator of my universe. I align myself with the creative forces of this alive and ever-evolving world. My life has meaning, I am a part of the stream of life; I am here, alive and willing to do my part.

I will stay a day longer

It is impossible to see how good work might be
accomplished by people who think that our life in this
world either signifies nothing or has only a negative significance.
If, on the other hand, we believe that we are living souls,
God's dust and God's breath, acting our parts among other
creatures all made of the same dust and breath as ourselves;
and if we understand that we are free, within the
obvious limits of moral human life, to do evil or good to
ourselves and to the other creatures—then all our acts have a
supreme significance. If it is true that we are living souls
and morally free, then all of us are artists.

—Wendell Berry

Neglect

I felt forgotten about in my alcoholic home. There just wasn't enough cohesion to hold my place intact. Everything was always fraying at the edges and I even wondered if I was loved. I personalized the lack of attention, imagining that something I had done or was doing was driving people and the attention I longed for away from me. I tried to correct myself, give more, work harder, be nicer but nothing worked. In fact, the squeaky wheels seemed to get more attention than I did. Being neglected was a powerful form of abuse. It left no obvious marks, but I bled on the inside. At least other forms of abuse are obvious, something to point to, something to feel like an actual victim over. At least I would have known I was there. But withheld love is a worse pain. It left me floating in space, wondering if I was there, shouting out into thin air but making no sound. Today I know that the love that was withheld from me was not personal. It was nothing I did or could have undone. It was part of a family that was dying on the inside.

I can feel and take in love, I can see myself

Being unwanted, unloved, uncared for,
forgotten by everybody, I think that is a much
greater hunger, a much greater poverty than the
person who has nothing to eat.

—Mother Teresa

Unplugging

I will have special moments, hours, or even a day when I disconnect from the world, when I unplug. I will not respond to each and every demand, each and every communication just because I can. Technology keeps me connected to absolutely everything twenty-four seven, but sometimes it just has me going in endless, unnecessary, and energy-draining circles. I need times of intentional unplugging, times when I can just relax and forget about everything, when I can drop down into nothing and nowhere. When I can just be, wander around my day with no particular purpose, ease up and unwind; when I can stay home. I need these times to shake loose of the bonds of the daily world, to not worry about who I need to contact and what I should say, to just veg out, to be unconstructive, to meander around with no particular agenda. I love it, lying around, doing as I please, hanging out, doing lots of nothing in particular or, particularly, a lot of nothing. I need to stop skimming the surface, scrolling down endless pages of whatever; I need time for me.

I refuel by unplugging

Before you become too entranced with gorgeous
gadgets and mesmerizing video displays, let me remind
you that information is not knowledge, knowledge is
not wisdom, and wisdom is not foresight.
Each grows out of the other, and
we need them all.

—Arthur C. Clark

Getting My Soul Back

My soul is coming back to me in drips and drops, meaningful moments in floods and flashes. My soul almost feels like an entity all its own, one that has its own substance, form, and energy. It is something I can get separated from, something from which I can become lost. Something that I can find and allow to find me. Just for today it is enough to know this, to feel aware of the presence of this part of me, to welcome it back and prepare a home for it within me. All that my soul seeks is in the moment, it is where all the waters meet, where the flow is, where life is. When I can be still and in the now, I do not question life, I experience it. I love it, it feels full and abundant, deep and wide. I have a quiet sense of being and knowing.

My soul is coming home to me

We're all on the journey of a lifetime.
God is our shepherd, and we have only to do what
He asks of us. Kindness for one another, love for each
other, that is what will change the world.
Medicine can heal the body.
But only God can make well the human soul.

—Lurlene McDaniel

Withholding

When those I love withhold from me, I all too often take it very personally. I wonder, "why don't they want to give to me, why are they making me feel small, needy, and undernourished?" But today I understand that this is exactly what they are experiencing inside themselves. It is they who feel small, needy, and undernourished, they who feel unseen and unvalued. They are acting out a state within themselves that they find unbearable, that they cannot allow themselves to feel. They are projecting that state onto me, unconsciously wanting me to feel helpless, needy, and unseen. Something must have happened to them when they were very, very small to be so withholding. Not a big trauma, but perhaps the ongoing trauma of feeling un-held, immobile, and alone in a crib, left to wonder if anyone knew they were there. Waiting to be picked up, waiting to be remembered, waiting to feel alive and connected. This can happen in the most privileged and affluent homes, in underprivileged homes, and everything in between. It reflects a lack of awareness of what a baby needs to develop emotional strength and resilience; it's a parenting problem.

I will not withhold from me

Withdrawal and projection are the natural outcomes of withholding. When you withhold, you keep inside yourself things that should be expressed. The very act of hiding these things takes you one step back from the relationship. A result of this withdrawal is that you will begin to project. In other words, you will begin to attribute to other people things that are actually issues of your own.

—Gay and Katie Hendricks

My Thoughts Are Alive in My Relationships

My thoughts become my life. My thoughts have power first over me, and next they fill the atmosphere. My thoughts shape my feelings and actions. What I have running through my mind all day becomes my day. If I imagine that I can think all sorts of negative, self-defeating, or resentful thoughts and they will have no impact on me or those around me, I am making a real mistake.

My thoughts are an alive and present force within my relationships; they are picked up on and felt by others. They are not confined to the limits of my head, they vibrate out and to the minds of those around me. They have power to affect people. Other people feel them and base their actions toward me on what they are picking up on. If I try to use words to mask my thoughts, I will feel incongruent or even phony to those around me. Today I will become aware of the thoughts that I think, the feelings I feel, and the impact that both are having on those around me.

I take responsibility for what I am thinking

[Richard] said, "Groceries, you need to learn how to select your thoughts just the same way you select what clothes you're gonna wear every day. This is a power you can cultivate. If you want to control things in your life so bad, work on the mind. That's the only thing you should be trying to control. Drop everything else but that. Because if you can't learn to master your thinking, you're in deep trouble forever."

—*Elizabeth Gilbert,*
Eat, Pray, Love

Controlling Others

When I try to control others I will ask myself, *Why?* Is it because I am feeling overwhelmed by *their* lives being out of order, or is it that *my* inner world feels chaotic, and I am trying to fix in them what really needs fixing in me? Sometimes I try to control someone else when I am feeling anxious because I imagine that this will allow me to be somehow calmer. I don't want to feel what I am feeling, so I make it about someone or something else; I project my troubled inner world onto another person, and then try to manage something I now perceive to be their issue. I try to get rid of what I'm feeling, get it away from me, and onto someone or something else. Then I can get busy analyzing them rather than myself. But when I do this, I don't grow. I may even regress and hold myself in a sort of trauma-think, circling round and round an unnamed wound without letting it go. When I am doing this today, I will recognize that I need to take a step back. I first need to ask myself what is going on with me, why am I having an overreaction? What needs attention and healing inside of me?

I will keep the focus on myself

Be not angry that you cannot make others as you wish them to be, since you cannot make yourself as you wish to be.

—Thomas à Kempis

The Mystery

Today, I accept that part of myself that will never be satisfied, and I comfort and tame it. There is a place in me that knows it will never necessarily solve the eternal questions of life: Who am I and where do I come from, and where do I go when I die? Part of me wants to know the answers to these questions. But I am beginning to feel that the answer is to live fully in the question, to open to the mystery. Perhaps meaning is not knowing and understanding, but an acceptance of mystery, an embracing of the unknown. After all, it is this evanescent sense of mystery that gives even the most ordinary circumstance an eternal sort of glow—a sense of depth, a feeling that there is more. And my ability to be present in the now is the key to unlock this mystery that surrounds me all the time, but I do not see.

I enter and embrace the mystery

Gratitude unlocks the fullness of life.
It turns what we have into enough, and more.
It turns denial into acceptance, chaos to order, confusion to clarity. It can turn a meal into a feast, a house into a home, a stranger into a friend. Gratitude makes sense of our past, brings peace for today and creates a vision for tomorrow.

—Melody Beattie

One Life

I have one life I can do something about and that life is mine. I have one mind through which to think the next right thought, one heart through which to experience the next feeling, and one body through which to take the next right action. I have spent too many years feeling overwhelmed by other people's problems, hurt by other people's actions, and baffled by other people's behaviors. When I feel stuck in that reactive mode of reasoning, I will say to myself *I don't have to stay here.* I will remind myself that other people's actions are theirs; they are about them and not me. If they are wrong actions, they will have to correct them. I am accountable and responsible for my actions only. I can do little about another's actions but I can do everything about my actions and reactions to others. Today, I will set my own course, based on my own inner impulses, needs, dreams, and abilities.

I can be me

I used to spend so much time reacting and responding to everyone else that my life had no direction. Other people's lives, problems, and wants set the course for my life. Once I realized it was okay for me to think about and identify what I wanted, remarkable things began to take place in my life.

—Melody Beattie

Shifting My Inner Awareness

Forgiveness doesn't require erasing my memories. I can forgive and remember. And I can forgive over and over and over again. I need to forgive myself and others for being human, for living slowly, for our collective ignorance, so that I can enjoy my day unencumbered by tiny thoughts of judgment, control, and revenge. Today I recognize forgiveness as the quickest road to freedom and serenity. When I forgive my past, I release myself from the grip that it has on my present and on my future. It is difficult to live in peace today if I am psychically engaged in yesterday's battles. I will do what I need to do today to fully process the issues in my life that remain unresolved, so that I can let them go, knowing that the resentment and pain I continue to possess against another person actually possesses me.

I meet my inner world honestly and with integrity.

Forgive and forget is a myth. You may never
forget AND you can choose to forgive. As life goes on
and you remember, then is the time to once again remember
that you have already forgiven. Mentally forgive again
if necessary, then move forward. When we allow it,
time can dull the vividness of the memory
of the hurt; the memory will fade.

—Larry Jones

Guilt

If someone I love is sinking, sinking, sinking, I want to
to STOP. If my life is better than theirs, I punish myself
this grinding guilt, this feeling that I am leaving someon
on the battlefield of the disease of addiction. But today I re
that I cannot help anyone who doesn't want my help. I cann
save anyone. People save themselves, fundamentally; oth
help, but others cannot do the job for them or as them. Som
I help because I feel so much survivor's guilt. What I reall
to do is run the other way, but I feel too guilty to do that.
really want is to just feel okay having a good life of my ow
somehow I feel that I should not have that if everyone I care
isn't okay. Today, I will allow myself to have what I have, to live
to follow my own path of renewal and recovery.

I can have a good life no matter what
is going on around me

No work or love will flourish out of guilt, fear,
or hollowness of heart, just as no valid plans for the
future can be made by those who have
no capacity for living now.

—Alan Watts

Secondary Gains

I will work through the pain of my past with the clear intent of allowing myself to live more fully in the present. When I work on my past simply to relive it over and over again, I strengthen its grip within me, I overempower it. I become preoccupied with reliving it under the guise of working it through, I become mildly obsessed with it. Talking about it has secondary gains for me; maybe it lets me off the hook when it comes to moving forward in my own life, maybe I use it to manipulate others into feeling sorry for me, maybe it's just gratifying to go over it again and again, or maybe it's just habit. When I work with my past in order to understand it, in order *not* to repeat or reenact it, I am speeding up my karma, I am living consciously, I am working something through in my conscious mind so that I do not have to live it out as "fate".

I work through my past in order to live more fully in my present

A lot of people feel like they're victims in life,
and they'll often point to past events, perhaps growing up
with an abusive parent or in a dysfunctional family.
Most psychologists believe that about 85 percent of families
are dysfunctional, so all of a sudden you're not so unique.
My parents were alcoholics. My dad abused me. My mother
divorced him when I was six . . . I mean, that's almost everybody's
story in some form or not. The real question is, what are you
going to do now? What do you choose now? Because you
can either keep focusing on that, or you can focus on
what you want. And when people start focusing on what
they want, what they don't want falls away, and what
they want expands, and the other part disappears.

—*Jack Canfield*

AUGUST

The Journey

One day you finally knew
what you had to do, and began,
though the voices around you
kept shouting their bad advice—
though the whole house
began to tremble
and you felt the old tug
at your ankles.
"Mend my life!"
each voice cried.
But you didn't stop.
You knew what you had to do,
though the wind pried
with its stiff fingers

at the very foundations
though their melancholy was terrible.
It was already late
enough, and a wild night,
and the road full of fallen
branches and stones.
But little by little,
as you left their voices behind,
the stars began to burn
through the sheets of clouds,
and there was a new voice,
which you slowly
recognized as your own,
that kept you company
as you strode deeper and deeper
into the world,
determined to do
the only thing you could do—
determined to save
the only life you could save.

—*Mary Oliver,* Dreamwork

Being with Life

Today, I allow myself just to be with life. Somehow it doesn't have to prove anything to me or give me any more than I already have to be okay. The lessons I have learned through sincere dedication to my own inner growth have taught me that I can face my most difficult feelings and still come home to a place of love and acceptance. Life is always renewing itself; nothing lasts, good or bad, and that is just the way it is. It is enough today to enjoy my coffee, to take a walk, to appreciate the people in my life. I can rest in a quiet sort of understanding that this is what it's all about; all the searching turned up such an ordinary but beautiful thing. This awareness allows me to roll more easily with change. I have an inner confidence that I will have the ability to enjoy many different situations, many different phases, and that I will be able to figure out how to live each phase in the happiest way for me and those close to me.

I enjoy the life I have

Life is a series of natural and spontaneous changes.
Don't resist them; that only creates sorrow.
Let reality be reality. Let things flow naturally
forward in whatever way they like.

—*Lao Tzu*

Meditation

Today, I recognize the source of light and wisdom that is within me. When I look outside myself to learn about what is actually inside, I need to exercise great discernment because some of what I see fits and some does not. But there is another source of information and wisdom available to me twenty-four-seven that I will take time to cultivate now that I am committed to personal growth. There is a fountain within me that is ever full and waiting to be discovered. When I can rest quietly in this inner place, I experience a sense of fullness, and my desire to go outside diminishes and gives way to a preference for undisturbed peace. Solitude takes on a different meaning when I can contact that quiet within. Life softens and external things become less important. My thoughts and attitudes become porous rather than rigid; there are spaces that weren't there before. I will look for this place within me on a daily basis. I give myself this present today.

Meditation is my medicine

If I had not been already been meditating,
I would certainly have had to start. I've treated my
own depression for many years with exercise and
meditation, and I've found that to
be a tremendous help.

—Judy Collins

My Interaction with My World

Who I am is a product of who I am. Those of us who had great starts in life are lucky, but all of us can do a lot about who we are. I elicit a particular response from the world about how it sees me based on how I see it, based on what I'm putting out there. If I see the world colored in dark and depressing hues, that is the world I walk around in. Much of my experience of my life consists of what is going through my head all day. If I see the world as a good place, a place in which I can find friendship and love, that is what I'll walk around with all day. What I vibrate into the world around me affects how others see me. Then they respond to me according to how I am being with them. I set up an active dynamic with those around me based on how I am feeling. In this way, I create my corner of the world, not completely perhaps, but significantly. Today I will try something new, I will act in a different way and see if I get a different result.

I take charge of my direction in life

If you do not change direction, you may
end up where you are heading.

—Lao Tzu

Becoming Real

Today, I will choose being real over being fake. This doesn't mean that I need to blab out each and every feeling I have whether appropriate to the situation or not. Nor does it mean that I will exaggerate negative feelings or thoughts because they are what I "really feel." This is a 360° kind of real. A willingness to live with life on life's terms, to manage my responses within me in an honest way that both allows me to feel authentic and allows me to move through my day and fit into my world in a constructive way. Being real means that I don't hide from myself, it gives me an opportunity to make choices as to how I interact with my day. Because I am allowing room within me to be where I am, I can decide what I want to let go of, what I need to act upon, or what I just need to let be. Being real also means that I understand how to pull meaning out of the life that I have rather than postpone living for another time or place. I can work with what I do, who I am, and my surroundings, and make the most of them.

I give myself space inside to be me

I realized a long time ago that a warrior in
search of his dream must take his inspiration from
what he actually does and not from what
he imagines himself doing.

—*Paulo Coelho,* Aleph

The Long and Winding Road

I have truly begun a journey of recovery. I'm facing my anger and hurt and bringing order and clarity to my inner world. I'm accepting the things I cannot change and changing the things that I can. Because I've shown the courage to face my inner demons and look them in the eye, I feel stronger and more competent. Grief has offered me a way out of pain and confusion, and now I find I have a renewed interest in life. I see things differently. I feel liberated from something that was tying up my energy. And I recognize and accept my own humanity, and the humanity of others. I am ready and willing to reinvest in the ideal of love. I want to find worthy projects and passions, and put my energy toward them. I have something to give to the world, and the world has something to give to me. I am right where I am supposed to be and I've met the challenges of my life. I am ready to live.

I am master of my own destiny

It is no good getting furious if you get stuck.
What I do is keep thinking about the problem but
work on something else. Sometimes it is years before
I see the way forward. In the case of information
loss and black holes, it was 29 years.

—Stephen Hawking

Taking Care of Business

Each of us has to learn our own lessons; that is what we are here to do. We can't learn anyone else's lessons for them, and learning our own is difficult enough. To plow through my own psyche and face the insecurity and wounds that are there is all that I can handle. To regulate my own responses to life, to find a way to keep the rich and deep parts of my reactions and tame the overreactions, requires a great deal of insight, discipline, and self awareness. Actualizing my own dreams, and taking meaningful steps toward them, is my responsibility alone, no one else's. To try to live other people's lives for them is to separate myself from my own responsibilities toward myself. I will naturally interact better with others as I improve myself, and if that doesn't make things better, I can't climb into them and make anything work. To try to live other people's lives is also to separate myself from God, because my first access to God is through and within me.

I accept my lessons

To laugh often and love much; to win the respect of intelligent persons and the affection of children; to earn the approbation of honest citizens and endure the betrayal of false friends; to appreciate beauty; to find the best in others; to leave the world a bit better, whether by a healthy child, a garden patch or a redeemed social condition; to know even one life has breathed easier because you have lived—this is to have succeeded.

—Bessie Anderson Stanley,
More Heart Throbs, *Volume 2*

Lesson and Life

I recognize today that I am in charge of my own learning. Life is constantly offering up circumstances that are useful in my personal growth, that I can use as my teacher. It is up to me whether I learn from life or live unconsciously. When I live unconsciously, I do the same thing over and over expecting a different result; I repeat behaviors even when they obviously don't work, exhausting myself and learning very little. Or I learn. I step back in my mind and ask myself what I need to see that I am not seeing, what I need to learn that I am not learning. I extract the wisdom that is hidden behind circumstances, and I grow in awareness and expand my capacity for living. The deepest and most appropriate things I need to learn in life are generally right in front of me. Life is my guru if I can use it as such. It is rich with subtle learning if I look for it. The real achievement for me today is to learn to be in my own skin, to see truth in all that surrounds me, to know that placing value and judgment is pointless and illusory—all of life is valuable.

I see beyond what is apparent

The world is indeed full of peril and in it there are many dark places. But still there is much that is fair. And though in all lands, love is now mingled with grief, it still grows, perhaps, the greater.

—J.R.R. Tolkien

AUGUST 8

Letting My Body Speak

I will let my body have a voice today and I will listen to what it's trying to say to me. Somatization was one of the ways trauma affected me—the pain, anxiety, anger, and fear that I couldn't express plowed itself into my body where I held it in stony silence. It stiffened my muscles, made me sore, and blocked my energy. Today when my body acts up, I will try to understand why. I will try to be open to seeing if it is expressing through tension, pain or sickness, frozen emotions, and stress that I have been ignoring for too long. If my body's voice has tears in it, I will allow those tears to come out. If my body is holding anger, I will allow myself to experience that anger so that it can dissolve and my cells no longer have to hold it for me. If my body wants to shiver and shake I will let it, knowing that it just needs to release something it doesn't want to hang onto anymore.

I allow my body to let go of the emotions it is holding

Pain (any pain—emotional, physical, mental)
has a message. The information it has about our life
can be remarkably specific, but it usually falls into one of
two categories: "We would be more alive if we did more of this,"
and, "Life would be more lovely if we did less of that."
Once we get the pain's message, and follow
its advice, the pain goes away.

—Peter McWilliams, Life 101

Dialoguing with My Inner Child

Sometimes I let my wounded inner child do all of my talking, and then I wonder why I drive people away. When I talk to the world *as* my wounded inner child, I blurt out whatever is on my mind, and I wait for someone else to contain it, make sense of it, or fix it. I feel and say things in an immature way because they are coming from an immature place inside of me. I am in an adult body but I am talking from a child place—then I get surprised and hurt when I get misinterpreted or misunderstood. But people expect an adult to talk like an adult: they don't necessarily want to have to do my adult reasoning for me, they expect me to do it for myself. Today, I will bring my inner adult on board in all of my communications with others; I will let my traumatized inner child talk to my reasonable inner adult before discharging at whoever is near. I will charge my inner adult with the job of listening to my wounded inner child and translating my feelings and immature thinking into more adult language and perspectives. Then I will let my adult do the communicating and in this way I have a shot at talking about my feelings thoughtfully rather than lacing them with blame, in this way I take responsibility for what's inside of me rather than make that someone else's job.

My inner child talks to my inner adult and my inner adult talks to the world

I'm a great believer that any tool that enhances communication has profound effects in terms of how people can learn from each other, and how they can achieve the kind of freedoms that they're interested in.

—Bill Gates

Freeing Me

Today, I understand that in forgiving someone else I free myself. I held back on forgiveness because it seemed too kind an act for those who had hurt me. Why should I make them feel good? Why should I let them off the hook? I understand now that forgiving someone else and letting go—when I am truly ready—releasing another person from my constant rumination and resentments, releases me; it dissolves the anger that is stored within me. I will not jump to forgiveness too quickly, forcing myself to do what I am not sincerely able to do. Forgiving doesn't mean that I will never again feel angry toward those who have hurt me, nor that I even wish to continue to be close to them. It does not mean that I condone their actions. I don't need to "forgive and forget"—that isn't real—but I can forgive and remember. When I forgive, it is to set myself free, to let go of the pain inside of me, to spring myself from the trap of chronic resentment. Part of forgiving is reframing; today I will ask myself what I learned from living with another's oppression, anger, or envy that has given me the courage to move past my own barriers and succeed. I will take hold of that learning as my gift. Then forgiving becomes a moot point; I learned what I learned, I can move on, I can drop my end of the rope—and if the person at the other end falls down, let them get up.

I forgive so that I can loosen up my compulsion to connect through pain

Never forget the three powerful resources you always have available to you: love, prayer, and forgiveness.

—*H. Jackson Brown, Jr.*

Making Room for More

Today, I will not hide my pain and suffering from myself or from my Higher Power. When I bring my most honest and pure self to the fore and understand my essential powerlessness over situations, when I am truly willing to turn over this angst to a power greater than myself, something changes. I let go and create space for a shift in perception. I experience a quiet awakening in my life. I allow healing winds to blow through my being; I invite forces that did not have space to enter, to come in to heal me. I create a spiritual void that the world quickly fills with better experiences; I leave room for growth. It is in letting go that I have a chance of achieving what I desire in my life.

I am finished living in mourning

It is our way to mourn for one year when one of our relations enters the spirit world. Tradition is to wear black when mourning our lost one. Tradition is to not be happy, not to sing and dance and enjoy life's beauties during mourning time. Tradition is to suffer with the remembering of our lost ones and to give away much of what we own and to cut our hair short. Chief Sitting Bull . . . represented an entire people, our freedom, our way of life, all that we were. For 100 years, we as a people have mourned our great leader. We have followed tradition in our mourning. We have not been happy, have not enjoyed life's beauty, have not danced or sung as a proud nation. . . . the heartbeat of our people has been weak and our lifestyle has deteriorated to a devastating degree. Our people now suffer from the highest rates of unemployment, poverty, alcoholism and suicide in this country.

—Maria Yellow Horse Braveheart, Ph.D,
Fifth Annual White Bison Wellbriety Conference

Telling Myself the Truth

Today, I accept that without truth there is no growth. Truth is the soil out of which nourishment comes: it feeds and nourishes me, it gives me simplicity, I can see more clearly. Lies have no food value and starve my spirit; but truth, though it can hurt, has a way of hoeing and tilling the soil of my soul so that some new growth can occur. Even though I may convince myself that I don't need to know it, or that it's better "to let sleeping dogs lie" who am I kidding? I know it anyway. Sunlight is the best disinfectant. Keeping things hidden allows doubt, insecurity, and shame to develop and propagate. Bringing truth out into the open gives me a chance to lift the veil of secrecy that has made a wound feel like a dark hole, like nothing is there. It allows angst to transform and break into a thousand little somethings that each contain usable and illuminating information. A thousand little bits of insight that can again nurture health and life once the alchemist's hand has extracted the wisdom from it, once my own internal healer has become aware and gained insight.

I will be authentic

Wanting to be someone else is a
waste of the person you are.

—*Kurt Cobain*

Being My Own Friend

Today, I will become aware of that part of me that is separate and observes all that I say, do, think, and feel. I have a witness within me, an inner observer who can become a very useful part of my life. I can be my own best friend once I come to terms with my inner enemy, my dark and accusing self-recriminations, all of the voices I use to beat myself up on the inside. Watching my behavior with a little bit of objectivity will help me to see myself in a more compassionate light. It will loosen me from my own unconscious trap and give me space and understanding to make new choices. I will look with a merciful eye. Just as I know it is not right to hurt others intentionally, it is equally not right to hurt myself. I recognize the godlike nature within me and others—we are all a part of the same Higher Power. By allowing my mind to observe itself, I can learn a great deal about the way I work. I can slowly heal myself.

I observe the inner workings of my mind

Self-observation brings man to the realization
of the necessity of self-change. And in observing himself
a man notices that self-observation itself brings about
certain changes in his inner processes.
He begins to understand that self-observation
is an instrument of self-change,
a means of awakening.

—*G. I. Gurdjieff*

AUGUST 14

Inner Sunshine

There is sunshine in this world. There is humor and grace and beauty. There is good and friendship and love. And it's all here for me. Today I will align myself with what is best and most nourishing about life. Everywhere there is evidence of an alive and magnificent universe if I open my eyes to see it and my heart to feel it. Sometimes it takes sickness to see wellness. Sometimes it takes pain to deepen my understanding of all that is good. I can see beauty in the world that is already surrounding me. I am part of that beauty and that beauty is part of me. I can let it into my pores and make it mine if I chose to, or I can reject it, see it as belonging to others, not me. Recovery has taught me to appreciate life, the world, the day, this hour. It has taught me to take responsibility for my own experience. If I don't like something, I can turn it around in my mind to see it in its most spiritual light, I can shift my mood, my awareness—and that will make the same life feel different.

I choose to see the glass as half full

The sun shines not on us but in us.

—John Muir

Becoming a Worker Among Workers

When I can see trauma in a larger context, as part of life, part of what has made me *me,* I can keep my sense of life's basic goodness intact. When I sink into a victim form of thinking, in which I play the starring role, I become that perpetual "nothing goes my way" person. It's a sort of convoluted way of being at the center of the universe, a dark narcissism, an unwillingness to recognize that we all have problems, and that we all need to work hard for what we get. Whatever negative characteristics may have become a part of me from living with unhealed pain, shame, and resentment are, unfortunately, mine to deal with now. Projecting and blaming will only confuse and hurt those close to me. If I do not own my feelings and bring them into consciousness, they will own me. Just for today, I will learn to see the past differently, to take the "boogeyman" out of it, to release its toxicity through reframing and understanding it. Today is the only day I know that I have, and I am going to live it.

I take a leap of faith and release what I am holding onto

We already have everything we need. There is no need for self-improvement. All these trips that we lay on ourselves—the heavy-duty fearing that we're bad and hoping that we're good, the identities that we so dearly cling to, the rage, the jealousy and the addictions of all kinds—never touch our basic wealth. They are like clouds that temporarily block the sun. But all the time our warmth and brilliance are right here. This is who we really are. We are one blink of an eye away from being fully awake.

—*Pema Chödrön,* Start Where You Are: A Guide to Compassionate Living

Getting Even

Today I will push myself through to letting go of some recent insult, knowing that if I don't, I bind myself to that energy—I attract more of it. Revenge only keeps me stuck at the place of wrongdoing. Better to let go the hurt or insult than the act of kindness. If I want to continue to grow my blessings in life, I will look up not down. Today I will look toward someone who has been good to me, and I will think of a way to repay their kindness, knowing that when I do that, my own life feels better, too. I connect myself to the energy of goodness.I step away from chronic revenge fantasies, some are alright and natural, too many just bog me down and become a place of attraction that just builds on itself.

I will not base my actions on the last bad action of another person

To see an enemy humiliated gives a certain contentment, but this is jejune compared with the highly blent satisfaction of seeing him humiliated by your benevolent action or concession on his behalf. That is the sort of revenge which falls into the scale of virtue.

—George Eliot

A Little Magic

Each day is a gift especially for me. I will look through innocent eyes at the world today and see the gifts that are meant just for me. Children think the sun rises for and because of them. They're sure that the moon hangs in the sky because they waved their arm towards the heavens, that flowers bloom for their eyes alone to see. They are magical thinkers. They take delight in the antics of a squirrel, in a balloon sailing in a bright, blue sky. They see the world fresh, in color and alive each new day, each new moment. Their senses ground them in the moment because they experience sights, sounds, textures, tastes, and scents so directly, as if they had never before been caressed by a warm breeze, surprised by the perfume of a flower, or jarred by a loud noise. They are constantly being drawn to the moment. Today, I think I'll borrow a little of their magic. Their magic and my maturity may just be a winning combination.

I see the magic that surrounds me, the mystery of life

Nothing can dim the light which
shines from within.

—Maya Angelou

Spirit at Work

I am waiting in pleasant anticipation for spirit to work its quiet magic in my day. My own deepest grief has opened a door inside my soul and allowed the healing forces built into this alive and vibrating universe to work their alchemy inside of me. There is nothing that I can think, feel, or do, that cannot be made lighter and truer by inviting spirit into it. I rest in the joyous awareness that spirit is with me. That spirit has never left me. If I feel an absence of spirit today, I will remember that it is not spirit that moves away from me, but I that move away from spirit. I am uplifted by the thought that I am not alone, nor ever was I. Today I need no proof that I am on a spiritual journey because the miracle of life surrounds me everywhere and this is proof enough.

I am living the gift

We must become so alone, so utterly alone,
that we withdraw into our innermost self. It is a way
of bitter suffering. But then our solitude is overcome,
we are no longer alone, for we find that our innermost self
is the spirit, that it is God, the indivisible.
And suddenly we find ourselves in the midst of the world,
yet undisturbed by its multiplicity, for our
innermost soul we know ourselves
to be one with all being.

—Hermann Hesse

Disappointing People

Disappointing people is hard for me. I fear retribution, I obsess about having done the "wrong" thing, I worry that I am starting a chain reaction that will double back on me. I feel selfish or bad, as if I am doing something that will get me into trouble somehow. Growing up in a family where there was not enough to go around meant that no one ever felt they got their fair share. Someone always appeared to get too much, others felt they were getting too little. Someone always had a long face or was blackmailing me behind the scenes. Things seemed always to be in chaos, and as a child, I blamed myself for that chaos. I tensed up inside and tried to think of things to do that would please people, make them happy, bring a look of relief to them, and keep me out of getting blamed. This kind of circular thinking sets off a chain reaction in my relationships today, in which I assume that those close to me *now* will have the same reactions as my family members did *then*. And when I get like this, I create confusion and anxiety in the other person. Today I can separate healthy attunement from this self-obsessed thinking, this fear of getting something wrong.

I can disappoint someone and not send myself to a horrible place for it

There are some things in this world you rely on,
like a sure bet. And when they let you down, shifting from
where you've carefully placed them, it shakes
your faith, right where you stand.

—Sarah Dessen

Self-Importance

I will get my mind off of the treadmill. There is more to life than my worries and obsessions. Just for today, I won't give every little thing that bothers me more importance than it deserves. In the scheme of things, all of my petty annoyances aren't all that important. I don't have to take them so seriously that they grab my mind and won't let go. When I am constantly preoccupied with all that's wrong, I forget to remember all that's right. I become glued to places inside of me, rather than process my thoughts and feelings, they take me over and I get hopelessly entangled, like a moth in a spider's web. Self-importance is different from valuing myself. Self-importance gets me tied up in mental knots, valuing myself is nourishing and loving. Self-importance, the not so good kind, makes me lose track of other people, my ability to empathize gets smaller as my self-absorption gets bigger. And I forget that other people are as important to themselves as I am to me; I forget to take their feelings, their personhood into account.

I am important to myself but not self-important. . . .

Self-importance can't be fought with niceties. . . . Self-importance is our greatest enemy. Think about it—what weakens us is feeling offended by the deeds and misdeeds of our fellow men. Our self-importance requires that we spend most of our lives offended by someone. . . . Self-importance is not something simple and naive. On the one hand, it is the core of everything that is good in us, and on the other hand, the core of everything that is rotten. To get rid of the self-importance that is rotten requires a masterpiece of strategy.

—Don Juan

A Loss of Self-Regulation

Stress and trauma create opposites. I shoot from zero to ten and ten to zero inside of myself with no speed bumps in between. I lose my ability to self-regulate, to modulate my thinking, feeling, and behavior. Addiction, dysfunction, acting out, rage, withdrawal, or shutting down all reflect a loss of neuromodulation, a loss of ability to self-regulate. Thinking becomes black and white; so does behavior. Today, when I am in that state, I will look for middle ground. I will watch my thoughts without getting lost in them, overreacting to them, or shutting them down. I will make the kinds of activities that literally rewire me, that create new, more balanced neural pathways, a part of my daily self-care. I'll journal, exercise, find a satisfying hobby, enjoy a network of relationships, go to meetings, relax, and share my feelings and thoughts with others.

I can bring myself back to four, five, and six

A loss of ability to regulate the intensity of feelings is the most far-reaching effect of early trauma and neglect. . . . Early [relationship dynamics] are imprinted into the biological structures that are maturing during the brain growth spurt that occurs in the first two years of human life, and therefore have far-reaching and long-enduring effects. . . . The period of early-forming [inter-personal] relation [dynamics] exactly overlaps the period of the brain growth spurt. . . . The caregiver is the most important [person] in the early environment. Human development cannot be understood apart from this affect-transacting [emotionally interactive] relationship.

—Allan Schore

Willingness

I will become willing. That is all I have to do. Once I become willing I will be guided by invisible forces, by unseen hands to the next place that I am supposed to be. Willingness is the key that unlocks my door of possibility for me. When I am not willing, I fold my arms, stand rigid and immovable, and challenge the world to budge me. I stick out my chin and tell life to go away. I invite toward myself exactly the energy that I am putting out; I am saying, "I want change, I want a better day, a better me, but I will not move anywhere to get it." It's as if a bowl of fruit were sitting on a table and I thought I should wait for a pear to walk over to me and jump into my mouth. I will walk over, reach out my hand, and move myself toward something I desire. Or at least I will be willing to consider it, so that it can move towards me.

I am willing

The gift of willingness is the only thing that stands between the quiet desperation of a disingenuous life and the actualization of unexpressed potential.

—*Jim McDonald,*
Who Would I Be Without

The Wind

Just as hot air and cold air generate wind, so do the hot and cold forces within me generate an inner shift in temperature; clouds that gather and become heavy burst inside of me and tears pour out. When I integrate my dark side with my light side, my cold with my hot, my chaos with my rigidity, my love with my hate, my intelligence with my ignorance, I experience an emotional wind. I have a pressure within me. I toss and turn inside and am pulled in opposing directions. I can do nothing about this but accept it; it's a natural combustion that accompanies change. But I can be less afraid of it, I can shelter myself, warm myself, find things that stabilize me as I move through this period of deep, inner change. Trying to avoid this kind of inner wind is like wishing for the weather never to change. It's not realistic or even desirable. If I am alive, I am subject to change.

I know an inner wind simply means change and integration is happening

Nobody, as long as he moves about among the chaotic currents of life, is without trouble.

—Carl Jung

My Attitude of Gratitude

Today I recognize that gratitude is one of my most important tools of recovery, of life, so I will daily list what I am grateful for. I am grateful for all the good that is in this world. I am grateful for a warm bed and a chance to wake up to one more day. I am grateful for my cup of tea or coffee, for a body that I can rely on to take me through this day. I am grateful for my walk, for my ability to enjoy what surrounds me, for the people in my life. As I am grateful something wonderful happens, my anxiety begins to lift, I am more hopeful, more alert to what is good. I am alive to the possibility that there might be good behind what I am fearing and I really have the feeling that I am giving that good a chance.

I co-create good in my life through gratitude

Be grateful for what you have now.
As you begin to think about all the things in your
life you are grateful for, you will be amazed at the never
ending thoughts that come back to you of more things
to be grateful for. You have to make a start, and then the law
of attraction will receive those grateful thoughts
and give you more just like them.

—*Rhonda Byrne,* The Secret

Emotions and My Health

My emotions affect my health. This awareness is now being daily proven by science. I used to think that my emotions were something that happened somewhere in the air, but neuroscience is telling us that emotions occur in the body and that they also travel in the space in between people. This means that how I feel gets plowed straight into my physiology and the physiology of those I am close to. My feelings, in other words, affect me physically and others as well. If secondary smoke can cause cancer in a nonsmoker, just by being exposed, then negativity and dysfunction can cause negativity and dysfunction in those around the "host." The good news is, I can do something about how I feel. Wherever I am, I can feel one notch better. I don't need to shoot for the moon, I don't need to be fake. My body will know the difference anyway—it won't let me lie. What I do need to do, is allow my mood to move slightly upward, to feel just a touch better.

I will do myself and those I love a favor by feeling better because I am contagious

Emotional contagion is very functional and has a good purpose—
it makes our interactions smoother, it helps us understand
one another better and it can be very motivating.
It's really good stuff, but then you have all this
collateral damage that happens.

—Heidi Grant Halvorson, Ph.D.

I Will Take Care of Me

Today I will renew my commitment to taking care of myself. For starters, I will make sure that I give myself the rest I need for my body to be healthy. So often I push myself too hard, and my body pays the price. I will eat the kinds of healthy foods that restore nutrients to all my cells and give me the energy that I need to meet the demands of my day. And I will exercise. I recognize that my body needs to move. I need to stay flexible and strong in order to be healthy. I need to feel as attractive as I am capable of being. Exercise has so many health benefits, I can hardly think of all of them. And I will sleep; without adequate sleep, all of my efforts towards health will be less effective. I will recognize and respect my body's need for rest. And I will have quiet in my day; just as my body needs rest in order to function well, my minds needs it just as much. Today I resolve to get enough good nutrition, exercise, and rest to feel good.

I do what I need to do to stay healthy

Keeping your body healthy is an expression
of gratitude to the whole cosmos—
the trees, the clouds, everything.

—Thich Nhat Hanh

Negative Thinking

Today I will take George Burns's advice when asked what his secret to a long and happy life was. "It's all about the attitude, you gotta watch that attitude, kid." He went on to say something about how easily it can slip. Negative thinking is the banana peel; start there and sail down fast. When I get into a pattern of negative thinking and talking, it's like throwing gasoline on a fire. Nothing grows but negativity: the people who like to stick around me all have bones to pick with life; the situations I am in get coated with my negative dust, a dust that they have to somehow shake off to look better. Negative thinking is not the same as being honest, although someone who doesn't want to face their own negative thinking might say that as their form of denial. Negative thinking is a sort of grudge in thought, word, and action. Honesty is just honesty, it can come out in one or two sentences. It's not a grinding, non-stop diatribe that attaches itself to practically any subject. Negativity never has enough to say. Today I don't want to be around my chronic negativity or anyone else's.

I see life through a positive lens

Once you replace negative thoughts with positive ones,
you'll start having positive results.

—*Willie Nelson*

Appreciating the Body I Have

I appreciate the body I have today. So many times I want my body to be different from what it is in one way or another. But today, I will love the body I'm in and feel good about the body I have. It may not be perfect, but resenting it is no answer. Nothing new can come to me if I don't appreciate what I already have. Nothing can transform if I don't accept and work with where I am now. I will send good and caring thoughts to my body , I will see it as beautiful no matter what state it's in. I will love it unconditionally; it doesn't have to be something else for me to love it. And each and every day, I will take actions to keep my body healthy, fit and attractive. My body is my only vehicle through which I can live my life. It is a gift to me and it's my responsibility and right to protect it, care for it, nourish and maintain it.

I make the body God gave me the best that it is capable of being

The man's body is sacred and the woman's body is sacred,
No matter who it is, it is sacred . . .

—*Walt Whitman,* Leaves of Grass

Codependency

Trying to get a deep attentive love from a distracted and disheartened parent can be difficult. Trying to find a secure spot in a family that is scrambling for secure spots can be a battle; there were so many factors that made the crazy or cut-off energy in my family feel more scary and serious because I was a child—factors that set me up for codependency, for fear of rejection, freezing on the inside, and getting very needy and pliable. I was trapped by my own size, unable to get support outside my family and stuck in some emotional no-fly zone, noise everywhere (but I could barely hear it), that sometimes made me feel alone and disconnected. I tried so hard to stay connected to my family, and sometimes twisted my personality out of shape to do so. I longed to be seen, bonded with, cared for, by my sober parent who was just too young, lost, and preoccupied by family addiction to give me that. I got the bonding I needed; after all, I was young, needy, and would have bonded to anything that walked upright. But the bond itself, the family bond, was not a calm and easy and reliable one.

Bonds in my family were traumatized: too tight or too loose

Gaze represents the most intense form of interpersonal communication, and the perception of facial expressions is known to be the most salient channel of nonverbal communication. . . . The most important visual stimulus for infant is mother's emotionally expressive face—"The infant's gaze, in turn, *reliably evokes the mother's gaze,* thereby acting as a potent interpersonal channel for the transmission of "reciprocal mutual influences."

—Allan Schore

Grateful for Life's Generosity

I appreciate the generosity of life. Everywhere I look, the world is spilling forth abundance. I open my hand to receive and the world fills it up with something. Whether it's sunlight, sweet smells or the gift of another day, this world is constantly giving forth. Today I say a quiet thank you for all that the world provides. For sunsets, fresh air and flowers. For rain and people and pets. My arms aren't big enough to hold it all, so today I will appreciate just what I have, knowing that appreciating what I can hold will feel more wonderful than running after more than I can carry. If I am alive then I need to look around me and feel thankful for the gifts that are mine. There is so much to be grateful for if I am willing to consider the blessings I already have. There is a wisdom in gratitude because what I focus on with appreciation has a way of expanding in my life. If I erase my blessings, I don't feed them with the grace of gratitude. If I give thanks for them, I show the creative force that brings forth all good things, that I am worthy enough to appreciate what has been so generously given to me.

I expand my world and myself by my appreciation of it

"Appreciation is a wonderful thing. It makes
what is excellent in others belong to us as well."

—*Voltaire*

Being Happy

I will remember the good times as well as the bad. I will take time each day to recall what worked in my past, what I loved, when I felt good or strong or warm or close to someone. When I remember those times, I will go over and over them in my mind. After all, that is often what I do with the bad times. I ruminate and go over them a hundred times. I blow them up inside of me, feel them over and over again, and in a way, I re-traumatize myself. I need to process my old pain and use my intellect to make new sense out of old, even frozen moments. I will do that as many times as it takes to chip away at old pain and make room for more pleasure. Then I will strengthen my ability to experience good feelings. I have been willing to face the dark night of my own soul. Today I will be equally courageous about facing the lightness of being, remembering all that went well. I will go over the good times as faithfully as I go over the bad. I will create and tolerate beauty, closeness, and happiness in my life each and every day, and I will be grateful for it. Gratitude will be my way of holding it and admiring it—like a butterfly that has perched on my hand, that will fly away and just as surely return over and over again. And in between times, I will carry the thought of beauty and I will hold my hand out for the butterfly.

I have the guts to be happy

It's so hard to forget pain, but it's even
harder to remember sweetness.
We have no scar to show for happiness.
We learn so little from peace.

—*Chuck Palahniuk*

SEPTEMBER

Autobiography in Five Short Chapters

Chapter One

I walk down the street.
There is a deep hole in the sidewalk.
I fall in.
I am lost . . . I am helpless.
It isn't my fault.
It takes forever to find a way out.

Chapter Two

I walk down the same street.
There is a deep hole in the sidewalk.
I pretend I don't see it.
I fall in again.
I can't believe I am in this same place.
But it isn't my fault.
It still takes a long time to get out.

Chapter Three

I walk down the same street.
There is a deep hole in the sidewalk.
I *see* it is there.
I still fall in . . . it's a habit . . . but,
my eyes are open.
I know where I am.
It is *my* fault.
I get out immediately.

Chapter Four

I walk down the same street.
There is a deep hole in the sidewalk.
I walk around it.

Chapter Five

I walk down another street.

—*Portia Nelson,* There's a Hole in My Sidewalk:
The Romance of Self-Discovery

The Treasures Within

Within me is the perfect life waiting to awaken. The gifts I seek are already inside of me. There for me to discover, to tap into whenever I wish. I get so lost in the superficial details and tasks of my life that I forget to live it, to drop down and contact the spirit that God has planted within me. It is the best kept secret that spirit lives within me, that vibrating, illumining, and bottomless sense of aliveness is present all of the time, but I am too distracted to know it. I will remind myself each and every time I think of it, that the way in which I come in touch with my inner light is through my breath, through stillness. I'll close my eyes and let the constant, preoccupying thoughts of my mind float by, not taking them so seriously, not trying to control them. Today I realize that the gold is not in my ability to control my mind, the gold is in what lies beneath. What emerges when my mind, for a precious moment, is stilled.

I am open to the miracle of the moment

Life is a song—sing it.
Life is a game—play it.
Life is a challenge—meet it.
Life is a dream—realize it.
Life is a sacrifice—offer it.
Life is love—enjoy it.

—Sathya Sai Baba

Feeling Good Inside

I will recognize the value of connectedness with others. Relationships with other people sustain and nourish me. They give me a place where I feel welcome and a part of all that surrounds me; they allow me the joy of feeling that I belong somewhere, that I have people in the world who are happy to see me. When I am overly preoccupied, I forget this need of mine to connect with others. When I am in the present, I can actually see what the next right action might be and I can take it seamlessly, easily, fruitfully. I see my day as an opportunity to grow, to give, to share. To let my light shine through to others, to be a connector rather than a divider. I can accomplish both large and small tasks naturally, quietly and without force. I become worthy of the life I have been given, grateful just to be alive for one more day. I let life work out. I let relationships be what they are, not perfect but real.

I take a relaxed and trusting attitude towards my life, towards my day

One of the most spiritual things you can do is embrace
your humanity. Connect with those around you today.
Say "I love you," "I'm sorry," "I appreciate you,"
"I'm proud of you" . . . whatever you're feeling.
Send random texts, write a cute note,
embrace your truth and share it . . .
cause a smile today for someone else . . .
and give plenty of hugs."

—Steve Maraboli, Life, the Truth, and Being Free

The Art of Balanced Living

I am willing to allow my life to happen. Life has taught me that the best laid plans can go awry. I know that I need to have goals and missions in order to give shape, meaning, and a sense of destiny to my life. However, when I let those goals run me, when I let them preoccupy me to such an extent that I stop living in the present, and I miss the beauty and spontaneity of each new day, then I am becoming a slave to my own plans. I will learn to take an action and let go of the result, to have a goal, then to move toward it in a relaxed manner that doesn't rob me of my pleasure and my day. And I will remember to use my breath as a tool to unite me with my body, mind, and spirit; I will breathe in and out, breathing out used up life and breathing in new life.

I breathe into my day, into the moment

Life is what happens to us while we
are making other plans.

—Allen Saunders

Do-Undo-Redo

Today I will see recovery as a process of doing, undoing, and redoing, of constant creation and experimentation. My life is my palette. I will blend and re-blend the various hues of my life into a momentary creation, look at it, admire it, love it, be dissatisfied, change it, look again, tweak again, and let it move and grow and transform constantly.

My life is in a constant state of transformation

Creativity isn't itself good:
Many of the ideas that take on the mantle
of creativity are bad ideas, and it is right to resist these!
Sometimes the new is much worse than the old and
should be rejected. But the spirit of wondering if some new
proposals just might be true, or have something interesting to say—
and then how can that dialectic play out . . . what if . . .
What if therapy wasn't to promote adjustment, but
reinventing oneself? What if spirituality was a little bit about
a re-birth of a fundamental mythic identity? What if many
of our personal habits and social norms need to be re-evaluated
and re-constructed? (And many are currently at issue.)
What if we give ourselves permission to re-evaluate, do,
and then, on re-consideration, do again a little differently?
To re-do? (and then again revise?)
What if the activity involves re-tooling and
re-transforming many of the methods?

—Adam Blatner, MD, TEP

Giving

Today I give with both hands. When I give with one hand and take with the other, I give only half of what I have and receive only half of what might be given to me. I limit myself in two ways. Somehow the universe responds to clear intention. When I fully release a gift, it goes to where it is supposed to go, and what returns to me comes when and how it is right. Giving is a circle, a channel, an openness to release something fully and without strings attached. When I attach strings to what I give, I entangle myself. Not giving is an option. Today, when I give, it will be freely knowing that it is up to me whether or not I choose to do so.

I give fully and with all my heart

This is the true joy in life—being used for
a purpose recognized by yourself as a mighty one;
the being thoroughly worn out before you are thrown on
the scrap heap; the being a force of nature instead
of a feverish, selfish little clod of ailments and
grievances complaining that the world will not
devote itself to making you happy.

—George Bernard Shaw

Learning My Own Lessons

I recognize today that I am in charge of my own learning. Life is constantly offering up circumstances that are useful in my personal growth. I can move through a situation, live it out, extract the wisdom that is in it—or I can ignore the lesson and keep repeating the same painful circumstance over and over again in my life. Repetition is one of life's ways of teaching me. The deepest and most appropriate things I need to learn in life are generally right in front of me. Life is my guru, if I can use it as such. It is rich with subtle learning if I look for it. The gift I can give myself today is becoming aware of what life is trying to teach me. When I accept the circumstances of my life as just where I am supposed to be, my personal learning skyrockets and my second-guessing and regret dissipates. I tune into what life brings to me in a whole new way.

I am with the constant richness of life

Think about what you have, not about what you don't.
Because what you have comes from
God's generosity, and what you don't have
is according to God's wisdom.

—*Author unknown*

Fear

Today, I allow myself to experience my fears as fears. They are real, and it is understandable that I have them. Healing mobilizes my deep fears, and they come up more intensely than ever. This is a part of my process of growth, and growth is not neat and tidy. It's not the remembering various situations or the getting close to someone that is, in itself, scary, it's that I am afraid of the feelings that feeling close might bring up in me that I won't be able to handle. Unconsciously, I'm scared I'll feel like that helpless, hopeless little kid all over again, trapped and alone. When I am very afraid, I will comfort myself or seek comfort from someone else. I will understand that I am afraid, and that even though I fear the worst, the worst will not necessarily happen. I am an adult today, in charge of my own life. My feelings feel very powerful inside me, particularly when they have been repressed and are surfacing after many years; but they are not facts. I can survive my fears and understand that they will pass.

I have compassion for the fearful part of me.

To lose focus means to lose energy.
The absolutely wrong thing to attempt when
we've lost focus is to rush struggling to pack it all back
together again. Rushing is not the thing to do.
Sitting and rocking is the thing to do. Patience, peace,
and rocking renew ideas. Just holding the idea and
the patience to rock it are what some women might call
a luxury. Wild Woman says it is a necessity.

—Clarissa Pinkola Estés, Ph.D.,
Women Who Run with the Wolves

SEPTEMBER 8

My Personal Time

Reexamining my life through recovery, makes me more aware of time. I slow down, and in slowing down I realize how fast I sometimes move. Some of the things I do are necessary. Some aren't. Sometimes I just overdo it because I'm in the habit of running all the time, because I learned to over-function to make up for my family's under functioning. I tried to fill the emptiness with anything I could fill it with. Sometimes I over-function because I'm afraid of down time, afraid I'll feel lonely or disconnected. But today I am seeing that when I move too fast, I forget to stop and smell the roses, I don't take in the soft beauty that surrounds me because I rush right past it. I miss the quiet pleasure of my day. Today, I will value my time and guard it. I need peace of mind in order to take in the subtle beauty and pleasure of the world.

There is a hole inside of me, inside of everyone, that I frantically try to fill

And above all, watch with glittering eyes
the whole world around you because the greatest
secrets are always hidden in the most unlikely places.
Those who don't believe in magic
will never find it.

—Roald Dahl

Accepting Abundance

Today I will dream. I'll use my capacity for visualization to imagine what I would like my life to be like. I will allow myself to see, in my mind, what I want to manifest in my life. Then I'll let the universe work its magic. Rather than stress and control and attempt to manipulate events, circumstances, and people so that they conform to my idea of what I want to happen, I'll hold my vision steadily and with faith, and trust that the universe will provide. This life is a gift, this world is a gift. Nature is abundant. I am part of the world, part of nature. Life means to fulfill me. Today I will take all of the steps that I need to take in order to manifest my vision, and let God do the rest. I'll take the action and let go of the result. I can imagine a better life. I can visualize what I would like to bring into my life. I can align my will with the source energy and quietly trust that what I see will come forth in its own time.

I have faith in my ability to manifest what I wish to have come towards me

You have to visualize a second or two ahead of your car what line you are taking, what you are going to do, before you get there because it comes too fast.

—Emerson Fittipaldi

SEPTEMBER 10

I Am Aware

Today, I see that my life is up to me. How I choose to live, what I will accomplish, how I conduct my intimate relationships, how I treat myself, all are in my own hands. They are gifts of awareness that I can give myself. I can process my most frustrating and difficult emotions and bring them into my conscious awareness so that I can put them into proportion. I can reframe and see things in a new and more helpful light. I can stop running from what clouds and confuses my inner being, what obscures my inner light. I am strong in the awareness that I can live as I choose to live. I am willing to walk a path of self-discovery that, though challenging, builds a strength in me and a knowledge that I can survive my most difficult feelings. I do not need to be afraid of my life if I am not afraid of my inner world. I am comfortable in my own skin.

I am aware of the temporary nature of life

A morning-glory at my window satisfies me
more than the metaphysics of books."

—*Walt Whitman*

Reframing

I will lift my own spirits today. I will look for that place in me that is still and serene, that isn't just constantly in response mode. Somewhere there is a constant, meditative place where the little, and even the big, concerns of the day slip away and become less important. A place where life is just life, and I can breathe in and out of a place of inner calm. Life doesn't have to prove itself to me today for me to treasure it. It is enough that I am here, that I have my freedom of thought and movement. I will appreciate the life I have. I will see the situations of my life in a way that makes new meaning out of them that I can use to better myself and my experience of life; I will reframe. I can see the life I have in a different light, getting the CEO of my mind/body, my thinking mind, to understand and reorder my experience, to make new meaning of it, to cull insight that can enhance my perspective.

I can always see things in a new light

Humans have the ability to shift perspective.
We can experience the world through our senses.
Or we can remove ourselves from our
senses and experience the world even less directly.
We can think about our life, rather than thinking in our life.
We can think about what we think about our life, and we
can think about what we think about that.
We can shift perceptual positions many times over.

—John J. Emrick

Seeing a New Life

I will visualize the life I want. I'll see myself moving around in it, operating as if living the life that I want is the most natural thing in the world. I will practice being the kind of person I want to be, imagining myself doing those things that are part of my day. I will fill the picture in with as much detail as my imagination can conjure up; I'll see, smell, taste, hear, and touch the day I am having, I will hug the people in it. I will give myself over to my visualization as if it were happening right now, over and over again anytime I think of it, each time releasing it. I see this as a mental discipline, as a recovery tool, as a way of reeducating myself into new habits, new beliefs about what my world can look like and how I can be within it.

I see myself living the life I wish to live

When you visualize you materialize.
Here's an interesting thing about the mind; we took
Olympic athletes and had them run their event only in their
mind and then hooked them up to sophisticated biofeedback
equipment. Incredibly, the same muscles fired in the same
sequence when they were running the race in their mind
as when they were running the race on the track.
How could this be? Because your mind can't distinguish
whether you're really doing it or whether it's just
a practice. If you've been there in the mind,
you'll go there in the body."

—Dr. Dennis Waitley

Simplicity

I will simplify my life today. I will do less, think less, and be more. When I let the basics of my life feel like enough, something wonderful happens: they become enough. When I get out of my head and actually let myself just be where I am, where I am takes on a kind of glow. I will simplify my life today so that it feels more livable, so that I am not living in the future or the past in my head, so that my mind is where my body is. When I slow down and remember to breathe, my life feels more manageable and the simple things take on a kind of radiance. They feel less dead and become more alive, less like a nuisance and more like the pleasures of my life. I sink into the moment, recognizing that the moment is all I really have and that it is sufficient onto itself. Knowing that if I allow it just to be there, it will fill me up. Knowing that a well-lived today is my best planning and practicing for a good tomorrow.

I will return to the simplicity of my daily duties, and do them with love

There is a tonic strength, in the hour of sorrow and affliction, in escaping from the world and society and getting back to the simple duties and interests we have slighted and forgotten. Our world grows smaller, but it grows dearer and greater. Simple things have a new charm for us, and we suddenly realize that we have been renouncing all that is greatest and best, in our pursuit of some phantom.

—*William George Jordan*

SEPTEMBER 14

Reaching Out

I will not require that my relationships be perfect in order to be good enough. When I need my relationships to be perfect before I can enjoy them, I am missing the point of stabilizing relationships in my life. What I need more than perfection is a sense of belonging—a place to be myself and to be challenged to grow beyond my own smallness. I cannot do that as effectively in isolation. Spiritual aloneness is a beautiful thing, but isolation and withdrawal are something quite different. Recovery can make me dissatisfied with my relationships because they don't match up with my newly acquired picture of health. Today when I want that picture more than a person I will remember that no one is perfect, least of all me, and that feeling loved and a part of the ongoing rhythm of life is part of what creates joy and stability in my life. Today I will not look to my relationships to fulfill me completely; I will recognize that they are only part of that picture and that I need many sources of fulfillment to be happy.

Love warms my heart and holds me to what is good in life

The greatest disease in the West today is not TB or leprosy;
it is being unwanted, unloved, and uncared for.
We can cure physical diseases with medicine, but the only
cure for loneliness, despair, and hopelessness is love.
There are many in the world who are dying for a piece of bread
but there are many more dying for a little love.
The poverty in the West is a different kind of poverty—
it is not only a poverty of loneliness but also of spirituality.
There's a hunger for love, as there is a hunger for God.

—*Mother Teresa,*
A Simple Path: Mother Teresa

Staying in the Game

Growing up with relationship trauma made me hypervigilant. I was always scanning other people's faces for their mood shifts; a raised eyebrow, a change in vocal tone, raised voices could make me shake inside. I swung into action to placate and please or to get out of the way of whatever might be coming next. I lived with a low hum of fear and anxiety. My hypervigilance makes me easily triggered: I react fast on the inside whether or not I express it—it creates stress within me. Today I recognize that program slogans like "a day at a time" or "easy does it" or "take the next right action" help me to manage my hypervigilance and live in the moment. Each and every day I will play the hand I'm dealt as well as I can play it. Each and every day I will wake up, place my hand in the hand of God, and move into my day with the confidence and comfort of knowing that I am not alone, that I have access to the greatest source of compassion and power in the universe. Each and every day I will put one foot in front of the other and try to make sense of the life I have been given. I will have faith; I will stay connected and alive while I'm living.

I am willing to constantly be reviewing,
reviving and restoring my life

The road to success is always under construction.

—Lily Tomlin

A Quiet Awakening

Today I will work my tools of recovery; I will journal, write an affirmation, listen to a guided imagery, do some spiritual reading, or meditate. Whatever fits most easily into my day, I will do. I will do my daily upkeep; I will work for my inspiration rather than expect it to fall on my head from the skies. I will work the tools of my program and my life tools. If I am not in a good place, I will run through a mental checklist of things I can do to help myself. I can pick up the phone, go to a meeting, take a walk, reach out and share, exercise, schedule time for me, get a massage, take a hot bath. I'll recognize that my mood is slipping and I'll quickly play the tape through to the end in my mind: *Where will this mood get me if I just keep indulging it? Where will this negativity land me if I keep feeding it. Where will this anger wind up if I keep winding it up?* I will *breathe*. I'll breathe in the spirit that is always there, vibrating just beneath the surface of my being, the membrane of my day. I will call to that part of me that has been waiting patiently for me to come to my senses and claim it. I turn and look, I quiet my mind and see, I rest in awareness. Spirit has never been far, but I have been asleep, right here, right now. Today I wake up to spirit.

I sense spirit at work within me, I feel imbued with spiritual light

Make your own Bible. Select and collect all the words and sentences that in all your readings have been to you like the blast of a trumpet.

—Ralph Waldo Emerson

Working It Till It Works

God has given me to me to take care of. I have been put in charge of my own self. I am the one who steers me through my day, who makes a myriad of tiny decisions that add up to a life. I am the eyes and ears behind each hour. I am the choice maker. If my day isn't going the way I'd like it to, I will remember that I am the one at the center of it, I'm driving the car. If my life isn't going as I wish it would, I will remember that it's my life, no one can live it for me and no one can change it for me. I am on a spiritual journey. And on this journey I am my own best pilot and my own best philosopher. No one knows me as I know me, and no one can synthesize all of the information that I receive each day into a coherent picture of my life as well as I can. If I don't take charge of my journey, no one else will, no one else can.

I can learn by personal reflections that lead to meaningful actions or observations

Man has three ways of acting wisely.
First, on meditation; that is the noblest.
Secondly, on imitation; that is the easiest.
Thirdly, on experience; that is the bitterest.

—*Confucius*

SEPTEMBER 18

Inner Light

Today, I will go within for the deepest sort of experience of joy, of ecstasy in being alive. I will get in touch with the deeper pulse of living—the thread that connects me with the divine experience. I will recognize that in order to be lit from within, I need to drop down inside of myself and be in the presence of inner light. Life itself has a purpose apart from any individual task or stage. Life itself is the experience. All of the things I have been trying to accomplish are both inner and outer goals. They are meant to bring me closer to myself, to develop me in ways that allow me to experience life more fully—to be more capable of pleasure. Today I will give myself these gifts of inner sight. I will observe the miraculousness of this life, this world, knowing that I am part of a divine mystery, a mystery of incalculable intelligence.

I observe the constant miracles of life and I am in awe

My religion consists of a humble admiration
of the illimitable superior spirit who reveals himself
in the slight details we are able to perceive
with our frail and feeble mind.

—Albert Einstein

Perfectionism

Dark forecasting was a residue of childhood dysfunction and trauma. I experienced a loss of trust and faith that the world was a predictable and safe place, that my needs were meet-able and not too much, that relationships could be fulfilling rather than disappointing. As a result, I sometimes seesaw between extremes, I want a perfect life and perfect relationships, or I want to throw them all over. I see that I need to seek balance rather than perfection or annihilation. Today I recognize that I need to consciously adopt better attitudes. I am a creative being. I have the power of reason, the ability to think, hope, and dream. I have the power to think my way into a better point of view, to see the glass as half full, rather than half empty. My mind can be my greatest enemy or my greatest ally. It depends on how I choose to use it. When my day goes sour, rather than try to manipulate others or complain about my fate, I will step back and observe what is going through my mind.

I have a powerful instrument at the ready;
my own mind

Perfectionism is not a quest for the best.
It is a pursuit of the worst in ourselves, the part
of us that tells us that nothing we do will ever be
good enough—that we should try again.

—*Julia Cameron*, The Artist's Way

Seeing Clearly

Today I will use my mind to actually visualize what I want my life to look like. I will give myself the gift of seeing my life through this beautiful lens. My thoughts have a creative power; they reach out, shape, and template my experience. What I see as true for me, can be true for me, if I am willing sustain my vision and do the work I need to do to get there. Today I will picture doors opening for me where there were none before. I will take my thoughts seriously. I'll decide on what I'd like to see manifest in my life, and I will carry it in my mind's eye and take daily steps toward actualizing it. I will see it as if it is already a reality. Then I'll let it go again and again and allow the wisdom of the universe to bring those experiences and opportunities toward me that allow me to take the next right action.

I see and release, I see and release, I see and release

It comes down to something really simple:
Can I visualize myself playing those scenes?
If that happens, then I know that I will
probably end up doing it.

—Jessica Lange

Living the Segments of My Day Intentionally

I will divide my day into segments of intention. When I wake up in the morning I will picture feeling good as I go about my early routines. When I move into the next part of my day I will see my morning going smoothly; whatever I have to do I will picture doing with ease and a happy feeling. I will be intentional about each segment of my midday, seeing myself operating effectively, competently, and enjoying my interactions with those I encounter. As afternoon approaches, I will imagine, in my mind's eye, a pleasant and peaceful evening. And as evening gives way to night, I will imagine myself enjoying a peaceful and restful sleep. Living with this intention not only sets good stuff into motion, it counters the dark forecasting, self-judgment, and negative jags I can get on. It makes me more conscious of all the junk that goes through my mind that locks me into just what I am trying to get free of.

I live intentionally

Visualize this thing that you want,
see it, feel it, believe in it. Make your mental
blue print, and begin to build.

—*Robert Collier*

Opening to What's Here

Everywhere nature brings forth. The clouds, wind, and rain draw me toward their eternal mystery. This world is designed to nurture and sustain life. I am part of that life, and I receive solace and comfort knowing that the world and I are both alive and vibrant, both imbued with the same life force. I am ready, willing, and able to open my mind and heart to the abundance that the world has to offer me. This world brings forth what I need. The sun shines, water from fresh springs makes its way across rocky slopes to quench my thirst, and abundant varieties of food germinate from seeds to nourish my body. This world is designed to nourish my body and my spirit; everything that I need to be healthy and strong is here, literally falling off trees. And all that my senses need to make them feel soothed and satisfied is around me all of the time—sunsets, fresh air, birds singing, warm caressing breezes, cleansing rainstorms—the world is amazing to me.

I plant the seeds in my day that I wish to see grow in my life

To accomplish great things we must first dream, then visualize, then plan . . . believe . . . act!

—Alfred A. Montapert

Accepting Responsibility for My Emotional and Psychological Health

Today I recognize that the way in which I live inside, impacts my experience of life, my relationships, my present, and my future. There are attitudes and practices that I can adopt, that can alter the course of my life. My integrity is a powerful and potent force. I will make certain that what I say matches what I do.

I live my principles

The Four Agreements

1. Be Impeccable With Your Word

Speak with integrity. Say only what you mean. Avoid using the word to speak against yourself or to gossip about others. Use the power of your word in the direction of truth and love.

2. Don't Take Anything Personally

Nothing others do is because of you. What others say and do is a projection of their own reality, their own dream. When you are immune to the opinions and actions of others, you won't be the victim of needless suffering.

3. Don't Make Assumptions

Find the courage to ask questions and to express what you really want. Communicate with others as clearly as you can to avoid misunderstandings, sadness and drama. With just this one agreement, you can completely transform your life.

4. Always Do Your Best

Your best is going to change from moment to moment; it will be different when you are healthy as opposed to sick. Under any circumstance, simply do your best, and you will avoid self-judgment, self-abuse and regret.

—Miguel Ruiz

Golden Moments

I have the gift of life. I am here. I am alive, with all of my senses and able to experience the magic of this incredible world. Whatever this day has in store for me—I am open to receive. I will act on my day and allow my day to act on me. I am open. I will take steps that I know will make my day feel good, productive, and pleasurable, and then I will let the rest happen. Each day presents me with gifts and surprises, if I know how to unwrap the present—if I remember how to be pleased, moved, and astonished by the wonders of this world. I will pay attention to guidance from within and without. There are moments when I know I am doing what lights my spirit and challenges me. Moments when I feel alive and in tune; in touch with a force beyond me that is guiding me toward something that's right for me. Those moments are golden. They carry me through my fears and hard times, they sustain me when inevitable doubts creep in, they give me strength to carry on and stay on course.

I see before me the life I am meant to live

Make sure you visualize what you really want,
not what someone else wants for you.

—Jerry Gillies

A Still Small Voice

I will look at the million little ways that I sabotage my day. The thoughts that I think are felt by others. Why do I set higher standards for others than I set for myself? There is a difference between being judgmental and having my own point of view. I need my own point of view, I need my own take on things. But grinding out the kind of judgment that's inevitably loaded up with baggage from my past, clouds my ability to see what is good. I see things as all good or all bad; I lose the in-between. Today I will have faith. I will follow that still small voice within me. When I have doubts, which of course I will have, I will reach down within myself and pull up something that I thought wasn't even there, I'll pull up faith that things will be all right. Whether or not things are going just the way I want them to, I'll have faith that they will somehow right themselves in the end. It will work out, or it won't work out, but still, all will be okay. I will give myself the gift of faith. With this faith I may not see myself surrounded by exactly what I want, but at least I won't make what I have worse by hating it, wanting to smash it, wanting to get rid of the life I have.

I have faith in what I cannot yet see

Don't judge each day by the harvest you reap
but by the seeds that you plant.

—Robert Louis Stevenson

Giving My Body a Voice

Relationship trauma takes its toll; my body holds frozen emotions, words that I could never say out loud, feelings that I had no safety to feel. This frozenness forms a block in my energy, a sort of lost emotional memory trapped inside of me. Today I will write in my journal as a part of my body. I might say something like, "I am your back and I want to cry. I am tired of being silent and this is what I want you to hear." Or maybe I'll say, "As your stomach I want to rebel. I want to relax, and let go of all this . . ." Or "I am your legs and I wish you appreciated me. I carry you all around the world but you are constantly wishing I were different." I will let my body parts have a voice and scribble their thoughts onto paper then I will read what they have said to me and wonder about what they have told me.

I will put pen to paper on behalf of my body

Illness is the most heeded of doctors:
to goodness and wisdom we only
make promises; pain we obey.

—Marcel Proust

Appreciating What I Have

Today I won't let my desire for more, blind me to what's already here. My life is full of blessings that I look right past when all I see is what's missing, rather than what is there. When I feel disappointed by life, I point toward what's empty, not understanding that I am only creating more emptiness. Desire is natural and good—I need to feel it to grow and reach beyond myself—but the kind of desire that keeps me stuck in a cycle of wanting and not having just creates more lack. I become wedded to the energy of "not enough." Today, I will appreciate what I already have before I ask for more. Appreciation is like water on a plant; it causes good to grow in my life. What I appreciate expands. It grows before my eyes, it deepens and widens. The mere act of appreciation somehow creates more of what I am already giving thanks for. It opens doors to the coffers of this generous world and invites the bounty to come in. Appreciation lets the creative universe know that I am grateful for what is being so freely given to me.

I appreciate what I have, what I see, what I am

When one door of happiness closes, another opens;
but often we look so long at the closed door
that we do not see the one which
has been opened for us.

—Helen Keller

Open to Receive

Today I will be open to what life offers to me. Instead of pushing away what's right in front of me, I will look at it as what life is trying to give to me today. I will experiment with receiving it gratefully and see what happens. The world comes to greet me like an old friend each morning. My daily habits comfort and ground me. The thought of moving into my day pleases me. Life unfolds one second at a time, and today I will be present to witness it. How much of my life do I let pass by unnoticed? How many of my feelings go unfelt? Today I will recognize that my time on Earth is limited. I choose to value my life a day at a time and embrace it while I have it. If I waste this day, it will simply be my wasted day, as if I squandered a thousand dollars on nothing. My time is more valuable than any possession I have; it is my greatest wealth. When I wish my time away, I am wishing away what I need to create the next part of my life.

I will appreciate and use my time productively, even if it is just smiling

Nothing is a waste of time if you use
the experience wisely.

—Auguste Rodin

Too Much Anger

Understanding and thought are distributed throughout all the cells in my body. Who I am is stored in my physical self. My body carries memory and knowledge about how I have responded to the circumstances of my life, about what I brought into this world to begin with. If my anger goes beyond what might be an appropriate response to a situation, I need to take a deeper look at what might be getting activated from my own personal history. Am I projecting my own unconscious anger and making today's situation worse than it is? If my anger is chronic I probably need to look more deeply to see if there's a piece of historical anger I'm carrying that might be getting mixed up with current anger and creating a ticking time bomb.

I will not add to my bed of anger,
I will look at it, process it, and let it go

If you are a highly sensitive or suggestible individual, receptive to mental imagery, and you have a lot of cortisol in your bloodstream (as when you're stressed), it is very possible for you to incorporate new "traumatic" memories into your brain and body that have no basis in your past experience. . . . Instead they may be the by-product of your current environment combined with the suggestions and imagery you picked up. . . . If someone or something in your environment seems to suggest that a certain thing happened at a moment when you are biologically susceptible . . . the scenario may then be encoded as a new trauma memory . . . one that you'll have to cope with on top of the original memories that have arisen on their own.

—*Christiane Northrup, M.D.*

Seeing Deeply

Every day I experience another piece of myself. Yes, I am laid low, but at the same time worlds are opening up to me on the inside. My body is struggling to heal and so is the rest of me. I am watching myself deepen inside and become more aware. It is forced upon me by illness, but I cannot help but feel a little bit grateful for the time to slow down and go within. I am seeing the subtleties of life, I am watching myself watch the world around me. I have a witness inside that is constantly with me, but I seldom take time to be with it. As I witness my own thoughts, I learn about who I am inside, what makes me tick. As I watch myself interact with others, I see how I act in relationships. As I notice the little things, life seems to matter more.

I am awake and aware, I get it

Wisdom comes with the ability to be still.
Just look and just listen.
No more is needed.
Being still, looking, and listening activates the
non-conceptual intelligence within you.
Let stillness direct your words and actions.

—*Eckhart Tolle,* Stillness Speaks

OCTOBER

Long ago all men were divine, but mankind so abused the privilege that Brahma, the god of all gods, decided the godhead should be taken away from them. But he had to hide it where man would never find it again. "Let us bury it deep in the earth," suggested one god.

Brahma said, "No, man will dig down until he finds it." "Then let us throw it into the deepest part of the biggest ocean," proposed another god. "Man will learn to dive and someday come across it," insisted Brahma.

"Then it can be hidden in the clouds atop the highest mountain of the Himalayas."

"Man will manage to climb that high some day," Brahma pointed out. "I have a better idea. Let us hide it where he will never think to look: inside man himself."

—Hindu story

OCTOBER 1

Self-Forgiveness

Today, I will forgive myself for not being perfect. I will have an attitude of acceptance toward myself and others for being other than what is expected. I forgive myself for being less than ideal, and for today, that's how I will love myself and others. Perfection is that celluloid image against which I measure myself and come out feeling lacking, that yardstick with which I hit my own backside. Truth be told, we're all just bumbling along, mostly doing the best we can, sometimes worse than we should, sometimes better. Just for this moment, I won't get hung up on imperfection and perfection. Beating myself up on the inside will benefit no one. In fact it will keep me stuck. If I have anger at myself, processing it will let it become less toxic to me. Hating myself will only create more hate and shame and anger. I'll take people as they come, life as it comes, myself as I come. I will focus on living today in the best way that I know how, confident that in this way, I am giving a good tomorrow the right foundation.

I forgive imperfection

Forgiveness entails the authentic
acceptance of our own worthiness as human beings,
the understanding that mistakes are opportunities
for growth, awareness and the cultivation of compassion,
and the realization that the extension of love to ourselves
and others is the glue that holds the universe together.
Forgiveness . . . is not a set of behaviors,
but an attitude.

—Joan Borysenko, Ph.D.

Unseen Hands

I have lost parts of me that I do not even admit to myself, little anxieties, worries, habits, behaviors, ways of thinking about myself that I hide from the world, from myself. And with them pieces of self seamlessly slip away and out of consciousness. I will pray to unseen hands to help me find these forgotten parts of me, to lift these fragments of self toward God and with loving hands and hearts, blow the dust and sorrow from them and tuck them carefully back into me wherever they belong. There are forces in this ever-alive and vibrating universe that want to help me if I can let them. I feel lifted by a million tiny and ever-so-light fingers upwards. When I pray, I am answered; I see that there is nothing that I need face alone or without more help than I could possibly want. My darkest hour can become my light. My lowest moment can become heavenly. When I am low, I will allow this legion of tiny hands to lift me in the blink of an eye. I will ask and then know that help is near, that help is here. I will take a leap of faith and know that I am anything but alone. I will free my mind so that it can include more experience than it normally does. I will allow the veil to be lifted so that I can see this spiritual and alive universe for what it is and people for the tender and vulnerable creatures that we all are.

I am lifted out of pain by a million delicate and tender hands

I call that mind free, which escapes the bondage of matter, which, instead of stopping at the material universe and making it a prison wall, passes beyond it to its Author, and finds in the radiant signatures which everywhere bears of the Infinite Spirit, helps to its own spiritual enlightenment.

—*William Ellery Channing*, Spiritual Freedom

Taming the Beast

Anger hijacks my thinking brain as it increases in my body. It can shoot through my limbs or ball up and tighten itself somewhere in my body. It's tense muscles, an overpowering urge to explode or withdraw, a sick feeling in the pit of my stomach. Sometimes I experience anger as sort of a psychic traffic jam, a mental gridlock. Other times anger is in the driver's seat and I am following it on a wild goose chase. Still again, I can cower in fear underneath my own anger, beating myself up for having those feelings. Then I have sort of a boxing match going on inside of me. For me, anger can be physical, emotional, or mental. When it is all of those at once, I better watch out—trouble is near. Anger takes so many forms. It pops up, down, sideways, straight ahead, or bursts like a fire cracker on the Fourth of July. Today I will take a step back when I feel this physical part of my anger taking me over, I will breathe, reflect, and let it pass. I can understand it if I feel my anger needs attention, or release it and just let it go if I feel my anger is just habit.

I explore the many faces of anger.

A man in passion rides a horse
that runs away with him.

—*Thomas Fuller,* Gnomologia

Feeling My Own Anger

When someone is angry at me all I can seem to do is question myself. *What did I do to offend? What should I have done differently? Why are they so mad?* But part of my near obsession is that I am mad too. I'm angry at their behavior, but not fully comfortable saying it. Why? Why do I hesitate so, to say what you did made me angry. It hurt me and made me mad. Saying those words feels so different. I fear they'll get mad back or twist the situation around and tell me I'm wrong, stupid, or bad for feeling angry. And so I create this confusion half denying my own anger and fearing theirs. Maybe it is my own anger that I'm afraid of.

I can let myself know that I am angry, even if I do not choose to tell the other person

"Anger is just anger. It isn't good. It isn't bad.
It just is. What you do with it is what matters.
It's like anything else. You can use it to build or to destroy.
You just have to make the choice." "Constructive anger,"
the demon said, her voice dripping sarcasm.
"Also known as passion," I said quietly.
"Passion has overthrown tyrants and freed prisoners and slaves.
Passion has brought justice where there was savagery.
Passion has created freedom where there was nothing but fear.
Passion has helped souls rise from the ashes of their
horrible lives and build something better,
stronger, more beautiful."

—*Jim Butcher,* White Night

Grief

People who I loved, I watched destroy themselves seemingly by their own hand; who said they loved me, but not enough to become someone safe to love. They made everyone sick at heart, and all too often, sick in mind and behavior. We disappeared, maybe not all at once, but by inches. But still I remember the love, the closeness, the goodness and decency that were there, and I cherish it. I cherish it because losing it made me realize with such stark clarity what I had. And I resolve to build it again.

I can have healthy relationships in my life

Grief can destroy you—or focus you. You can decide a relationship
was all for nothing if it had to end in death, and you alone.
OR you can realize that every moment of it had more meaning than
you dared to recognize at the time, so much meaning it scared you,
so you just lived, just took for granted the love and laughter of each day,
and didn't allow yourself to consider the sacredness of it.
But when it's over and you're alone, you begin to see that it wasn't
just a movie and a dinner together, not just watching sunsets together,
not just scrubbing a floor or washing dishes together or worrying
over a high electric bill. It was everything, it was the why of life,
every event and precious moment of it. The answer to the mystery
of existence is the love you shared sometimes so imperfectly,
and when the loss wakes you to the deeper beauty of it, to the sanctity
of it, you can't get off your knees for a long time, you're driven
to your knees not by the weight of the loss but by gratitude for what
preceded the loss. And the ache is always there, but one day
not the emptiness, because to nurture the emptiness,
to take solace in it, is to disrespect the gift of life.

—*Dean Koontz,* Odd Hours

Life Is a Spiritual Journey

No one can learn the alphabet for me. And no one can develop wisdom, appreciation, or inner strength for me. These are things I have to do for myself. What is life but growth and expansion, increasing my understanding so that I can deepen my experience of feeling alive? There are gifts in healing if I am willing to see them, lessons I can learn, awarenesses that I need in order to appreciate what I already have. Sickness can be my teacher if I let it. Even as I wait for strength to return to my body, still my spirit and my character can grow stronger and better and more refined. I am not doing nothing as I lie here; I am growing on the inside. Today I will use this moment that puts me into a deeper part of myself to come in contact with an openness to grow. I am in touch with a part of life that I normally don't get in touch with.

I am understanding and expanding my inner world

Always remember:
happiness is not a side matter in your
spiritual journey—it is essential.

—Reb Nachman of Breslov

New Life

I can feel my body, my mind, and my spirit trying to come back to health. I am breathing in and out with relaxed, complete breaths, and with each breath I take, I feel more serene. I sense the life within each pore of my body and it feels good, it feels right, it feels alive. My body and mind needed to fall apart a little, they needed to get my attention and tell me they needed tender, loving care. They want to tell me to treat them better, with care, attention, and love. Parts of my life that aren't working are calling out to me for healing. Today, I will pay attention to what my body is trying to tell me it wants and needs, and I will give it what it is calling out for. I will care for my mind by not burdening it with unnecessary weight; I will get help and support because recovery has taught me that going it alone, toughing it out, white-knuckling it, only leads to loneliness and isolation. I will accept the messes that I have created and clean them up one at a time, I will clean them up in a way that is organized and maintainable. In exactly the same way that an organized room is easier to keep clean, an organized life is easier to keep clean, too.

I will have an orderly mind and an orderly life

Everyone who is born holds dual citizenship,
in the kingdom of the well and in the kingdom of the sick.
Although we all prefer to use only the good passport,
sooner or later each of us is obliged, at least for a spell,
to identify ourselves as citizens of that other place.

—Susan Sontag,
Illness as Metaphor, *1977*

Co-Creation

I live in a world of possibilities. I live in a world in which my imagination walks ahead of me. What I can see in my mind's eye can manifest. First, I have to see it, feel it, experience it as real. Then I open a door within me through which my vision can manifest in God's time. I create space in my life for experiences to enter and when they do, I recognize the opportunity that's before me. I listen, think, and take the sorts of actions that are appropriate and right-sized for the day I am in. Bringing my good into being is a daily process, and the more I do it, the better I get at it. I am limited only by what I am willing to accept as possible. I can expand my vision of what feels possible, seeing it in my mind's eye with clarity and detail, and feeling my vision with excitement and a fulfilled, happy feeling. Life is a creative process in which I am the co-creator. God and I work together to make this world a better place to be.

I know that today I plant seeds in a fertile universe

First comes thought; then organization of
that thought, into ideas and plans; then transformation
of those plans into reality. The beginning, as you
will observe, is in your imagination.

—Napoleon Hill

OCTOBER 9

Being Authentic

I will stop fighting with myself and give my mind, body, and heart the rest and inner quiet that they are craving. I'm not going to rush myself into wellness, or force my thoughts into a phony sort of gaiety. I will accept myself as I am and feel what I feel. Thoughts and feelings won't kill me. Resisting the ones I don't want to experience puts me in a constant struggle with my own insides. My random thoughts and feelings are trying to tell me something. If I turn away and refuse to listen, I only hurt myself. Instead I will let the adult in me listen to those younger, fearful, or anxious selves that are bubbling up inside of me—just as a loving parent would allow a child who is hurt to pour out all of his feelings, knowing that the simple act of pouring, is in itself the cure. I will hold my inner child and let her cry, listen to his childlike voice with an attentiveness, give to her, nurture him. I will take care of the vulnerable part of me that needs to be protected and heard in order to feel safe.

I am willing to know myself

When tears come, I breathe deeply and rest.
I know I am swimming in a hallowed stream where
many have gone before. I am not alone, crazy,
or having a nervous breakdown . . .
My heart is at work. My soul is awake.

—*Mary Margaret Funk,*
Thoughts Matter

Accepting Caring from Others

I will soak up any extra attention that those around me give ne when I open up or reach out. Even if I don't need it at the moment, I will soak it into my pores and store it up for a time when I do need it. I will let the attention feel good. I will allow it to restore my faith in, and affection for, people. I enjoy the little things people are willing to do for me, going a bit out of their way, worrying about how I'm doing. It feels good if I let it. It restores me, if I willing to be restored. Feeling grateful for what is coming my way has a healing power all its own. When I am rested, I won't spend all of my energy the moment I get it; I will keep it, enjoy the feeling of health and well-being, and store up reserve power for another day. I will feel so that I can heal. And then I will let feeling go, pass through me, become big, then medium sized, then small. I am in charge of regulating my mind and body and hence my thoughts and actions. I will take care of me, so that I am not a burden or danger to myself or anyone else.

I drink up the care and concern of others

The power of love to change bodies is legendary,
built into folklore, common sense, and everyday experience.
Love moves the flesh, it pushes matter around. . . .
Throughout history, "tender loving care" has
uniformly been recognized as a
valuable element in healing.

—Larry Dossey, M.D.

OCTOBER 11

Inside My Mind

I am changing, I can feel it. I am learning and growing just by being still. I am sensing more than I normally sense and feeling more than I normally feel. I am grateful to feel alive and to recognize that life is a spiritual journey. All my life, circumstances are spiritual challenges, opportunities to see new sides of myself, new sides of life. Life surrounds me; it is inside, outside, and everywhere. If I am open and still on the inside, life is there. If I am not lost in a million unnecessary distractions, life is there, spirit is there—waiting to be seen and felt. Trauma in my family can make being happy seem like a bad idea; unconsciously I fear that if life feels good, it will only hurt more when it blows up in my face. But this belief keeps me from my own enjoyment of the life I do have, right now—the life I have earned and am working for a day at a time.

I trust this moment and will be happy just this moment.

I believe that the very purpose of life is to be happy.
From the very core of our being, we desire contentment.
In my own limited experience I have found that the more we
care for the happiness of others, the greater is our own
sense of well-being. Cultivating a close, warmhearted feeling
for others automatically puts the mind at ease.
It helps remove whatever fears or insecurities we may
have and gives us the strength to cope with any obstacles
we encounter. It is the principal source of success in life.
Since we are not solely material creatures, it is a
mistake to place all our hopes for happiness on external
development alone. The key is to develop inner peace.

—H.H. the Dalai Lama

Prayer

Prayer helps me to heal. Study after study scientifically prove that prayer is beneficial to my health. I will pray for my healing throughout my day whenever it occurs to me. I will accept and be grateful for the prayers of others knowing that they are being carried to me by unseen hands. Just as radio waves pulse through the air and become voices, prayers come to me in an inner voice. I will ask my body to hear the prayers that are coming toward me and to invite them into each and every cell.

I accept the power of prayer to heal

There are a great many studies now looking at
the role of intercessory prayer and proving clinical outcomes
in sick people. Many of these studies have used Buddhists
as the people doing the praying just as they have used
fundamentalist Christians. And there isn't any evidence that
anybody's prayer works any better than anybody else's.
I know that may sound rebellious and even heretical to a lot
of people in our culture but I'm impressed by these studies.
I think we ought to pay more attention to them because they
show that prayer does work and that nobody's cornered
the market on prayer. I think it points like an arrow to the need
for religious tolerance. If there's one thing our culture is in
great need of now, it's tolerance between religions.
So one thing I like about these studies is they
really do stand up very strongly
for religious tolerance. . . .

—Larry Dossey, M.D.

Think, Think, Think

Today I recognize the power of my own thinking mind to heal myself. Moments of intense fear, stress, and pressure made me freeze inside. My thinking mind, my prefrontal cortex, froze when I geared up for fight or flight. But I could do neither in the family I grew up in, and so I froze. Part of my healing is to go back to those frozen moments, feel the feelings that went unfelt and translate them into words so that I can bring them to a conscious level. I can use my thinking to make sense of what I am feeling and place it into the overall context of my life. I can use my adult mind to make mature meaning of the childlike interpretation of events that I made when I was young, trapped, and scared. I can grow up on the inside. I can heal myself. My thinking mind is my friend, my powerful tool, the CEO of the rest of me. It has the power to perceive, to self reflect, to order thought and direct action, to interpret emotion and experience. Without it I am an animal, all limbic, reacting unconsciously without thinking through the implications and long range consequences of my actions. I'm driven by emotion and sensation. With my clear thinking, I am a human being.

I treasure my God given ability to think

"You know, I once read an interesting book which said that, uh, most people lost in the wilds, they, they die of shame. . . . Yeah, see, they die of shame. 'What did I do wrong? How could I have gotten myself into this?' And so they sit there and they . . . die. Because they didn't do the one thing that would save their lives. . . . Thinking."

—Charles Morse, character in the film The Edge *(written by David Mamet)*

My Feelings Have Force

Today, even though I am feeling out of sorts, I will take responsibility for what I am putting out to others. Actions speak louder than words, and silence is not always golden—sometimes it's controlling and manipulative. My feelings vibrate out into the atmosphere and are felt, even carried, by others; particularly my unconscious feelings have force. My unprocessed, disowned feelings are felt by others. When I then deny them, those people picking up on them feel crazy: they feel one message but I am telling them something completely different. In this way, I make them the carriers of my unfelt pain, anger, or insecurity. Today I will own my own feelings, take responsibility for them, and even accept caring and support from others. Then I will ask myself if I'm appreciating the efforts people are making for me. Am I looking into and beyond their faces as they are looking into mine? Am I giving them half a chance to help me, and am I giving myself half a chance to be helped? As I move through the experiences of my day, I will try to remain conscious of others' efforts and well as my own. I will appreciate what is being done for me.

I let good in

The *I* in illness is isolation, and the crucial letters in wellness are *we*.

—Author unknown, as quoted in Mimi Guarneri,
The Heart Speaks: A Cardiologist Reveals the Secret Language of Healing

Thinking Positively

Today when I think positively, I will allow and invite my entire body to carry a positive thought. I will instruct each cell within me to be active, healthy, and vibrant. Each time that I feel I am getting low on reserves, I will open my body to receiving uplifting light and energy from the universe. I am not a talking head. I am a body, mind, and spirit. I tune in to my body, I scan it for areas that my intuition tells me might be weak or in need of a little TLC, then consciously bless whatever part of my body needs blessing. As I breathe deeply, I picture a light pouring into each and every part I have blessed, extending itself to envelop all of me and imbuing each cell with healing energy. I am confident that this energy is filling and restoring me. In this way, I give to myself, I care for myself, I show myself love through actively demonstrating that feeling toward myself. I rest when I am tired, sleep all night, and exercise to stay loose, fit, firm, and flexible. I take care of the only body I have.

I do daily self care

I believe in pink. I believe that laughing is the best calorie burner. I believe in kissing, kissing a lot. I believe in being strong when everything seems to be going wrong. I believe that happy girls are the prettiest girls. I believe that tomorrow is another day and I believe in miracles.

—Audrey Hepburn

The Healing Universe

Everywhere I look life is in a process of healing from something. A plant that has been stepped on fights to come back to life. A tree that has lost branches sprouts new growth. An animal that has lost a leg learns to run on three. Life is always reaching for life. It's an unbroken circle. Life is programmed to heal itself and it will strive towards that with all its will. I will allow this powerful force that's built into my DNA to work its magic on me. I won't resist my own healing. I will allow it in. My psyche has healing forces built into it by nature—when I cleanse emotional wounds, purge pain, or lance a turgid emotional boil, my mind and heart can begin to heal themselves. I experience a catharsis of pain relieving me of inner blocks and pressure, making way for a catharsis of integration. Things begin to make sense. When my feelings are less blocked, I can begin to let them flow, use my thinking mind to make sense of them; I gain access to my inner world. I see with greater clarity what I have been carrying and make new and mature sense of old, perhaps immature pain. I gain insight, strength and resilience. I see the same situation with new eyes.

My heart and mind heal just as a cut finger heals

We shall not cease from exploration
And the end of all our exploring
Will be to arrive where we started
And know the place for the first time.

—*T. S. Eliot,* Four Quartets

Unexpected Gifts

My family disease brought so many unexpected gifts to me. A new freedom from convention: so many things that were supposed to work, just didn't. The life we were supposed to live had so many holes in it that I had to look for new solutions, new ways to live. I became open-minded by default. It was great. I felt a new sense of freedom seeing that my parents' solutions were so far from perfect. It gave me the impetus to take my own risks, to try out my own ideas. What I learned is that my own ideas about how to live my life were good ones—they worked much better for me than following someone else's ideas, however good. I learned from a young age that if I didn't do something myself, chances were it would not get done. If I didn't make my own plans, there would be no plans. If I didn't take care of myself, no one was likely to step into the breach and take care of me. Even though depending on myself was lonely and I felt forgotten at times, I learned so many important lessons on taking care of myself that have actually made me a real choice-maker who has the will to shape my own life. After all, if I don't, no one else really can.

Dysfunction had so many liberating gifts

Life is like arriving late for a movie, having to
figure out what was going on without bothering everybody
with a lot of questions, and then being unexpectedly
called away before you find out how it ends.

—Joseph Campbell

More Isn't Better

I will let my thoughts float today; it's time for me to let go, to just be. I will visualize my life just as I want it to be. I will see myself enjoying the activities of my day, doing more of the things I enjoy and fewer of the things I don't enjoy. Sometimes I create my own stress doing things I could just as easily not do. I push too hard. I work things too much. It's a carryover from my overfunctioning; though I come by that trait honestly, I need to learn when to stop making things happen and enjoy all that I've already got going. More isn't necessarily better. Today I will visualize what my life would look like if I were to let go of extraneous activities and have more time for me, more time to have fun, to play, to enjoy my home and my family and friends. Today I will picture my life the way I would like it to be and I will remember how important it is to just have fun.

I can create a better me, a better life

Now, on this road trip, my mind seemed to uncrinkle,
to breathe, to present to itself a cure for a disease
it had not, until now, known it had.

—*Elizabeth Berg,* The Year of Pleasures

OCTOBER 19

The Twenty-Four Hour Plan

There is peace within me that I can draw on each and every day. Today, I will pay attention to the myriad of ways in which I am thrown off balance. When I feel myself losing my serenity, I'll take a moment to center myself, to breathe, to connect with that part of me that is eternal and unchanging. I'll remind myself that when I can calm my body, mind, and spirit, I interact differently with the people, places, and things of my day. I will remind myself to take a few moments today to center myself. I will breathe. I will sit. And when I go about my day, I will carry that peace around with me. There is nothing in my day that is more important than my serenity. I am here. My spirit is here. My serenity is at my fingertips. I am in charge of my deeper experience of living. I connect with my divine self and the divine energy that is ever present. I give myself the gift of inner peace.

I find peace within

Better than a thousand hollow words
Is one word that brings peace.

—*Buddha, from the* Dhammapada

You Only Get Out of It, What You Put Into It

So often I feel that it's my life that needs to change, when it's actually how I see the life I already have that needs updating, revision, and upgrading. Reframing is a powerful tool for happiness—it puts satisfaction a few minutes away rather than a few years away. What will it hurt if I see my life in its best possible light? Who will be the wiser if I see my own life as just the life I enjoy? Why not reframe past events as shaping the person I am today—purposeful and meaningful? This is one of the gifts of recovery, it puts me in a state of mind to see things differently. This is a moment of change in my life, when the deep and rigidly held beliefs I have are challenged. Part of that is painful, part of that is sort of wonderful. I can use this moment to take risks, to create new habits, to try new ways of being. I can use my thinking to create new awareness that can guide my future. I will embrace this moment in my life, knowing that if I see what is there in a life-enhancing light, my future will reflect that. And I will learn to see this day, this moment, my life, in its most spiritual and positive light.

I have faith in my day

One of the secrets of life is to make
stepping stones out of stumbling blocks.

—Jack Penn

I Can Soothe the Self

I can calm and nourish my heart by regularly meditating or praying. These activities produce the "relaxation response"—a physiological state that is exactly the opposite of stress—a state that reduces blood pressure and increases blood flow to my heart. This state is within my reach each minute of each day. I can take a break and breathe in and out for two or three minutes. I can say a prayer. I can meditate on love or peace or a calm scene in my mind. Not only will this create soothing feelings in my mind, but in body as well. Today, when I am feeling stressed, I will (1) take a break and mentally disengage from the situation, (2) bring my attention to the area of my heart, and (3) recall an experience with a loved one in which I felt happiness, love, or appreciation—or I'll just meditate for a moment on those kinds of thoughts and feelings. I will take a break and breathe.

I can calm my body through calming my heart

Spirituality does not lie in meditating on
the body of an ex-master.
Spirituality exists in mediating
on your own inner body.

—Amit Ray

Growing Old Is Mandatory; Growing Up Is Optional

Today, when I am irritated by another person's actions I will let myself feel my feelings without judging them or trying to change them. I will observe them and try to understand what they are teaching me about me. Why does this particular behavior bother me so? Why is it so effective in tugging at my inner world? Do I feel manipulated, rejected or intentionally punished? What is getting triggered in me that I can take a deeper look at?

As a child who grew up with addiction and dysfunction, I experienced a lot of vying for love, vying for place and power in my home. There was anger, envy, and resentment that was never spoken. There were acting out behaviors that made home feel unpredictable and unreliable. Often I gave over my power just to feel safe. I did what I was manipulated into by those stronger than me so as not to be rejected, so as not to have what little rug I was standing on pulled out from under me. I am very vulnerable to manipulation—in my home it was real—but I can overreact to it. When I can pay attention to what is getting triggered in me, if I feel I am overreacting I can use life and relationships to learn about what I am carrying from the past that still may have power to explode into, or undermine my present.

I will use my overreaction to tell me where I have been hurt

Everything that irritates us about others can lead us to a better understanding of ourselves.

—Carl Jung

OCTOBER 23

Serenity Is Not Freedom from the Storm, But Peace Within the Storm

I am part of all that is alive, sacred, and divine. I am alive, accounted for, created by an intelligence and life force far greater than me, far greater than anything I can imagine. I have meaning woven into the cells of my being because I am not some random accident. I am woven into the fabric of all of life, part of a divine order. I have a purpose simply by being alive and having each day, each hour, a choice of who and how to be. If I can trust the day, I will see that my life is unfolding as it should, that experiences are coming to me, sent to me from a source as I can accept them. I don't have to be constantly pumping meaning into life because life itself has such poise, beauty, and magnificence. The experience of living is incredible when I tune in on it. I sense that I am one with all things, made of the same stuff that everything is made of, something that carries life in its seed form, that manifests into all that I see, feel, and know. This is a strange and mysterious experience that we call life, and all that is alive is meant to be here, including me.

I co-create along with a life force that breathes as and through me

I called the world of phenomena an illusion, I called my eyes and my tongue an accident, valueless phenomena. Now, that is all over; I have awakened, I have really awakened and have just been born today.

—*Hermann Hesse,* Siddhartha

Paying It Forward

Today I will show my gratitude for the many kindnesses I have received by paying it forward, by giving what I have so appreciated getting, to another individual. I know how good it feels to have someone reach out to me in generosity. I will do that for someone today. I will see an opportunity to give, and I will give. Whether it's a smile, an encouraging word, an extra moment of my time, or some kind of object, I will not hang on to it, I will give it. And when I do give it, knowing "I can only really keep what I have by giving it away," I will say a quiet thank you to the person who gave to me. I will see the gift going full circle. Each day I will count my blessings and give a little something. Each day I recognize the positive role that gratitude plays in my life. Some days it isn't even what I do for another person, but who I am able to be, how I am learning to live. When I make a positive contribution to the world I am born into, I am saying thank you to God for giving me life. I am creating a good patch of earth for myself and my family to stand on, by sowing the seeds of good deeds and good karma for all of us to enjoy for a long time to come.

In giving I grow

My friends, Dr. King realized that the only real wealth comes from helping others.

—*César Chávez*,
Lessons of Dr. Martin Luther King Jr.

OCTOBER 25

An Attitude of Gratitude

What I appreciate tends to persist and grow in my life. It's exactly the same as watering a plant, because the universe is alive and growing and so am I. Appreciation is like Miracle Grow. It nourishes and feeds, it helps something to take root and get strong. If I want something in my life to expand, I will silently send it my good thoughts, prayers, and energy. I'll daily develop an attitude of gratitude. Gratitude is a feeling that energizes me and motivates me toward life-enhancing ways of thinking, feeling, and acting. Because of this, it's is a good antidote for sadness. While sadness or depression can make me feel as though I'm falling apart, gratitude can help pull me together. Gratitude helps me to organize and mobilize my thoughts and emotions in a positive direction. It helps me to appreciate the life I already have.

Today I am grateful for . . . (I will make a list)

Begin to weave, and God will
give you the thread.

—German Proverb

When All Else Fails, Follow Directions

Goals organize and mobilize—they help me consolidate my skills and talents and realize them in some concrete form. Self-esteem is enhanced by a feeling of competency and a sense of engagement in meaningful activity. I know that once I have accomplished one thing, I can set new goals to work toward. Today I can set a goal without becoming that goal. I can take baby steps towards something I want and derive a sense of accomplishment in simply having taken that step. Many small steps in a good direction will enhance my self-esteem. I will have the nice feeling of just knowing that I am on a positive track. It's not the goal that is such a big deal, it's simply my ability to see something good ahead of me and take steps toward it each day.

I can walk in a good direction

A man is but the product of his thoughts.
What he thinks, he becomes.

—*Mahatma Gandhi,* Ethical Religion

Life on Life's Terms

One of the powerful effects of trauma is a loss of trust and faith. I lose faith in the people nature intended for me to depend upon. I can carry a sense of disappointment that I can brood on, that can expand like yeast inside of me and I can use that sense of disappointment as a reason not to trust, not to engage, not to live the best life I can live. Today I will remember that I, too, have disappointed people. Today I will be aware that life is full of disappointment. But I will have trust and faith anyway. As others have let me down, I have also let them down. Just for today, I will let all of us off the hook. I will shake loose of this dark cloud of disappointment and move into my day with an open and expectant feeling. If I want to grow free of my past mistakes, if I want to learn from them rather than repeat them, I will not hold someone else to a standard I am not maintaining myself.

I will be human and let others be human

When you find your path, you must not be afraid.
You need to have sufficient courage to make mistakes.
Disappointment, defeat, and despair are the
tools God uses to show us the way.

—*Paulo Coelho*

Time with Me

I will take time. Time to renew myself, to come back to me. Time just to be. Time to reflect on how I'm living my life, what I want to keep, and what I want to change. Sometimes, grappling with serious problems is an opportunity to reassess. It lets me slow down enough to pay attention, to tune into my life long enough so I can really feel it. I have images floating through my mind. If I pay attention, they tell me what I'm doing that's too much for me. And they quietly point the way toward what I'd like to experience more of, if I pay attention. The images that make me feel a little frantic, I will take a closer look at. Am I pushing too hard? Does my attitude need to change, or is it the activity itself that's out of balance? The intuitions I have about what activities and directions feel right, I will listen to, I will become quiet enough inside so that I can hear my own, inner guidance.

I will learn to listen and listen to learn

Our bodies have five senses:
touch, smell, taste, sight, hearing. But not
to be overlooked are the senses of our souls:
intuition, peace, foresight, trust, empathy.
The differences between people lie in their use
of these senses; most people don't know anything about
the inner senses while a few people rely on them
just as they rely on their physical senses,
and in fact probably even more.

—C. JoyBell C.

Taking Responsibility for My Own Anger

Today I am willing to take responsibility for the anger that I carry within me. I am not a bad person because I feel angry. No one wants to think of himself or herself as an angry person, and I am no exception. But when I refuse to acknowledge the anger and resentment that I have stored within me, (1) I turn my back on me and refuse to accept a very important part of myself, and (2) I ask the people close to me to hold my feelings for me, to be the containers of my unconscious or the feelings inside me that I do not wish to see. Because I deny my anger to myself does not mean that it goes away. Today, I am willing to consider that there might be something more to it, that I may be carrying feelings of anger that I need to accept.

I am willing to experience my own anger

It is easy to fly into a passion—anybody can do that—
but to be angry with the right person to the right extent at
the right time and with the right object in the
right way, that is not easy, and it is
not everyone who can do it.

—Aristotle

Stick with the Winners

"Although we are not responsible for our disease we are responsible for our recovery" (slogan).The thoughts that I think affect my body. Scientific research shows that the kinds of thoughts I think affect the way that I feel. Stressful thoughts release stress chemicals into my body that make me feel jumpy and tense. Stress chemicals, like cortisol and adrenaline, though helpful in the right dose, can have negative impacts on my health in an overdose. If I stay on a treadmill of thinking, feeling, or behavior, I stimulate too many stress chemicals and too few soothing ones. On the other hand, when I think positive, upbeat thoughts, my body actually releases the kinds of chemicals that make me feel good and enhance my health and well-being. This new research shows me that there is something I can do right here and now in order to feel better. I can be aware of the thoughts I'm thinking and guide them toward a positive place.

Resentment is like drinking poison
and expecting someone else to die

Despite that we've learned a lot about
healthy exercise practices, healthy diets, and good
medical care, the bottom line is that the most significant way
of contributing to our own good health is through the quality
of our thought processes. This power is a valuable gift,
in light of the lack of control we have over other aspects of life.
. . . Every thought and every perception you have changes
the homeostasis of your body. Will it be the brakes or
the accelerator, a health account deposit
or a health account withdrawal?

—*Christiane Northrup, M.D.,*
The Wisdom of Menopause

Experience, Strength, and Hope

I am open to receiving today. The acts of kindness that are directed my way during these days of healing are meant for me. I will let them in. I am open to receiving the pleasant energy behind the smile on someone's face, the gift I am given. I take in the nourishment in my food and I let it build strength and energy in my cells. I allow my body to grow healthy, strong, and attractive through good nutrition, exercise, rest, and positivity. If I can create and receive the good that is out there for me, I can pull what is best from my surroundings. Sometimes I ward off what is being given to me. The world is so intense and feelings can be so strong that they are too much to take in. I get anxious that if I let life feel too good, it will blow up on me, betray me, or I will somehow lose what I love. Today, I will not push my good away. I will let it in. Life is full of loss but that doesn't mean that I shouldn't take in all the good that I can; it will fortify me for loss and bring me daily pleasure, nourishment, and health. And I will remember to be kind to others when they need me, trusting that what goes around comes around.

I let kindness and goodness in

Right from the moment of our birth,
we are under the care and kindness of our parents,
and then later on in our life when we are oppressed by
sickness and become old, we are again dependent on
the kindness of others. Since at the beginning and end of
our lives we are so dependent on others' kindness,
how can it be in the middle that we would
neglect kindness toward others?

—H.H. the Dalai Lama

NOVEMBER

From The Paradoxical Commandments

People are often unreasonable, illogical, and self-centered;

Love them anyway.

If you are kind, people may accuse you
of selfish, ulterior motives;

Be kind anyway.

If you are successful you will win some
false friends and true enemies;

Succeed anyway.

If you are honest and frank, people may cheat you;

Be honest and frank anyway.

What you spend years building, someone
could destroy overnight;

Build anyway.

If you find serenity and happiness, they may be jealous;

Be happy anyway.

The good you do today, people will often forget tomorrow;

Do good anyway.

Give the world the best you have, and
you'll get kicked in the teeth;

Give the world the best you have anyway

—Kent Keith, 1968
(Mother Teresa hung these words on a
wall in her orphanage in Calcutta.)

Awakening into a New World

Recovery and spiritual seeking has allowed me to see a new world within and without. The world so often conforms to my vision of it; I see the same life through new eyes and I ask myself, *What is in my heart that I now see surrounding me? What feels new that once felt old? What feels smoothed out inside of me, that once cut me with its jagged edges?* Today I understand that much of what life offers me is what I offer it. And that's a quiet thing—it has more to do with what my heart projects than exactly what's around me, more to do with an inner glow than an outer one. I see a kind of radiance that life, that the world gives off; it was always there but I had to prepare my mind, eyes and heart.

I have learned "Nobody ever found recovery as a result of an intellectual awakening"

A kind of light spread out from her.
And everything changed color.
And the world opened out.
And a day was good to awaken to.
And there were no limits to anything.
And the people of the world were good and handsome.
And I was not afraid any more.

—John Steinbeck, East of Eden

Other People's Arrows

People will aim their arrows at me sometimes; it will just happen, it's the way of the world. And I will unwittingly, or even on purpose, do the same. When I have an arrow come to me, I will keep my focus on myself. I will ask myself what I am meant to see and learn from this. Surely, I will examine the other person and wonder why, but more than that, I will wonder why it hurts me so particularly, why I feel so vulnerable in this spot and unable to protect myself. Why I did not see this arrow coming, or how I may have even participated in its finding me, are questions I will explore. What in my thinking, feeling, or behavior, if anything, drew this towards me? And why does it sink so deep?

I will grow from each experience I am given

If someone comes along and shoots an arrow into
your heart, it's fruitless to stand there and yell at the person.
It would be much better to turn your attention to the
fact that there's an arrow in your heart . . .

—*Pema Chödrön,* Start Where You Are:
A Guide to Compassionate Living

Only One Space

There is no space between me and God because I am one with God. There is no separation, no asking, begging, or distance, because God lives in me, as me, through me. When I pray, I pray to my best friend, my higher self, my beloved, my creator, and my baby. All wrapped into everything and everything wrapped into all. Why should I go looking for something that I already am and why should I not quietly, like a good child, know that I have been found? I am only as far from God as my mind allows. There is no negative image, no double exposure, no misalignment, unless I see it that way. I am created in the image of God and that is God's intention.

I am one with my creator

Jesus Christ knew he was God.
So wake up and find out eventually who you really are.
In our culture, of course, they'll say you're crazy
and you're blasphemous, and they'll either put you in jail
or in a nut house (which is pretty much the same thing).
However if you wake up in India and tell your friends
and relations, 'My goodness, I've just discovered
that I'm God,' they'll laugh and say,
'Oh, congratulations, at last you found out.'

—*Alan W. Watts,*
The Essential Alan Watts

The Grand Adventure

Life is my grand adventure; my boat, my ship, my plane into the wilderness and back home again is me. My mind is the cockpit of my adventure: I sit in it and look out. I navigate, I glide and go with the forces of the wind so that I can float on air, move in a direction, and be carried. I work with the forces that exist and they allow me even to defy something that seems like it cannot be done. There is always a path open to me if I learn to find the right airstream and altitude. If I tried to carry myself through this world, I would never get off the ground. I work with the world and let the world work with me, I find wind that is right for me and then allow it to push me from behind, to lift me, to caress and carry me to where I long to go. I work with natural forces, waiting for favorable wind and weather; I work hard when the sun shines, live off stores when things are inclement, and work again when the long, light days return.

I am part of the world's natural forces

Live to learn to love.
Learn to love to live.
Love to live to learn
so that you may live the life that you yearn.

—Rico Dasheem

Caught and Freed

Life does not only happen in my brain, in my thinking the right thought, or doing a series of deeds. Though my thinking mind is essential in making sense of experience; there is also a spiritual part of my mind that is connected to my higher self. Much of life is a mystery. There are spiritual laws that govern life—they appear in layers, like an onion; I peel back one layer only to meet with another layer. First I attend to the basics, my body, my thoughts, and my emotions. I learn to guide my thinking, feeling, and action along healthy lines. I exercise, eat well, and rest so that my body is a fit vehicle for living. Then I peel back more layers of the onion. I access a path to my higher self, a path to conscious contact with my Higher Power. Today I will allow my mind to float beyond what it absorbs with its five senses and engage my sixth sense, my sentient intuition. I will move into a wordless place to comprehend the mysterious and magical quality of life. I will allow my steps to be guided by something much larger than me, something that naturally expands who I am on the inside, which then becomes the outside, which then no longer has a place or time.

I expand into the mystery

As soon as you look at the world through an ideology
you are finished. No reality fits an ideology. Life is beyond that. . . .
That is why people are always searching for a meaning to life. . . .
Meaning is only found when you go beyond meaning.
Life only makes sense when you perceive it as mystery and
it makes no sense to the conceptualizing mind.

—Anthony de Mello

Acting As If

When I first try something new, it may feel as if I am trying on an article of clothing that doesn't quite suit me. But there is nothing wrong with acting *as if*. Sometimes, when I allow myself to act *as if*, the old me sort of falls away and makes room for a new me to come forward. Children do this all the time, trying on different roles and playing with them. There is no reason to commit myself to a limited view of who I am. Acting *as if* lets me play with new behaviors, it acts as a bridge between an old way of being and a new way. It gives me time and space to catch up with who I am becoming. Acting *as if* allows me to experience myself as someone who can try on a new way of thinking, feeling, and behaving, someone who can change and grow. If others who know me well or who are invested in my staying as I was won't play ball at first, I won't worry about it; there will always be people in the world who will be glad to see me change or who don't know me yet. I will practice with them until I feel my new approaches to life are a part of who I am.

I can be who I want to be

What we achieve inwardly will change outer reality.

—Plutarch

Easy Does It, but Do It

I am capable of experiencing and understanding the anger that may be inside of me, knowing that shutting it down, denying it, or splitting it out of consciousness does not make it go away. When I hide my anger from myself I learn nothing from it and it leaks out in less-than-functional ways. Experiencing my anger doesn't mean I have to act it out or dump it all over my life. Nor does it mean that I give up my right to feel it. There is something in between wanting to scream, resist, or act out, and wanting to disappear, medicate, or go numb. I have more options than these. I can tolerate the strength of my angry feelings without acting out or collapsing under their weight. I can be angry and talk about it, journal about it, or let it scramble my thoughts momentarily—then breathe, step back, and think about it. Knowing that I have the strength to experience my own feelings builds confidence and strength within me.

Recovery is a discovery, not a destination

The thing about long-term or unresolved anger is we've seen it resets the internal thermostat. When you get used to a low level of anger all the time, you don't recognize what's normal. It creates a kind of adrenaline rush that people get used to. It burns out the body and makes it difficult to think clearly—making the situation worse. . . . When the body releases certain enzymes during anger and stress, cholesterol and blood pressure levels go up—not a good long-term disposition to maintain the body in.

—Dr. Frederic Luskin, Director of the Stanford University Forgiveness Project,

NOVEMBER 8

Building Resilience

I can mobilize my supports and make use of them. I can make small changes that have a big result. I can get something to work that's not working, if I am willing to look my life squarely in the face. I will know what to do. I am capable of radical acceptance, the kind that just takes what the day, the month, the year is dishing up and makes peace with it. Once I accept it, I can take the next step, I can put one foot in front of the other. Reaching out is part of resilience, learning to access help and support and use it to feel better, to be seen or understood, to see myself. I can look back and remember all of those wonderful people and experiences that buffered me as a child; the people who just seemed to understand and provide safe haven. I had a lot of angels in my life and today I say silent prayers to thank them. Their help along with my ability reach out for it, and absorb it into me, made me resilient. They reminded me, just by being there, that there was a such a thing as "normal," as "business as usual." Today I realize what a resilient person I have learned to be and this is a gift of meeting adversity and dealing with it. I don't wait for life to plop onto my doorstep, I go out and find it. I deal with what is in my path rather than pretend it isn't here. I meet life on life's terms and I live it.

I can look around me and figure out what to do next

Resilience is accepting your new reality, even if it's
less good than the one you had before. You can fight it,
you can do nothing but scream about what you've lost, or
you can accept that and try to put together something that's good.

—Elizabeth Edwards

Creating My Own Inner Turmoil

I will stop being so hard on myself on the inside. I give myself a ridiculously tough time. What do I think it will get me if I tear at my own insides? If I undermine my own peace of mind by obsessing over nothing, finding things to feel bad or guilty about, or blaming myself unnecessarily, it will only hurt me and leak out on those close to me. Addiction has no conscience. It creates monsters who fall apart all over the place, sober up, feel guilty and ashamed, and try to make over-the-top reparations to compensate for their awful behavior, in the hopes of forcing a connection with those who want to run from them. Then they do it all over again. And again. And again. It is a seesaw world: up/down, up/down, up,/down. It is crazy making. It creates uncertainty, mistrust, and guilt—a feeling of always being in the wrong place at the wrong time, of never getting it right. It trains everyone around it to have all those same behaviors, even if they aren't using. It creates overfunctioners and underfunctioners, to fill in all of the holes left both by the addict and the people around the addict who are so worn out they jump ship, too.

I recognize the source of why I churn and churn on the inside

When she can't bring me to heel with scolding,
she bends me to shape with guilt.

—*Libba Bray,* The Sweet Far Thing

My Inner Stress

What I do with stress on the inside is even more important than what I do with it on the outside. Sometimes I throw yeast on situations that stress me out and they grow and grow inside of me. I make the feeling and thoughts surrounding what stresses me unnecessarily large and overblown. I give them too much life, breath, and attention. In an effort not to suppress my feelings, I blow them up instead. I go from zero to ten on the inside with no speed bumps in between, the trauma extremes of chaos to rigidity, of overwhelm to shut down. I get my own little stress factory working overtime inside of me. This inner stress that I create puts pressure on every organ of my body; it stresses my heart which is connected to my other organs. It taxes my lungs because I hold my breath. I tense my muscles and constrict my easy flow of energy. Today I will become aware of what I am doing to myself through my own, internal stress.

I work through and let go of stress rather than manufacture more

When we are unable to find tranquility
within ourselves, it is useless
to seek it elsewhere.

—François de la Rochefoucauld

Giving Back

Today I give something to the community of people in which I find myself. I look around me and wonder what I might add to the world, to someone else's day, and I do it. I recognize that giving and receiving are one channel, that when I open my heart to give, I simultaneously open it to receive as well. I experience the good feeling of getting out of my own way and letting a gift be given through me, as me, because of me.

I feel good when I let go and give

Lord, make me an instrument of your peace,
Where there is hatred, let me sow love;
Where there is injury, pardon;
Where there is doubt, faith;
Where there is despair, hope;
Where there is darkness, light;
Where there is sadness, joy.
O Divine Master, grant that I may not
so much seek to be consoled, as to console;
to be understood, as to understand;
to be loved, as to love.
For it is in giving that we receive.
It is in pardoning that we are pardoned,
and it is in dying that we are born to Eternal Life.
Amen.

—Prayer of St. Francis of Assisi

Cultivating and Living by Good Values

Values are the road map for my journey through life. Values ground me. They provide a solid foundation upon which I can build a self, relationships, and a life. They also keep me steered in the right direction when I'm having weak moments or can't think clearly; they carry me through so I don't have to keep reinventing the basics. They make me fit company for the kind of people I choose to be around. When I have good values and live by them, I have a certain congruency; my actions on the outside match who I am on the inside. Having and practicing the kinds of values that are part of basic human decency and care toward others and myself, give me strength and a good feeling about myself and my world. These values give me self-respect and a feeling that I am someone worth taking good care of, they let me sleep at night, and they let me wake with energy and light. Having good values, in this way, is its own reward, just having them enhances my sense of well-being and self-respect. And, as what I believe and live by tends to manifest in my life, I'm creating my own, better world to live in, attracting those experiences toward me that fit my sense of a good life.

I have values that I can feel proud of

The first principle of value that we need to rediscover is this: that all reality hinges on moral foundations. In other words, that this is a moral universe, and that there are moral laws of the universe just as abiding as the physical laws.

—Martin Luther King Jr.,
"Rediscovering Lost Values," from A Knock at Midnight

The Now

I can only live in the now, and when I do, the now gives way into the forever. I can only breathe into this moment, and when I do, this moment breathes into my soul. I can only act in this time and space, and when I do, my actions carry ripple and resonance because past and future are part of the now. I can only experience where I am, and when I do, I am everywhere. Today, I recognize that when I am present in this moment, I am present in all moments. The now is my gateway into the experience and meaning of life itself; when I miss it, I miss my life. I am enough today. I can breathe into this moment, into this day, into this life, and relax. I am enough. I don't have to be something better, different, or even renewed to be okay. I can enter this day with an inner confidence that whatever the day brings, I can handle; and if I feel anxious, scared, or not enough, I can reach out for a little support and I will get through. I am enough today, the day is enough, my life is enough, my understanding is enough, I am enough.

It's all right here: I do not have to be something different to be okay

Forever is composed of nows.

—*Emily Dickinson*

Surrender: Turning It Over

Today I will let God work to make me better. I will surrender. Surrendering is very different from giving up. Giving up is a helpless, hurting feeling filled with fear and resignation. Surrender is a spiritual letting go. I place my life and health into gentler, wiser hands than mine. Surrender is an act of trust and faith. Surrender is, in itself, restorative because it gets me out of my own way so that other forces can be free to work in my life. When I surrender I leave room for higher forces to enter, I create space inwardly and outwardly, I move my circular thinking and obsessing to the side, so that it doesn't block anything new from entering. Though I may not be able to successfully stop self-destructive thinking, I can surrender it. I can turn it over and place it in the hands of a loving Higher Power. Surrender brings me relief from the feeling that I have to constantly do, do, do in order to make something happen. Surrender lets me allow rather than force; it is its own kind of freedom and deep relief. When I turn it over, I let God work and trust that all will come right in God's time.

I surrender, I let go, I release

In trying to control everything, we make our world smaller.
Instead, we can open into a larger world where we are
not in charge, but are a part of something much larger—
something deeply wondrous.

—*Philip Martin,*
The Zen Path through Depression

Asking for Help

I will ask for help when I need it today. One thing that recovery teaches me is that I cannot go it alone. I have to let others in, sometimes into my very private self. But in doing this I become freer, I let go of the tightly wound me and move toward a lighter, more open me. People are so often willing to help me, if only I can let them. If one person can't or won't, there are others who are more than willing. If I can get myself to ask, and show gratitude and appreciation for anyone who is willing to help, I have done what I am supposed to do—I have created some room in my life to let help in. And I will do my part. I will be someone easy to help because I pull my own weight, make necessary changes. In this way, I will earn and deserve more help, each bit of help I get will move me forward because I will make good use of it. My way of saying thank you will be in more than words: I will demonstrate that I was worth helping, rather than collapse and ask others to hold me up and drag me along. I will stand up and move forward, knowing I can lean in for support as I need to and stand on my own when I wish to.

Today I call out to a benevolent universe and ask for help

If you get up one more time than you fall,
you will make it through.

—*Chinese Proverb*

Mistakes

Today I will let go. I can be so hard on myself if I feel I've gotten something wrong, or screwed a situation up, or done something stupid. Today I will treat this part of myself like an inconsolable child who needs love, support, and acceptance. After all, what good does it do for me to turn a problem into a crisis inside of myself? The world is rarely as hard on me as I am on myself. But the truth is, when I can't be forgiving of my own stupid mistakes, I am less forgiving of others, too. Everybody makes mistakes. When I am too hard on myself, eventually, I pass on the pain and am too hard on others. Today, I will soothe myself and right-size my self-recrimination, I will breathe and remember that I am going for *progress not perfection*, I will keep things in proportion. I will hold my inner discouraged self, my wounded child self, my angry adolescent self, or my blocked young adult self, when they throw their little tantrum. I will understand that they need some form of expression for their frustration and consoling for their upset, and then I will stand next to them until they pick themselves up, dust themselves off, and continue to move forward.

Everyone makes mistakes, it's okay

When I let go of what I am,
I become what I might be.

—Lao Tzu

My Inner Critic

My inner critic can really take off on me. If I put a foot wrong in any direction, my inner critic can really go nuts—blaming me for screwing things up, getting down on me, and generally making me feel terrible. It doesn't help anything. In fact, it makes things worse. Not only am I feeling bad about what happened, but I am compounding it and digging myself even deeper into a hole. What's the point? What happened happened, it can't be undone. But beating myself up just makes it so big that I have two things to recover from: first, the screw up itself, then, the bruises I inflict on myself because of it. Beating myself up doesn't help anything. Today, I will find a kinder and more tolerant inner voice to replace the chiding, judging voices in my head. I will examine where the negative voices come from that I have internalized as my own—are they parents, authority figures, peers? Wherever they came from, I need not carry them any longer. I will substitute each negative voice with a positive one. I will be a friend, cheerleader, and supporter, to me.

I can speak to myself with kindness

All you really need is the courage to be yourself.
Your real value is rooted in who you are, not what you do.
The only thing you need actually do is express your
real self to the world. You've been told all sort of lies as to
why you can't do that. But you'll never know true
happiness and fulfillment until you summon
the courage to do it anyway.

—Steve Pavlina, author of Personal
Development for Smart People

NOVEMBER 18

Wholeness

Today, I recognize my essential wholeness. While I see myself as deficient and look to others to complete me, I condemn myself to a life of reactivity. A life in which I constantly measure who I am by the thoughts, ideals, needs, and wishes of others. In this mode, I can only spend my days trying to bend myself into the shape that I feel will make me lovable to those whom I wish to please or appear worthy to. Then, if I succeed in gaining their acceptance or approval, I am both full and terrified that the feeling will go away. I construct a world to live in, in which I see others as being in charge of my feeling bad about myself, or good about myself; and I go about pleasing, placating and manipulating to keep my supply of good feeling on tap. I put the on/off spigot in their hands. I get stuck in an immature, needy place. If they in any way reject me, I feel belittled or even furious at having compromised myself. Then that becomes an excuse to hole up and feel bad. The only solution is to seek wholeness within, to see myself and my life, as mine to build, nourish, and sustain with the help of willing others.

I keep myself full and reach out where it works

When we're young . . . our experiences tell us
that we're less than whole, that something is wrong
with us, we're not enough, or we're not doing "it" right.
And from those events a core belief of fear is created. . . .
The journey into Oneness includes identifying
and dissolving those limiting beliefs
that were created early on.

—*James Twyman with Anakha Coman,* The Proof:
A 40-Day Program for Embodying Oneness

Forgiving Myself: Making Amends

I forgive myself because I know that it's the wisest course of action for my own healing. I release my own bad actions and give myself a chance to heal my self-recrimination. That way I don't act out my self-hate on those close to me. And I forgive another person, not for the other person, but for myself. I forgive, not to erase a wrong, but to relieve the residue of the wrong that is alive within me. I forgive myself, and another person, because it is less painful than holding on to resentment. I forgive myself and others because without it, I condemn myself to repeating endlessly the very trauma or situation that hurt me. I forgive because, ultimately, it is the smartest action to take on my own behalf. I forgive because it restores me to a sense of inner balance. I make amends for the same reason, to free myself from the anxiety and shame I carry from having wronged another person. I make amends so that I can move forward with a clean conscience, so that I can give a damaged relationship a chance to begin to repair, so that I can be the kind of person I want to be.

I complete the circle of amends and forgiveness

It is the highest form of self-respect to admit
our errors and mistakes and make amends for them.
To make a mistake is only an error in judgment,
but to adhere to it when it is discovered
shows infirmity of character.

—Dale Turner

Learning

Today, I do not accept other people's truths as my truth. Even if what they believe seems better or more obvious, I need to give myself credit for feeling and seeing what I feel and see. I am the learner behind the information; I am the seer behind the seen. I learn by direct experience. And I incorporate that learning into my mental schemas, I use it in my own, unique way. I apply what I learn to my life. I have a unique contribution to make to this world, a distillation of knowledge held only by me that I can build on. If I create something, I have my own little area of passion and expertise. I become the expert simply because I have the courage to see things in my own idiosyncratic way, the guts to combine this with that to make a whole new something. Having my own point of view, my own combination, unlocks something that I own. As so few people think for themselves, it makes me a sort of leader or model of something unique, something that is mine.

I learn to trust the perceptions that I gain from my own observation of life

Often what we think are "wrong" with us are only our expressions of our own individuality. This is our uniqueness and what is special about us. Nature never repeats itself. Since time began on this planet, there have never been two snowflakes alike or two raindrops the same. And every daisy is different from every other daisy. Our fingerprints are different, and we are different. We are meant to be different. When we accept this, there is no competition and no comparison. To try to be like another is to shrivel our soul. We have come to this planet to express who we are.

—*Louise Hay, author of* You Can Heal Your Life

Aligning Myself With God's Plan

If I miss today, I will not get it back. If I allow it to work its beauty inside of me, it will fertilize tomorrow's garden. Today is what I know I have. All of life is here, woven into the atoms of the world that surrounds me. If I am with this day, I am with all of life. Trauma can undermine a sense of faith in a predictable and orderly world. As I witness the mystery of birth, a tree that bears fruit, the sun rising, and the moon shining bright in a night sky, I see only too clearly that the kind of order I am a part of far supersedes the sense of order I lost. I can align myself with a deeper sense of order, rhythm, and goodness. I will live in the present, grateful to be alive and in this radiant world for one more day. Living in the present brings its own perspective. What is not worth getting preoccupied about falls away, while what is truly meaningful and important rises up and into focus. I am here to appreciate and live life, to grow, to share my heart and soul with those around me.

Life is not an accident

The most important lesson that I have learned
is to trust God in every circumstance. Lots of times we
go through different trials and following God's plan
seems like it doesn't make any sense at all.
God is always in control and he
will never leave us.

—Allyson Felix,
2012 Olympic Gold Medalist

Intuition

Today, I will trust my own heart. The clear message that whispers within me has more to tell me than a thousand voices. I have a guide within me who knows what is best for me. There is a part of me that sees the whole picture and knows how it all fits together. My inner voice, my intuition, may come in the form of a strong sense, a pull from within, a gut feeling, or a quiet knowing. My intuition may simply be there moving in and out of my mind with a special pull. However my intuition comes to me, I will learn to pay attention. My intuition is part of my emotional and spiritual guidance system. I have a guidance system built into me that finds those experiences that feel right. When I ignore my deep intuitions, I generally wish I had at least listened to them; they are there for a reason, they are trying to tell me that something about my life is either the right direction to go into now, or not to do something for now. Though I am conditioned by the world to look constantly outside myself for meaning, today I recognize that it is deeply important for me to listen to my inner intuition.

I will trust my inner voice

When I examine myself and my methods
of thought I come to the conclusion that the gift
of fantasy has meant more to me than my
talent for absorbing positive knowledge.

—Albert Einstein

My Joy

There is joy within me that I can find and expand upon. My joy. My joy burns away my pain, and my pain burns a path to my joy. When I resolve the blocks that keep me stuck in repeating cycles of pain and blame, I make room for joy. When I recognize the relationship dynamics that I repeat and repeat, in spite of knowing better, as flags that mark the spot of my pain, I mine there. I mine for gold. I sift away a lot of stone, pebble, sand, and even fool's gold, but I find me. I find my joy. When I am willing to own my negative projections, rather than slather them all over the faces of other people, when I pull them back and question what is going on with me, rather than obsessing about what is going on with me, I clear out the underbrush that tangles up my feet. And I make room for joy. I turn the lake of my unconscious into something clear and still and beautiful, and I see what lies on the floor of my mind. And my joy is there. Once I have this experience of joy, I know what it means to experience the majesty of being alive, I experience God. No one can talk me into or out of anything because I have my own direct experience of spirit within, spirit at work in my life, spirit at work in my relationships. And I know my own path to my joy, so that even when I am off course, I have the experience within me and I can find my way back in time.

I access joy and let it grow within my being

I say, follow your bliss and don't be afraid,
and doors will open where you didn't
know they were going to be.

—Joseph Campbell

Friendship

I choose my friends. The people, or even animals, I choose to spend time with are very important to me, and the relationships that I begin, I wish to respect and nurture. Friends are meaningful to me. I enjoy their company, I can talk with them, play with them; we have fun together. I can call them with a deep personal need to just have a pal to hang around with. I choose to share myself where I feel a return of good feeling. I want both to have a friend and to be a friend. One of the unexpected gifts of growing up in a dysfunctional household was that I learned the value of friendship, because I had to turn to my friends to meet very deep needs. I am grateful for my friends, and for what I felt for and from them.

I value friendship

When we honestly ask ourselves which person
in our lives means the most to us, we often find that
it is those who, instead of giving advice, solutions, or cures,
have chosen rather to share our pain and touch our
wounds with a warm and tender hand. The friend who can
be silent with us in a moment of despair or confusion,
who can stay with us in an hour of grief and bereavement,
who can tolerate not knowing, not curing, not healing,
and face with us the reality of our powerlessness,
that is a friend who cares.

—*Henri J. M. Nouwen,*
The Road to Daybreak: A Spiritual Journey

Patience with Myself

Today, I will be patient with myself. When I do not do as well as I wish I would, I will not make that a reason to get down on myself. I will instead recognize that the fastest way to bring myself out of a painful funk is through understanding and being good to myself. I needn't get caught in my own cycle of shame, resentment, and blame. If a child is upset, I comfort the child because I understand that is what will makes things better. Today, I will give myself the same kind of comfort I would extend to that hurt child, knowing the comfort will help me have the strength to forgive and move on. I will hold the child within me, and give her love and encouragement. The simple act of holding, of letting the child within me lean into me, sob, hurt, adore, and need without shutting it down, will be enough.

I will cuddle up with the child inside of me

Don't run from your weakness, you
will only give it strength.

—Stephen Richards

NOVEMBER 26

Chronic Anger

My family had trouble managing anger in healthy ways. We all suffered for my parent's difficulty with this and eventually it became our own difficulty. Our anger seeped out in less obvious passive aggression; teasing, withdrawing, over-controlling, lateness, silence, chronic disagreement, constant sloppiness, or even just "having an attitude." Depression also grew out of anger that never got processed or expressed, but instead fueled a sort of negative self-concept and a dark inner dialogue. We walked on eggshells to keep anger from bursting out. I now recognize that some of the anger we carry today may be a late reaction to these early relationship wounds. Anger's half-life: radioactivity from buried pain, fallout from hidden wounds that seeps up through the emotional ground years after it's been buried. This bleeding half-life of pain becomes part of a post-traumatic stress syndrome, part of how unprocessed, compacted, or frozen pain expands or thaws out and fertilizes new, and too often dysfunctional, growth. The codependency, low self esteem, depression, or anxiety grows out of the conditions of this toxic soil.

Misery is optional

Anger is an acid that can do more harm to the vessel
in which it is stored than to anything on which it is poured.

—*Mark Twain*

Jump-Starting a Good Mood

I have body chemicals that are meant to smooth me out, to nourish me and to help me feel good inside. They're my natural mood menders, they take the edge off a jagged mood and calm me on the inside. When I engage in my feel-good activities, I can sense them coursing through my system, elevating my mood. I can jump-start these self-soothing mood chemicals in so many ways: a brisk walk, thinking uplifting thoughts, spiritual reading, journaling, or sharing what I am feeling with friends are all proven by research to release serotonin into my bloodstream. When I consciously use the chemicals nature put in my body to lighten my mood, I am using the natural power of my body/mind to soothe and care for itself.

I access my natural mood managers consciously throughout my day

Serotonin is a naturally occurring substance in the body that makes us feel more comfortable, peaceful, and even blissful. In fact, the role of most anti-depressants is to stimulate the production of serotonin chemically, helping to ease depression. Research has shown that a simple act of kindness directed toward another improves the functioning of the immune system and stimulates the production of serotonin in both the recipient of the kindness and the person extending the kindness. Even more amazing is that persons observing the act of kindness have similar beneficial results. Imagine this! Kindness extended, received, or observed beneficially impacts the physical health and feelings of everyone involved!

—*Wayne Dyer*

A Healthy Soul

Today, I will pray for a healthy life, a healthy spirit, a healthy me. My prayers have power in unseen realms. I will rely on the intelligence of the unseen; invisible hands will guide my prayer. There is a peace within me that surpasses all understanding, and today I am willing to access that peace. I do not have to do this alone because there are so many angels waiting to hold and guide my prayers, so many waiting hands, willing to carry them, hearts willing to blow them toward where they need to go, higher minds making sense of them and creating what will appear to me as "coincidences" in my day-to-day life, "coincidences" that somehow answer my prayers. My prayers have power. They connect me to something outside of me, something awake and waiting to hear my voice, something waiting and willing to help.

I turn to prayer at the drop of a hat

Prayer is not asking. It is a longing of the soul.
It is daily admission of one's weakness.
It is better in prayer to have a heart without
words than words without a heart.

—Mahatma Gandhi

The Peace Within

Today, I will cultivate inner peace by taking time to go within. The world within me is as real as anything I see outside of me. It sustains and nurtures me. It is of more value to me than I can imagine. I need this part of me to be alive and well. I need a healthy inner world, so that I can create health in my outer world. This peace is available to me any time I wish to drop down within me and experience it. When I am frazzled, when I am far away from myself, I will remember that this pool of calm is waiting for me. I will create a little time and space in my day so that I can be with this place inside of me. I will tune in and tap in to a wellspring within me that is always there.

I take time to go within

We can only help make our lives and our
world more peaceful, when we ourselves feel peace.
Peace already exists within each of us, if we only
allow ourselves to feel its comfort. Peace of mind begins
when we stop thinking about how far we have to go, or
how hard the road has been, and just let ourselves feel peace.
Peace of mind gives us the strength to keep trying
and keep walking along the path that we
know is right for our lives.

—Robert Allen

Keeping Myself Safe

No one can really keep me safe but me. When I wait for the world to take responsibility for my safety, I ask them to perform an impossible task. I am with me all the time. If I repeatedly allow someone to mistreat me, what service can swoop down from above and pull me out of my misery? It is a myth that the government, or even other family members, are the ones who can keep me safe if I do not do my part and get myself to safety. If I continue to put myself in harm's way, what I will get is trouble. I need to understand my own resources. I need to learn to remove myself from a situation that is hurting me, whether it's just walking into the next room, leaving the house, or making a life change. I need to learn to stand up and take care of myself, and to do the internal recovery work to find out why I put myself at the other end of harm. I am not to blame, but I am responsible for taking care of me. If I don't, no one else will. No one else can.

I am capable to taking care of myself

The guarantee of safety in a battering relationship
can never be based upon a promise from the perpetrator,
no matter how heartfelt. Rather, it must be based upon
the self-protective capability of the victim.
Until the victim has developed a detailed and realistic
contingency plan and has demonstrated her
ability to carry it out, she remains in
danger of repeated abuse.

—*Judith Lewis Herman, M.D.,*
Trauma and Recovery

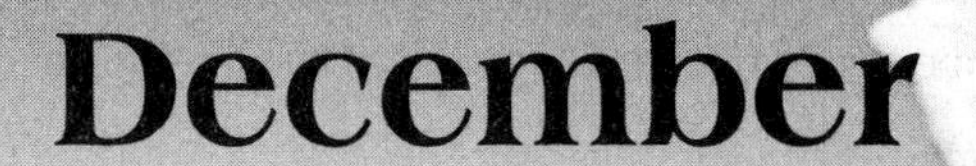

December

Desiderata

Go placidly amid the noise and haste,
and remember what peace there may be in silence.

As far as possible without surrender be on
good terms with all persons.

Speak your truth quietly and clearly; and listen to others,
even the dull and the ignorant; they too have their story.

Avoid loud and aggressive persons,
they are vexatious to the spirit.

If you compare yourself with others, you may become
vain or bitter; for always there will be greater
and lesser persons than yourself.

Enjoy your achievements as well as your plans.

Keep interested in your own career, however humble;
it is a real possession in the changing fortunes of time.

Exercise caution in your business affairs;
for the world is full of trickery.

But let this not blind you to what virtue there is; many persons
strive for high ideals; and everywhere life is full of heroism.

Be yourself.

Especially, do not feign affection.

Neither be cynical about love; for in the face of all aridity
and disenchantment it is as perennial as the grass.

Take kindly the counsel of the years,
gracefully surrendering the things of youth.

Nurture strength of spirit to shield you in sudden misfortune.

But do not distress yourself with dark imaginings.

Many fears are born of fatigue and loneliness.

Beyond a wholesome discipline, be gentle with yourself.

You are a child of the universe, no less than the trees
and the stars; you have a right to be here.

And whether or not it is clear to you,
no doubt the universe is unfolding as it should.

Therefore be at peace with God, whatever you conceive
Him to be, and whatever your labors and aspirations,
in the noisy confusion of life keep peace with your soul.

With all its sham, drudgery, and broken dreams,
it is still a beautiful world.

Be cheerful. Strive to be happy.

—Max Erhmann

Breathe

I will breathe into this moment. I will lean into this day. I will embrace, with all of its uncertainties, the mystery of now, trusting that a guiding hand will move me through it, separating the chaff from the grain. I will have faith. I will stay with my breath, and let it be the silver thread that connects me with the infinite, the all: eternity. I am a part of all that is, was, or ever will be. I am grateful for one more day on my spiritual path.

I am breathing, I am here, I am alive in God's presence

Take a breath . . . and lean into it
Lean into that power and presence behind the breath
That creative force at the center of our very being.
And it is from this place that we are linked,
linked by the goodness, the power and grace
that calls for us to be present to one another,
to serve and to share, for the goodness of all.
I am so grateful for this moment of recognition
of the presence of the Presence that has gathered
us together to do our work today.
And for it all, I say thank you, thank you, Sweet Spirit.

—Michael Ingersoll

DECEMBER 2

I Am Whole

Today, I see that my life is up to me. How I choose to live, what I will accomplish, how I conduct my intimate relationships, how I treat myself, all are in my own hands. I am no longer afraid that pain and anxiety will return me to a state of helplessness and vulnerability. Let it come; I am ready to meet it head-on. I am strong in the awareness that I can live as I choose to live. I have been willing to walk a path of recovery that, though difficult, has built a strength in me and a knowledge that I can survive my most painful feelings. I do not need to be afraid of my life, if I am not afraid of myself. I have met and tamed the monsters that live inside of me. I am comfortable in my own skin.

I am free to be who I am

Know your magic, trust your magic, use your magic and know that you are a manifestation of life's magic.

—Rasheed Ogunlaru

A Dialogue with My Heart

I will journal as my heart. I will give my heart a voice, I will allow it to speak to me. Putting pen to paper I will let everything that needs to spill out, spill out. I will simply free-write as my heart says what it needs me to hear; I'll let all of my feelings and thoughts pour out onto the page, unedited. Then I will write a letter back to my heart from me, I will tell my heart I understand, I will take my heart by the hand and talk to it with a steady, calm, loving, and mature voice. This kind of writing lets things come out of me that I hardly knew were there. It allows my thinking and my feeling to integrate and become more clear and coherent. When I let my feelings flow out of my heart, they flow out of my body, too. My body is a container for emotion. I feel my emotions in my body as well as my mind. They make me want to take an action. Today I will take that action on paper, I will give my heart a voice.

I let my feelings flow

Health is a large word. It embraces not the body only,
but the mind and spirit as well; . . . and not today's
pain or pleasure alone, but the whole
being and outlook of a man.

—James H. West

Reinvestment

I am ready and willing to reinvest in the ideal of love. I want to find worthy projects and passions, and put my energy toward them. I have something to give to the world and the world has something to give to me. I will allow the shapes, images, thoughts, and urges within me, just to be. I have wonderful things inside of me, I want to make this world a little better. I am positive today and have ways of being that are good ways. Recovery has taught me so much, and I am a different person inside. I don't even have to say anything because who I am speaks louder than what I say. I am willing to give life the love and energy and gratitude that it deserves—I am renewed. I am right where I am supposed to be, and I've met the challenges of my life. I am ready to live.

I invest my energy with care and gusto

You are one thing only. You are a Divine Being.
An all-powerful Creator. You are a Deity in jeans and
a T-shirt, and within you dwells the infinite wisdom
of the ages and the sacred creative force
of All that is, will be and ever was.

—*Anthon St. Maarten,* Divine Living:
The Essential Guide To Your True Destiny

My Journey

I have been through a journey of finding myself. I've faced my anger and hurt and brought order and clarity to my inner world. I've accepted the things I cannot change and changed the things that I can. Because I've shown the courage to face my inner demons and look them in the eye, I feel stronger and more competent. I have a renewed interest in life. I see things differently. I feel liberated from something that was tying up my energy. And I recognize and accept my own humanity, and the humanity of others. Recovery is a rebirth of hope, a reorganization of thought, and a reconstruction of dreams; meaning has been extracted from the difficult experiences and used to create a new set of moral rules and a new interpretation of life's events. Once recovery begins, dreams can be rebuilt.

I have the will to live an aware life

We may get knocked down on the outside, but
the key to living in victory is to learn
how to get up on the inside.

—*Joel Osteen*

DECEMBER 6

Keep Expectations Realistic

I will have realistic expectations. I do not want to ask more of life than I am willing to give. If I do not love life until it meets some idea I have in my head of what it should be, I am missing one more beautiful day of living, loving, and appreciating it. This world is, in itself, such a miracle. My life, the energy in my body, the experience of feeling a part of this alive and ever-evolving universe is reward enough. I don't want to set myself up for disappointment by creating shallow hurdles for life to leap over. I don't want to sabotage my own joy. I don't want to walk right by happiness because it doesn't conform to some picture I have of what it should look like

I keep my expectations realistic, I have pleasure in what is

In studies done on animals, the relationship between expectation and the body's release of dopamine (also known as the pleasure or feel-good hormone), was explored. Dopamine levels went up when the animal received a pleasant surprise. The more unexpected the pleasant stimulus, the higher the rise in dopamine. However, when a stimulus was expected but did not come, the animals' disappointment could be measured by a drop in dopamine levels. Stable expectations produced stable levels, pleasant surprises elevated ones, and disappointed expectations a drop in levels of feel-good hormones.

—*Tian Dayton, Ph.D.,*
The Magic of Forgiveness

Rage

Rage is not the same as anger; it is an attempt not to feel anger, to discharge stored pain at someone else's expense. Rage may get rid of something for me, but it plants it firmly into the soul of another—it is passing on the pain. When I rage, my brain is temporarily hijacked, my thinking mind shuts down, and I am all white heat and fury. It's a moment of total self-absorption with no empathy as to what it might be like to be on the receiving end. My rage gets me nowhere. It works nothing out, it terrifies those around me, and because my thinking was on the blink, many times I don't even remember what I have said. Today, I take responsibility for facing and processing feelings I have dissociated, so that they don't burst out as rage. I see rage as a symptom of disowned pain that overwhelmed me; I own it as mine and heal my pain so that I don't traumatize another person, another generation. And if I am near another person's rage, I remove myself, I do not stand there frozen and take it.

I see rage as a symptom of being traumatized

Dissociation is the common response of children
to repetitive, overwhelming trauma and holds the untenable
knowledge out of awareness. The losses and the
emotions engendered by the assaults on soul and body cannot,
however be held indefinitely. In the absence of effective
restorative experiences, the reactions to trauma will find expression.
As the child gets older, he will turn the rage in upon himself
or act it out on others, else it all will turn into madness.

—*Judith Spencer,* Satan's High Priest

It's All in the Game

Painful experiences are a part of anyone's life. What makes them traumatic for one person and less so for another is a combination of factors that buffer the effect. Today, I will ask myself questions like, how old was I when these events occurred, who was around to provide relief and support, how much access did I have to other, ameliorating experiences? Was I trapped by my size, my age, my basic make up, or position in the family? Was there anyone around who could help me process and make sense of frightening or chaotic experiences? I understand today that at moments of extreme stress I may have frozen; my thinking may have shut down, but I was still absorbing the sounds, sights, and smells around me. I kept the memories but not the "story" of my experience. But I can ameliorate through recovery my childhood experiences. I can process what didn't get processed. I can revisit, re-experience and reframe old events with new purpose and meaning. I can create a new story, a new narrative. I am not stuck with anything I don't want to be stuck with, I may not get 100% of it processed, but I can process enough to learn, grow, enrich myself, and move on. I can recapture something beautiful and enjoy my life today.

I don't create unnecessary trouble for myself today

Many deeply hidden memories have come flooding back. The important message here though is that it is possible to heal and survive. Everyone has survived their own kind of emotional or mental trauma. We all have our inner fears and misplaced feelings of guilt.

—*Lynette Gould,* Heart of Darkness: How I Triumphed Over a Childhood of Abuse

Helping Others

I am paying it forward as a part of my journey. So many have helped me with their knowledge, skills, and passion. I thank them in my heart and honor them in my thoughts and actions. And I pass it along. Part of my healing is to help others to heal, to keep doors open that were open for me, and to open new ones. Helping others keeps my recovery green and alive and growing.

I give what I got

I hold the hands of people I never touch. I provide comfort to people I never embrace. I watch people walk into brick walls, the same ones over and over again, and I coax them to turn around and try to walk in a different direction.
People rarely see me gladly. As a rule, I catch the residue of their despair. I see people who are broken, and people who only think they are broken. I see people who have had their faces rubbed in their failures. I see weak people wanting anesthesia and strong people who wonder what they have done to make such an enemy of fate. I am often the final pit stop people take before they crawl across the finish line that is marked: I give up.
Some people beg me to help. Some people dare me to help. Sometimes the beggars and the dare-ers look the same. Absolutely the same. I'm supposed to know how to tell them apart.
Some people who visit me need scar tissue to cover their wounds. Some people who visit me need their wounds opened further, explored for signs of infection and contamination. I make those calls, too.
Some days I'm invigorated by it all. Some days I'm numbed.
Always, I'm humbled by the role of helper.
And, occasionally, I'm ambushed.

—*Stephen White,* Critical Conditions

DECEMBER 10

Survivor's Pride

I am strong, resilient, and alive. I have made some great choices and I have figured things out. I am so proud of myself for having the courage and wisdom to seek out the help I needed, in spite of what anyone else said or did to encourage or discourage me. I knew there was a better life out there for me and I took baby steps, gigantic leaps, and solid strides toward it. I am so proud of myself. I have wisdom that is mine, a story of my life that I am scripting each and every day, a practice of well-being that I maintain because I know that it's good for me, that it heads me in the direction that I want to go. I looked trouble in the eye and did something about it, I faced my tiger in the night. I am the kind of person I always wanted to be and growing more into that person each day. I love and am loved. I have a life I feel good about.

Good for me!

We define survivor's pride as the well-deserved feeling of accomplishment that results from persisting in the face of hardship or adversity. It is a bittersweet mixture of pain and triumph that is usually under the surface, but is sometimes readily visible in many youth and adults who have gone through difficult circumstances. It develops over time in the course of a struggle that typically goes unnoticed in professional and lay circles more likely to document problems and deficits in people than their strengths. It is not a rare feeling; nor is it limited to those with dazzling success. In our work, we have been able to find survivor's pride even in young people with on-going struggles and whose claim to a satisfying life is far from secure.

—Steven Wolin, M.D., and Sybil Wolin, Ph.D.

I Believe in Love

Love is that little germ of faith, hope, and charity. It's the shaft of light in darkness, the reason to live. Love is what changes whatever it touches; it transforms. Love is hope. Love points the way by providing that inner knowledge, that feeling that I want to reach out for and repeat and repeat and repeat. Love is the wisdom at the core of life; it is the life in life. In it is wrapped wisdom, truth, and the promise of a better tomorrow. Love is at the core of everything that works, it is our weapon of mass construction, it makes everything grow and reproduce itself in the right way.

Love will find a way

You survived by seizing every tiny drop of love
you could find anywhere, and milking it, relishing it, for all it
was worth. And as you grew up, you sought love, anywhere you
could find it, whether it was a teacher or a coach or a friend
or a friend's parents. You sought those tiny droplets of love,
basking in them when you found them. They sustained you.
For all these years, you've lived under the illusion that somehow,
you made it because you were tough enough to overpower the abuse,
the hatred, the hard knocks of life. But really you made it because
love is so powerful that tiny little doses of it are enough to
overcome the pain of the worst things life can dish out.
Toughness was a faulty coping mechanism you devised to get by.
But, in reality, it has been your ability to never give up,
to keep seeking love, and your resourcefulness to make
that love last long enough to sustain you.
That is what has gotten you by.

—*Rachel Reiland,* Get Me Out of Here:
My Recovery from Borderline
Personality Disorder

Self-Care

Growing up with narcissism and addiction taught me to put other people's needs first, to take care of them as number one. If there was something left over for me I could have it, or if I could twist my needs around and experience taking care of them as meeting my needs, that was okay, too. This taught me not to take responsibility for taking care of myself. It taught me to take care of myself surreptitiously, to hide what I really wanted, eventually even from myself. It taught me to feel guilty when I was getting what I wanted. Watching narcissism was a negative example of self-care, my narcissistic parent made it seem like taking care of myself meant leaving everyone else feeling alone in their needs. Watching an addicted parent made it look like self-care meant checking out, falling off the radar, being unresponsive and irresponsible. Today, I will look for healthy examples of self-care.

I can take care of myself in a way that is good for me and for those who need me

Information overload (on all levels) is exactly WHY you need an "ignore list." It has never ben more important to say "No."

—*Mani S. Sivasubramanian,* How to Focus

Being Me

I will not know how to be, what to do, or how to act, if I am constantly preoccupied with being someone other than myself, ever living in my head, trying to figure out what's expected, trying to think my way through my day rather than actually live it. I have one shot at being me—I don't want to lose it by trying to be a thousand "somebody elses." If I develop one mediocre talent in myself and work daily to refine it, use it, and apply it, I will get so much farther than if I try to be everything to everyone, to live up to someone else's ideas of what I have to offer. I know me. I know what I like doing and what I am good at doing. I know what skills and talents the world seems to be choosing me for and where I feel I am in synch with me and the world. When I am reasonably connected with me, I can sense where I am and where the current of life is taking me. I can allow the alchemy of my life to work its magic and draw me in directions that are right for me. Today I will get out of my own way and go with the flow, trusting that what the world sees in me, what I feel chosen for, and what I choose, will match up and make music together. There is a stream waiting for me to float down and I am going to find it and let myself go with it.

Today I live the life that I actually have

Live life fully while you're here. Experience everything.
Take care of yourself and your friends. Have fun, be crazy, be weird.
Go out and screw up! You're going to anyway, so you might as well
enjoy the process. Take the opportunity to learn from your mistakes:
find the cause of your problem and eliminate it. Don't try to be
perfect; just be an excellent example of being human.

—Anthony Robbins

DECEMBER 14

The Medicine Chest Inside of Me

There is a medicine chest inside me and I want to let it help me heal. Nature has designed me to heal. If I cut myself, nature knits my skin back together so well that I hardly know I was injured. If I break a bone, nature, along with rest and quiet, gives it back to me. If I get a disease, my own body tries to fight it off and bring me back into health and balance. My mind and heart, too, have a natural drive towards unity, balance, and integration. Feeling out of balance and overwhelmed can lead me to self-medication, acting out, depression, anxiety, shame, and any number of defenses against feeling pain. My mind will create such complex defenses, or circular thinking, to ward off feeling fragmented and unbalanced. It's my attempt to stabilize something that feels lopsided; a misguided, but well-intended effort to restore equilibrium. Today I will find healthy ways to maintain and nourish a daily balance. I will put emotional, psychological, physical, and relational balance at the top of my list, knowing that my life flows more smoothly when I do.

I trust my psyche's ability to restore its own balance when I don't over stress it

The power we discover inside ourselves as we survive a life-threatening experience can be utilized equally well outside of crisis, too. I am, in every moment, capable of mustering the strength to survive again—or of tapping that strength in other good, productive, healthy ways.

—*Michele Rosenthal,*
Before the World Intruded

Constant Change

I will accept the changing rhythms of my life. I will be open to new blends of people, experiences, and circumstances. I will allow the seasons of my life to reveal themselves, and I will make room for them. If recovery has taught me anything, it is to appreciate what I have right now, to make good use of the moment and to bank the good memories and hold them close to my heart. It's so easy to make unnecessary stress and trouble—just for today I won't. Just for today, I will make each glitch easier by not multiplying whatever is bothering me, and I'll expand on what is working, what feels right, what feels good. Each day, each season, each decade is different; wanting them all to look alike, only means that I miss most of them. I will change along with the times, I will let things be different, welcome new combinations. Some of my previous routines and lifestyles will keep going; some will shift to make room for new experiences, while still others might become distant memories.

I am getting good at living

Your hand opens and closes, opens and closes.
If it were always a fist or always stretched open, you
would be paralyzed. Your deepest presence is in
every small contracting and expanding,
the two as beautifully balanced and
coordinated as birds' wings.

—*Rumi,* The Essential Rumi

Say Thanks

Today I will say thank you. If someone does something for me, I will say thank you. If I feel good when I wake up, I will say thank you. When I have food that gives me pleasure and nourishment, I will appreciate its flavor. If the world provides me with another day of what I need to keep going, I will say thank you for being alive, for my health, for my family and my friends. I will appreciate the little things others do for me, and I will thank them for doing them, rather than leave them feeling as if I don't even notice. As I show appreciation, a curious thing happens: I get more of what I am saying thank you for. People want to be appreciated; saying thank you allows them to give with pleasure. Life wants to be appreciated; saying thank you allows life to give with pleasure. God wants to be appreciated: saying thank you gives me many more moments of conscious contact.

I not only feel but express my appreciation

Be thankful for what you have; you'll end up having more.
If you concentrate on what you don't have,
you will never, ever have enough.

—*Oprah Winfrey*

Healing

Sometimes, healing doesn't feel good. Sometimes, it involves deep pain. The effect of healing is gentle, freeing, and wonderful, but the road leading to it can be hellish. Now, I understand what Psalm 23 means by the "valley of the shadow of death." It is referring to a spiritual enlightenment involving a death and a rebirth. In order to be born into enlightenment, it is necessary that I face the dark and scary parts of myself. Just looking at them will transform them, just dragging them out of hiding, out of cowering in shame, out of numbness and wordlessness into words, that will change everything. I need all of me for a life of spiritual freedom.

Today, I know that I was never alone along the way, and that I need never feel alone again

If you want to shrink something,
You must first allow it to expand.
If you want to get rid of something,
You must first allow it to flourish.
If you want to take something,
You must first allow it to be given.
This is called the subtle perception
Of the way things are.

—*Lao Tzu,* Tao Te Ching,
translated by Stephen Mitchell

Looking on the Bright Side

Looking on the bright side doesn't mean that I deny what is right in front of me, that I am making nice or playing Pollyanna and refusing to face "reality." Looking on the bright side takes guts, heart, and character. It takes faith. In fact, it can actually strengthen my confidence and sense of self to look at a situation as it is and make conscious choices about seeing it as part of my spiritual path, part of my life, which after all *is* my spiritual path. It weakens me inside to rely on denial or self-medication in order to make a situation livable. It shows a lack of character and emotional intelligence. Spiritual strength allows me to live with the truth and transcend my circumstances. My willingness to see my life in its best possible light, and doing the daily work it takes to stay clear and clean inside, are my commitments to God and my ways of showing gratitude for the life I have been given.

I enjoy being me, that's part of being healthy

If you celebrate your differentness, the world will, too.
It believes exactly what you tell it—through the words you use
to describe yourself, the actions you take to care for yourself,
and the choices you make to express yourself.
Tell the world you are a one-of-a-kind creation who came
here to experience wonder and spread joy.
Expect to be accommodated.

—*Victoria Moran,* Lit from Within: A Simple Guide to the Art of Inner Beauty

A Clear Conscience

Other people's negative projections of me no longer run me. I am the one who makes the decisions about who I want to be. I need not defend and explain myself again and again. I need not ask permission to be who I am. I allow myself to be happy in my own skin today. I think well of myself, no matter what others think of me. Today, I keep my house clean and let go of the rest. I will keep my own scorecard clean and not worry about the results. I will act in a way that makes it easier for me to live with myself—that keeps my own conscience clear. Some of the ways that I wish to live as a recovering person will not be readily understood by others. I will live them anyway, confident that how I am now and what I do now, will reveal itself over time to be a worthwhile approach to life. If I don't help myself today, no one else will, no one else can.

I am my own best friend

There is nothing like returning to a place that
remains unchanged to find the ways in
which you yourself have altered.

—Nelson Mandela

Born to Thrive

I am born to thrive. Like the trees, grass, birds, and flowers, the equipment to thrive is built into my DNA. Everything in nature thrives or it wouldn't be here. Plants grow through cracks in a wall or sidewalk. Birds build nests in roofs and animals find what they need in the wild. Everywhere there is evidence of life's ability to adapt and thrive. I am no different. I am one of nature's and God's crowning achievements. Born to thrive. My job is to keep myself rested, watered, and fed; to give myself food, quiet, love, and spiritual sustenance. The rest will happen naturally if I don't get, or can overcome, disease when it does occur. And I am in good company: every tree, flower, breeze, shaft of light, dog, cat, horse, and human is also here and now thriving with me. We're all of us thriving together and in balance. Nature intended me to be part of an ever-alive and adaptable universe full of wonder and life.

I am designed to adapt and thrive

Sometimes you need a little crisis to get
your adrenaline flowing and help
you realize your potential.

—*Jeannette Walls,* The Glass Castle

Spirit Calls

I will dare to be more. To take a flying leap into the life I would like to live. Hiding my best qualities, my talents, and my dreams only means that they remain hidden. I do myself no favors when I don't actualize the gifts that are in me—and I do no favors to those around me, either. There is plenty room in this world for me to shine, plenty of need for a little extra light here and there, plenty of longing for song and dance, plenty of room to move and grow and become. The idea of shortage is manmade. I have a will and a wish and a responsibility to access, express, and enjoy the beauty that is in me.

I pay attention to the gifts sewn into the lining of my life

Our deepest fear is not that we are inadequate.
Our deepest fear is that we are powerful beyond measure.
It is our light, not our darkness that most frightens us.
We ask ourselves, Who am I to be brilliant, gorgeous, talented,
and fabulous? Actually, who are you *not* to be? You are
a child of God. Your playing small does not serve the world.
There is nothing enlightened about shrinking so that
other people will not feel insecure around you. We are all
meant to shine, as children do. We were born to make manifest
the glory of God that is within us. It is not just in some of us;
it is in everyone and as we let our own light shine, we
unconsciously give others permission to do the same.
As we are liberated from our own fear, our presence
automatically liberates others.

—*Marianne Williamson,* A Return to Love

The Power of a Safe Space

Knowing that I have people in my life who carry my personal history as I carry theirs, with whom I can share my deeper self, helps me to face the world with more courage and less fear of failure because, no matter what happens on the outside, I have somewhere I belong. The same is true for knowing that I have an inner space where I feel at one with a higher life. Meditation can be a safe space for me, an inner space, a space where I am one with an inner world. Having a safe space provides me with a sense of belonging that I carry around with me. It makes the rest of the world feel like a safer place. It frees me up to succeed in the world, because I need the outside world less, I am less dependent on its approval. How the world does or does not receive me feels somehow less worrying when I have a secure place of my own. Program can be this safe corner of the world for me. If I have been let down in personal relationships, I can find pieces of what I missed in the rooms. I can feel held and safe, as if I have a place to go to, to feel okay. And I can also go within to experience my safe and sacred place. I have ways of creating beauty and safety in my life.

I use what I have on a regular basis to create a personal sense of sacred safety

Your sacred space is where you can find yourself over and over again.

—Joseph Campbell

Faith in What I Cannot See

Nothing in the world is certain. The kind of certainty I want, in order to feel safe, just isn't available. The only certainty is that I was born and I will die. Between these two ends, I am part of a movable feast that changes, shifts, and regroups all the time. It is the nature of things. But I want to take a leap into the unknown and trust that there will be a net, I want to step out and let my feet find the foot bridge, I want to learn to fly. Otherwise, I will never know what it means to talk a leap of faith. I want to see something in my mind, and believe that it can be a part of my life, and that it can be better than I even imagined. Today I will have faith in what I cannot see and what I do not know for sure.

I move into the unknown with faith

When you walk to the edge of all the light you have
And take that first step into the darkness of the unknown
You must believe that one of two things will happen:
There will be something solid for you to stand upon,
or, you will be taught how to fly

—Patrick Overton

DECEMBER 24

Inner Light

Today, I will go within for the deepest sort of experience of joy, of ecstasy in being alive. I will get in touch with the deeper pulse of living—the thread that connects me with the divine experience, I will recognize that in order to be lit from within, I need to drop down inside of myself and be in the presence of inner light. Life itself has a purpose apart from any individual task or stage. Life itself is the experience. All of the things I have been trying to acccomplish are both inner and outer goals They are meant to bring me closer to myself, to develop me in ways that allow me to experience life more fully—to be more capable of pleasure. Today I will give myself these gifts of inner sight. I will observe this miraculous life, this world, knowing that I am part of a divine mystery, a mystery of incalculable intelligence.

I observe the constant miracles of life and I am in awe

My religion consists of a humble admiration of the illimitable
superior spirit who reveals himself in the slight details
we are able to perceive with our frail and feeble mind.

—Albert Einstein

A Christmas Affirmation

Life is a gift. Everywhere we look, we see evidence of God's creative power. In this season, I will remember where I truly come from. I will remember that my place is to stand in awe of the divine mystery—to recognize, celebrate, and praise all the beauty that surrounds me constantly, waiting for me to notice it. Today we open our hearts to receive the blessing of God's love, here on earth. As I open my heart to divine love and guidance I become purposeful, my life becomes meaningful, and my world feels safe and warm. I respect and appreciate the life that I have been given and place my heart and day into the loving hands of my Higher Power.

I breathe in the collective spirit affirming life

This is what rituals are for. We do spiritual ceremonies as human beings in order to create a safe resting place for our most complicated feelings of joy or trauma, so that we don't have to haul those feelings around with us forever, weighing us down. We all need such places of ritual safekeeping. And I do believe that if your culture or tradition doesn't have the specific ritual you are craving, then you are absolutely permitted to make up a ceremony of your own devising, fixing your own broken-down emotional systems with all the do-it-yourself resourcefulness of a generous plumber/poet.

—*Elizabeth Gilbert,* Eat, Pray, Love

A Safe Harbor

The rooms are a safe harbor for me where I can drop anchor; they keep a lighthouse burning so that I can navigate in darkness or find my way back to safety when I am out, or even lost at sea. They provide a haven of caring and support that I can lean into. The power of love in the rooms helps to restore me to sanity. It lets me surrender and have faith. It gives me a place to open up and share what I would not feel comfortable sharing in many other places. This process of listening, identifying, getting triggered and feeling my feelings, translating them into words and reflecting on them and sharing them, right-sizes them. As I right-size my emotions through feeling and understanding them, I integrate them into the overall context of my life. As I integrate this new personal knowledge I become clearer to myself, and others become clearer to me. I become capable of personal growth and expansion. It teaches me emotional stability. The rooms humble me and right-size me, which allows me to confront my demons and grow as a human being without feeling threatened by my own flawed character: because—so what?—we're all flawed. I learn a new way to right myself when I get off balance, and I can let other people into my process, I can learn new ways of being with people.

I do not have to be right or wrong in the rooms, I can just be

> The kind of man who always thinks that he is right,
> that his opinions, his pronouncements, are the final word,
> when once exposed shows nothing there. But a wise man
> has much to learn without a loss of dignity.
>
> —*Sophocles*

Using My Tools

I can write out all my thoughts and feelings in my journal. As I do, something wonderful happens—I begin to make sense to myself. I pour out what is in my inner world without reservation, restriction, or revision. I let the editor in my mind take a rest. I simply free-write and let what wants to come out, come out. Parts of me wriggle their way to the surface of my mind, parts that I had ignored, forgotten, or never even met. Sense impressions and the feelings woven into them burst forward into words where my mind can see them neat, clean, and audible At first glance I am reading about me as if meeting me anew, and I am fascinated by the internal workings of my own mind, the forgotten details of my own story. I will write in my journal today to explore the interior of my own mind.

My journal reveals me to myself

Our dreams and stories may contain implicit aspects of our lives even without our awareness. In fact, storytelling may be a primary way in which we can linguistically communicate to others—as well as to ourselves—the sometimes hidden contents of our implicitly remembering minds. Stories make available perspectives on the emotional themes of our implicit memory that may otherwise be consciously unavailable to us. This may be one reason why journal writing and intimate communication with others, which are so often narrative processes, have such powerful organizing effects on the mind: They allow us to modulate our emotions and make sense of the world.

—*Daniel J. Siegel,* The Developing Mind: How Relationships and the Brain Interact to Shape Who We Are

Pushing Myself Too Hard

I am not a machine. I cannot just keep pushing myself beyond my natural capacity. I need rest, quiet, ease, and nourishment. I need to relax and take it easy. I need to go with the flow of my day rather than jerk, push, and pressure my way through it. What am I doing to myself by pushing, pushing, pushing? Why do I think I have to pressure myself like this? Why do I think more is always better? Why don't I understand that relaxing and taking it easy is part of what allows me to give more to life, to see more clearly, to act more efficiently? When I treat myself like a machine, I lose myself, my ability to tune in, to be me and let others be them. I see the world as less alive.

I recognize that my day needs a peaceful rhythm

Life should be touched not strangled.
You've got to relax, let it happen at times,
and at others, move forward with it.

—*Ray Bradbury*

Where the Treasure Lies

I see today that the door within myself that I was so afraid to enter, the feelings I was so afraid to feel, the pain around me I tried so hard to ward off, were the passage into my own soul, once I surrendered to them. Whenever I have bumped up against parts of my life that I thought I could not bear or handle, that is where the gold turned out to be. The hardest times in my life were what launched me into the best of myself and my most alive, deep, and productive times. Today I see with a sort of surprise and wonder what these periods in my development as a person did for me. What I thought were the problems foisted on me by life were, in some way, the gifts given to me. Some were the fault of others, some were my own making, but they all were just me; much of my pain has been my own blindness, what I would not or could not see. Liberation is in seeing and just being.

I use where I stumble as a point of entry into more of life

Where you stumble, there lies your treasure.
The very cave you are afraid to enter turns out to be
the source of what you are looking for.
The damned thing in the cave, that was so
dreaded, has become the center.

—*Joseph Campbell*

Little Dreams, Little Magic

I will invite magic into my day. I believe in magic, why not? I feel surrounded by so much that appears to come out of nowhere, so why can't I close my eyes and make three wishes and expect one of them to come true? Why should life lose its magic for me, the magic that I was so aware of as a child? As adults we say there is a "mystery." As children we see the hand of an alchemist, and angels extending themselves into our life especially, just to make our dreams come true. I have dreams too, dreams that I truly do feel can be actualized, dreams that I love to dream, that make me feel good inside. A dream of a garden, of a meal, a beautiful kitchen, a long walk, the house I'd like to live in, a business. Dreams for my family, for a life together that's happy and good for all concerned. Today I will have my beautiful, little dreams, they are not so little after all. They make up a life.

Because I am alive, I am in this life, in this magic, in this mystery, in these dreams

Magic exists. Who can doubt it, when there are rainbows and wildflowers, the music of the wind and the silence of the stars? Anyone who has loved has been touched by magic. It is such a simple and such an extraordinary part of the lives we live.

—Nora Roberts

One Foot, One Step, This Step

Today I continue to put one foot in front of the other, I take baby steps when baby steps are necessary, long strides regularly; some days I walk briskly, some days slowly. Some days I take leaps and some I hardly move at all. I take my steps, through my world and into my day, confident that I have the tools to manage what comes along. I am confident that I know how to get out of trouble when I'm in it, and that I know how to embrace, appreciate, and taste the wonder of being alive. I am here. My life is today. Everything that surrounds me gets my attention, in my hands are my colors with which to paint my day, my stage to bring myself to the moment. Today I love the life I have been given, and I will respect, take care of, and appreciate it. I will have fun with my life, enjoy it, and move through it with an attitude of gratitude. I will create and express this feeling inside of me, I'll connect with others, and I'll be alone. I will love my food, my flowers, my friends and family, and my simple activities as they onfold. Today is my day. This is my life.

I hold my life like a baby, I see the world as exciting and filled with possibility and beauty

But somewhere, a child surprises himself with his
endurance, his quick mind, his dexterous hands. Somewhere a
child accomplishes with ease that which usually takes great effort.
And this child, who has been blind to his past, but his heart
still beats for the thrill of the race, this child's soul awakens.
And a new champion walks among us.

—*Garth Stein,* The Art of Racing in the Rain